Failsafe IS Project Delivery

To Sally, Thomas and Elizabeth

Failsafe IS Project Delivery

ANDREW HOLMES

Gower

Published by
Gower Publishing Limited
Gower House
Croft Road
Aldershot
Hampshire GU11 3HR
England

Gower Publishing Company
131 Main Street
Burlington
VT 05401–5600 USA

Andrew Holmes has asserted his right under the Copyright, Designs and Patents Act 1988 to be identified as the author of this work.

British Library Cataloguing in Publication Data
Holmes, Andrew
    Failsafe IS project delivery
    1. Information storage and retrieval systems 2. Computer
    system failures
    I. Title
    005.7'4

ISBN 0 566 08255 1

Library of Congress Cataloging-in-Publication Data
Holmes, Andrew 1965–
    Failsafe is Project Delivery/Andrew Holmes.
    p.cm
    ISBN 0-566-08255-1 (hardback)
    1. Information Technology. 2. Information resources management. 3. Computer
    software – Development – Management. I. Title.

T58.5.H67 2001
658'0546–dc21   00–044276

Typeset in Utopia by Bournemouth Colour Press, Parkstone and printed in Great Britain by MPG Books Ltd, Bodmin.

Contents

List of figures

List of tables

Preface

A number of years ago I was sitting in my tutor's office at the London School of Economics (LSE) discussing the dissertation for my MSc. At the time I was working on an information systems project which had not gone as well as planned. Indeed, the system failed to function properly, caused immense problems to the organization, and was personally a painful experience.

At the time, I had no clear understanding of why it had been such a disaster, and as a means of dealing with it, externalized it by blaming management, the users – anyone but me. But was it purely down to my own incompetence? My tutor had a research interest in information systems project failure, and recommended I look into the issue in greater detail. The touch-paper had been lit.

The dissertation came and went, but my desire to try and understand why information systems projects fail remained. From personal experience, research with the LSE, and discussions with those who had experience of failed projects, it was clear that there were no simple answers. It also became obvious that there were some serious issues that had to be resolved within the wider business and technology communities, before the regularity of failure could be reduced. I also noticed that there had been no attempt to describe or manage the issues from a holistic perspective.

There have been many texts, processes, methods and management techniques that purport to solve the problems once and for all. Suffice it to say, none of these has been truly successful, universally applicable to understanding, and able to resolve the problems associated with software project failure. The majority have failed to provide anything more than motherhood statements and arguably inappropriate solutions. From my research, I recognized that software projects present unique problems to organizations and require a concerted organizational effort to resolve them. They cannot be tackled in a piecemeal fashion.

Six years later, having conducted further research into the problems, I have finally put pen to paper; I am continually depressed by the lack of understanding of the key issues associated with failure, and the continued search for the elusive silver bullet, that is, the catch-all solution to all the ills associated with software, and particularly software development projects.

Whenever I am in a position to discuss the issues covered within this book, I am often confronted by the usual 'why concentrate on failure?' question. Surely, it would be far better to discuss what constitutes a successful information system project? Indeed it would, but there seem to be so few of these, that it is difficult to draw out common themes without reducing them to trite and simplistic statements such as 'involve the users'. Success also has the tendency to breed complacency, which is a danger in itself. With the larger number of failures, and the vigilance that failure can bring, understanding why failures occur may be one of the surest ways to breed a successful information systems project. Also, in raising the level of awareness of failure, it is hoped that fewer project managers and organizations will suffer the ignominy of failure in the future.

ANDREW HOLMES

Acknowledgements

Writing a book is always, to a lesser or greater extent, a collaborative exercise. I would like to thank the many people who have given me the necessary encouragement required to maintain the high levels of effort to produce this book. There are, of course, one or two people who are worthy of a specific mention. In particular, I would like to thank David Jacobs of *profit for information*, and Shan Shanthakumer of the Executive Studio at the West London Tech. who kindly contributed their thoughts and ideas on how the culture gap between business and IT might be resolved. I would also like to thank Mike Woodman, of Sema Group Consulting, who, back in the summer of 1998, gave me the push I needed to start writing the book.

Furthermore, writing this book has not been without its trials and tribulations; loss of confidence, creative blocks, and so on. Throughout the last twelve months, my wife Sally has provided me with immense support not only through encouragement, but also in reviewing each chapter as it was completed. I would live in fear of her reviews, as I knew she took it seriously, and would provide me with valid, and often brutal criticism. This has, in my opinion, allowed me to provide the reader with a higher quality product; thank you Sally.

AH

Introduction

Computers were probably the most important technology to have emerged in the twentieth century. In the relatively short space of forty years, they became central to the efficient operation of most industrialized nations. It is now recognized that many industries, organizations and government bodies could not operate efficiently, and in some cases not at all, without them. Therefore, a significant proportion of organizations can now be considered information technology (IT) centric. That is, their ability to function within the increasingly competitive global economy is only possible through the effective and continued application of IT. Furthermore, the general trend towards greater computerization, and the merging of information and communication technologies, is creating an environment in which technology is becoming the dominant component of almost any modern enterprise.

Thus, organizations, through their increasing dependence on IT, seek out the latest technological solution that will provide them with, or maintain, their competitive advantage. But technology and its application presents a paradox – the more you have, the more you need, because without it, competitive advantage can be very short-lived. Product and service life cycles have been reduced by IT's ability to increase the immediacy of product and service need. Thus, the application of IT has created an environment that both encourages dependency upon it, and speeds up the already frenetic pace of change.

This move towards greater computerization and dependency is reflected within investment trends, for example:

- Research in 1994 aimed at the world's largest economies by Brunel University in the United Kingdom estimated that spend on IT including software, hardware and staff stood in the region of 4 per cent of Gross National Product. Of greater interest was that they also expected this figure to double by 2002.[1]
- In his book *Computer Ethics*, Forester estimated the 1995 global spend to be in the region of $450 billion.[2]
- In 1997, an International Data Corporation study of 55 nations that accounted for 99 per cent of the world's IT expenditure, estimated global spend to be $680 billion.[3]
- In 1999, Gartner predicted that the global spend on IT in 2002 will be in the region of $3.3 billion, significantly larger than the estimated 1999 spend of $2.2 billion.[4]

With dependency comes hope and promise – hope that the next wave of technological advancement will bring bigger benefits, better opportunities (especially global), and larger market share; promise in that the IT industry will be able to meet these expectations. But, just as there are winners, there are a significant number of losers.

A typical organization's experience with IT has not been as comfortable as one might imagine. Many experience difficulties in harnessing IT, especially in managing the increasingly complex projects required for its implementation. Late, over-budget and failed projects are an endemic problem. One only needs to read the computer press to see, almost on a weekly basis, the tip of the project failure iceberg. Furthermore, survey after survey since the early 1970s points to the depressing truth that only a small percentage of information systems projects can be considered successful against the standard measures of time, cost and quality. Viewed in isolation, such surveys can be easily dismissed, but viewed collectively, and as a longitudinal study of failure, they provide an important insight into the software crisis that still remains.

For a long time organizations have been led to believe that unravelling and correcting the failure of information systems projects is a simple task requiring a single-shot solution and only limited effort. After all, if the project manager is a good one, who understands the technology, and follows good engineering disciplines, there should be no problems, should there? In reality, project failure is a difficult problem to unravel. Indeed, ever since the 1970s software crisis, attempts made to improve information systems projects have had little success because they have tended to deal with isolated parts of the problem and, in many cases, just those associated with technology. Silver bullet solutions to a complex problem will not provide the answers, which do not lie solely in the technological domain either. The problem is an organizational one, which requires an organizational response. Therefore, it is not sufficient to have a good project manager, as there are other factors which must be managed outside of the project that are necessary to provide an environment which facilitates success.

Recognizing that IT has taken on a key role for most organizations, every senior manager should have the management of IT projects within an environment that is conducive to success at the top of their agenda. Naturally, when times are good, and money is awash within the enterprise, project failure may be less of a concern. But with increasing pressures to deliver projects faster, and successfully within an increasingly competitive environment, it is necessary to reduce, and if possible eliminate, those factors which can cause an information systems project to fail.

Such factors extend well beyond the management of the project itself, and one only needs to witness the continued problems with IT projects, to recognize that these cannot be resolved through strong project management skills alone. Therefore, this book will focus on those factors outside of the project management domain that contribute to project failure, and in discussing these, I will assume that there is a professional project manager running the project. Consequently, there is no intention to discuss the general principles of project management *per se* – there are plenty of books

and journals dedicated to the subject. However, any discussion of failure cannot be made in isolation of project management because the two are inexorably linked, so the reader should expect the occasional reference to both the project manager and project management throughout the book.

I believe this book to be essential reading for all senior managers and executives who are trying to come to terms with, and tackle the problems associated with, the delivery and management of IT. Moreover, its coverage makes it compulsory reading for all business and IT professionals on whom the delivery of an effective information system depends. It is equally applicable to the student population who will be the business and IT professionals of the future. Ensuring they have a complete understanding of why information systems projects fail should allow them to become sensitive to the problems that persist within organizations today, and prevent them from happening in the future.

The purpose of this book is to:

- raise the reader's awareness of the factors which can lead to project failure;
- force the recognition that this is an organizational, and not just a technical issue;
- demonstrate there are no silver bullets by describing the complexities of the problem;
- outline in detail the significant contributory factors associated with information systems project failure;
- introduce approaches that can be used to minimize and eliminate the worst effects of these factors, and hence improve the success rate of information systems projects; and
- suggest a blueprint for the optimization of information systems projects.

Within the book, I will concentrate on information systems rather than information technology, as this is fundamental to the analysis and understanding of the problems. In the latter, technology is the focus, whilst in the former, it is the application of technology within the wider organizational setting that is of interest. It is the human and organizational interactions with the IT system that are linked to the majority of failed information systems projects. That said, I will tend to use both terms quite frequently.

For the purposes of this book, 'project failure' will refer to:

- the termination of an information systems project during its development – that is, at some stage within the development or project life cycle; and
- the rejection of an information system at implementation – that is, as it is passed to the business users, or some time soon after implementation (after limited operational use).

There is, of course, a further form of failure which is caused by the long-term dependence on poor systems: many badly created information systems are forced into production, leading to major headaches for those organizations which then become dependent upon them. In addition, the issues raised and discussed within this book are equally applicable to the innumerable projects which are completed late and often substantially over-budget.

The book is divided into three parts. Part I introduces the problem by way of a two-chapter reprise of what we know about failure to date, followed by separate chapters which introduce the failure model and analyse each of the contributory factors. Part II mirrors the key issues identified within Part I, and introduces approaches to minimize and eliminate them. Finally, Part III provides a blueprint for optimizing information systems projects, highlights the much-needed changes in attitude required to make them successful, and provides some general advice to those having to grapple with the problems associated with IT.

The result – a comprehensive understanding of the problem, how it can be resolved, and ultimately a higher degree of success – is something all organizations should be interested in.

PART I

THE PROBLEM WITH INFORMATION SYSTEMS PROJECTS

The information systems community faces a paradox: despite impressive advances in technology, problems are more abundant than solutions; organizations experience rising costs instead of cost reductions, and information systems misuse and rejection are more frequent than acceptance and use.[1]

It is said that in order to be cured of alcoholism you must first recognize that you are an alcoholic. Maybe it is the same for information systems project failure. Superficially, organizations understand there are significant problems, but is this true at the detailed level?

Certainly, at a more detailed level, I would argue that there have been insufficient attempts to understand the full extent of the underlying components of information systems project failure. Generally, there do appear to be problems associated with the general competency of project managers, but there is more to failure than just poor project management. Without a deeper understanding of what else impacts the viability of an information system project, organizations end up addressing the wrong problem, and at the wrong level. Instead of resolving it, they tend to create further problems – what is often termed the 'bite-back'.[2] For example, the knee-jerk reaction to failure is usually the generation of a catch-all approach to its prevention – the silver bullet – itself often based upon a superficial understanding of the issues involved.

Unfortunately, this tends to increase the severity of failure, because, as organizations focus on one part of the problem, it allows other components to become more dominant.

The purpose of Part I of this book is to raise the awareness of failure beyond that of technology and project management by introducing and discussing other issues that may appear familiar but which have not been fully articulated before. At times this will appear quite negative, in that it will seem to pour out nothing but bad news. There is a purpose to this: awareness. Realizing that the problems associated with the management of software projects are not easy to resolve is a dawning realization that must be had by all chief executives, IT and business professionals alike. And, until this happens, the pain of failure will continue to dog organizations everywhere.

Once the extent of the problem is recognized, the approaches to its resolution can be discussed from a much firmer footing, and as a result have a much better opportunity for success.

Read on.

CHAPTER ONE

A fifty-year context

Any organization faced with the immediacy of an IT problem wants to solve it now, and they will grab anything available to help them. This is of course a natural reaction, but they would do well to take a step back and recognize that some of their current problems with IT and information systems projects have as much do with how IT has evolved and been applied over the last fifty years as with the modern day. I believe there is benefit from understanding the past, as the study of history allows the past to be analysed, interpreted and, ultimately, explained. History also allows us to generalize, derive theories and learn lessons from which the present and future can be interpreted and improved upon. Therefore, understanding the history of IT, and how it has become such a dominant force within the modern enterprise, is valuable because it allows us to interpret and explain some of the present-day problems with IT, and hence derive a much better understanding of how these problems can be rectified.

Three historical perspectives are worth analysing. The first is how information technology has advanced over the last fifty years, the second is how organizations have grappled with the tensions that have arisen from its application, and the third is how the relationship between the developers and users of information technology has developed. Each generates understanding and awareness that we are dealing with a problem that has distinct historical roots.

TECHNOLOGY: THE COMPUTER GENERATIONS

There have been phenomenal changes in computer technology since its birth during the 1940s. These changes have been labelled the first, second, third, fourth and fifth generations of computing[1] (see Figure 1.1).

The first generation of computing consisted of vacuum tubes and electromagnetic relays. To ensure these large, and very bulky machines

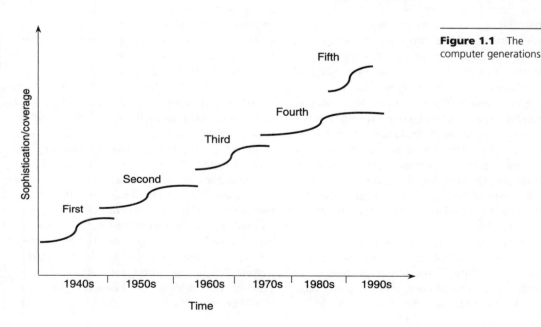

Figure 1.1   The computer generations

operated without malfunction, special environmental conditions were required, as well as expensive specialist knowledge and maintenance skills. The first ever stored program computer, BABY, was completed in 1948, and ran its first program in June of that year. This machine had a limited memory of 128 bytes, weighed one ton, was over 16 feet long and required over 3500 watts of electricity to power it.[2]

The invention of the transistor in 1948 allowed the speed of these early computers such as BABY to be significantly increased. More importantly, with the transistor came reliability, smaller size and lower cost. This improvement in the price–performance ratio – more power for less money – made these devices more affordable, whilst at the same time more practical for meeting organizational needs. They also made it easier for organizations to consider the replacement of manual systems. This transistorization of computers has been labelled the second generation of computers.

The third generation of computer technology was heralded by the development of the integrated circuit board in the mid-1960s. Additional gains in performance were realized with a further improvement in the price–performance ratio. The integrated circuit board made it possible to simplify the construction of the computer and, in doing so, made it more reliable and easier to repair. The size and speed of the computer's core memory was also enhanced, making the processing of data faster. The increase in capacity and efficiency allowed the hardware developers to consider ways of making storage more accessible, resulting in the development of the magnetic disk. This combination of hardware performance improvements, plus advances in storage media encouraged the development of more sophisticated operating systems which in turn led to the rapid expansion of computer use within organizations.

It was however, the miniaturizing of electronics – resulting from the discovery in the 1950s of the semi-conducting properties of silicon – that allowed computers to make their most significant impact. The mini computers of

the mid-1960s to the early 1970s had all the advantages of their larger mainframe cousins, but at a fraction of the price. They were also smaller, faster, more powerful and more reliable.

The technological developments associated with the electronics industry continued well into the 1970s and 1980s with the development of the large-scale integrated circuit – a small chip that contained thousands of miniature electrical components. These micro-computers were lightweight, powerful, cheap, portable and widely applicable within organizations, and particularly suited to office automation. So began the fourth generation of computing.

Despite the emergence of the personal computer and associated desktop applications, the 1980s also saw the continued dominance of the large centralized information systems driven by the need to process vast quantities of corporate data. This was especially the case within the financial services sector, which was at this stage, and arguably still is, the most IT-dependent sector.

Towards the end of the 1980s, ever-more powerful mini and personal computers, together with workstations, began to emerge and provide greater capability to distribute powerful computer technology throughout the organization. Continued advances in both power and miniaturization have produced even smaller, more powerful devices including the laptop, the pen-based and the notebook computer, all of which are now being marketed with an ever increasing range of facilities and functions. Such devices have high-speed chips, large memory capacities and are cheap, making entry-level computing highly attractive to all organizations.

In October 1981, Japan's Ministry of International Trade and Industry (MITI) sponsored a conference to announce the Fifth Generation Project. The Japanese believed that the next, fifth, generation of computer technology would revolutionize the computer industry and society in general. The philosophy behind the project was that a radical departure from traditional computer systems was possible. The systems which the Japanese proposed would be more like the humans that used them, in so far as they would be able to associate, make inferences and navigate through masses of information and data. The main aim of the Japanese initiative was therefore to design and develop computer hardware and software for knowledge engineering that could be used for a whole range of applications. Underlying this initiative was a belief that there was to be a shift from data processing to the intelligent processing of knowledge, with artificial intelligence forming the backbone. The ultimate goal of the project was to create, by the early 1990s, a super artificial intelligence computer capable of processing up to a billion logical inferences per second, with a massive knowledge base. This failed to materialize partly because of the lack of interest in artificial intelligence at that time, but also because of over-ambitious timescales and technical problems. Despite the results of the Fifth Generation project being somewhat disappointing, the march of technology continues, and there are those that still hold on to the belief that the age of the smart machine is still possible, and that one day technologists will be able to create artificial intelligence. Indeed, some futurologists predict by the year 2019, $1000 worth of computing power will have the computational abilities of one human brain, by 2029, this will have increased to 1000 human brains, and by 2060 to the collective brains of the entire human race. Perhaps artificial intelligence is not that far away.[3]

Further advances in computer technology are driven by the software companies, who, in attempting to remain competitive, have had to develop newer, faster and more widely applicable products, which are no longer restricted to automating existing business processes. Today, such products are more integrated, provide intuitive graphical interfaces, run on client/server and enterprise-wide architectures, and are more widely available in package form. In addition, the advent of the Internet and e-commerce is having a profound effect on the way technology is applied within organizations. It is therefore fair to assert that this technological change will continue pretty much unabated, especially if we are to believe the many books and articles on the subject of continuous technology-based change. Indeed, only very recently, an article appeared in the United Kingdom's *Computer Weekly* that heralded the end of the silicon chip. The article highlighted research being conducted by the University of California which had demonstrated that it is possible to replicate the silicon chip molecularly. The scientists believe that this will allow computers to be 100 billion times more efficient than those currently available – within only ten years.[4]

Returning to BABY for one moment, comparing this machine to modern-day equipment makes for an interesting comparison. The microchip on which the modern computer depends is 25 million times more powerful, and has 64 million times more memory, than BABY. Clearly, the last fifty years have seen incredible advances in power, reliability and price, and it would be reasonable to expect the next fifty to see much the same.

But, with such improvements, why do we see so many projects falter and fail? It would seem the problem does not just lie in the technology itself, but more in how it is applied.

ORGANIZATION: A DIFFICULT INTEGRATION

Initial developments within information technology largely concentrated on the underlying hardware, and were largely laboratory based. Such work took little account of the organizational effect of technological change and innovation. However, once technology had advanced far enough to become useful, organizations were quick to latch on to its possible applications. Unlike the laboratory, where the technology was used in isolation, the introduction into the wider organization proved to be far more problematical.

Very few commercial IT applications existed prior to the 1950s. Those that did tended to be used by the mathematician or researcher who were more concerned with the number-crunching abilities of the machines than anything else. The earliest applications of computers within organizations tended to concentrate on formalized and repetitive tasks, such as payroll and accounting. Automating such tasks was attractive primarily because of the advantages associated with the economies of scale. As this coincided with the first and second generations of computing previously described, the expensive nature of the systems meant that organizations had to focus their attention on those limited number of areas that lended themselves well to automation, and hence were easy to justify the enormous costs.

As the principal repetitive tasks lay within the finance division of the organization, it was the natural place to start automating the business, allowing the business to gain valuable experience and expertise within computing and systems development. At that time, the expense of establishing and operating these new systems prevented other departments from purchasing and developing their own – they had to rely on the finance division's expertise to develop systems for them. And, because Finance controlled all the systems and their associated development activities, this made it difficult for other functions to gain the level of service they required. This meant that a significant percentage of the organization was unable to exploit information technology to the degree they wanted.

In order to diffuse the problem, many organizations decentralized their computing facilities. Unfortunately, this caused more problems than it cured, as it encouraged the proliferation of expensive hardware in areas where computing experience was very limited. It also resulted in the fragmentation of the systems portfolio, and in the duplication of corporate data. As a reaction to this, a centralized data processing unit was established that reported directly to senior management. This unit was designed to provide all departments with an effective, centralized approach to meeting organizational computing needs.

During the late 1960s and early 1970s, the development of new operating systems and programming languages resulted in more reliable systems, which, in turn, resulted in a greater demand for systems from the users. By the late 1960s, most companies had acquired a large mainframe computer. This was not without its problems: although businesses sought to establish the merits of introducing information systems based on hard financial measures, using headcount reductions as their favourite tool, these merits rarely materialized. Organizations were clearly immature at managing the benefits realization process, and any savings that materialized were largely offset by the increasing costs of managing the systems portfolio, as more expert staff and an increasing proportion of activity focused on maintaining the existing systems.aging the systems portfolio, as more expert staff and an increasing proportion of activity focused on maintaining the existing systems.stems portfolio, more expert staff and an increasing proportion of activity focused on maintaining the existing systemsnifested themselves in an increased dissatisfaction with the centralized data processing department and in the way in which systems were being developed. To tackle this, new development methodologies and engineering approaches were adopted to ensure systems were delivered successfully.

By the early 1970s, the mini-computer was becoming more widespread throughout the organization and was effectively superseding the mainframe as the main hardware platform. These were more versatile, required less demanding environmental conditions, and were cheaper than their mainframe equivalent. Furthermore, they had the major advantage of dealing with on-line applications and required fewer professional staff to operate and maintain them. The lower hardware costs meant that smaller user departments were able to purchase their own computers without going over their local budgets. This allowed them to circumvent the internal data processing department's procurement process, and hence create an invisible wave of IT investment.

Further advances in technology during the 1970s and early 1980s, particularly the database, led to a new emphasis on data and information, especially corporate. This was believed to allow universal access, and more importantly, remove the inconsistencies caused by the duplication of data rife within most organizations at that time.

In principle, all functions would have access to information belonging to the whole organization, but this global provision of management information failed to materialize. There were a number of reasons for this failure, but it was principally because of the difficulty in modelling the business: with a constantly changing organization, it was impossible to stabilize the data model long enough to create the stable information systems to go with it. This problem was compounded by similar problems with external data.

At about this time, organizations were considering how to integrate their existing IT infrastructure in order to leverage their information needs. This system integration activity resulted in the linking of corporate information systems through networks, databases and associated feeder/receiver systems, and provided clear advantages, not least in data and information access. But again there were some unforeseen problems, this time associated with increased complexity, and the impact of minor changes made in one system on another, usually unrelated to the first. In extreme cases, this could lead to the failure of one system because of a seemingly innocuous change in another. Such systemic impacts were difficult to locate and correct, and put a premium on excellent documentation and testing, something that was notoriously poor.

During the mid to late 1980s, as the importance and dependence on IT increased, the board of directors became worried and very conscious of having to rely on IT specialists. To address this, they appointed a manager to look after IT, and, in the majority of cases, they appointed this manager to the board. Although the appointment of an IT director, or chief information officer, was seen as a strategic move by the chief executive, there appeared to be a problem with the acceptance of a technologist by the rest of the board. Expected to integrate IT with the corporate objectives, many of these early IT directors fell short because they were typically excluded from many strategic discussions, and were rarely involved with setting the direction of the business. In addition, because the majority of these directors came through the traditional IT career route, they retained some of their fundamental beliefs about IT: instead of broadening IT into the mainstream business arena, they concentrated on the operational aspects of managing a major IT function. This culture gap between the business and IT executives at the highest levels was symptomatic of the underlying problem that IT was experiencing with the rest of the organization.

As the 1980s gave way to the 1990s and beyond, the level of IT investment within companies continued to increase, for example, from 1.8 per cent to 2.75 per cent of turnover between 1993 and 1998.[5] As well as installing a personal computer on every employee's desktop, organizations found they were having to invest in massive enterprise-wide systems. Such systems were (and still are) very complex and costly to implement, but without them, organizations felt they were unable to maintain their competitive edge, or even operational efficiency.

IT AND THE BUSINESS – THE CULTURE GAP IS BORN

THE IT DEVELOPER

Up until the early 1960s, the information systems developer had to be a technical expert, either in systems or applications programming. This was primarily due to the unsophisticated programming languages available at that time. But even when computing graduated from the research office into the organization, these practitioners still required an in-depth knowledge of how the underlying hardware operated. Furthermore, the techniques and tools available to them were very limited, and required a high degree of technical know-how to use them. There was little need, or even time, for these specialists to acquire business knowledge.

It was during the early 1960s that practitioners started to develop their own theoretical base for their work. The different activities that made up the process of systems development gained recognition and the discipline of systems analysis emerged as a key activity. In terms of hardware improvements, the main emphasis lay in making the operations closely associated with the computer as efficient as possible. At the same time, the creation of new programming languages and specialized operating systems greatly enhanced development practices.

With the advent of the mini-computer, and the subsequent increase in demand for more systems, project management techniques were introduced to cope with the higher workload that was generated. Projects at that time were suffering from the problem of frozen specifications which, together with the formalized approach to the development and maintenance of the systems, led to them being large and unmanageable – usually resulting in their late delivery at higher cost, and often failing to meet their requirements.

By the late 1960s, the problems associated with large system developments came to a head, culminating in the 1968 NATO Conference on the Software Crisis. Although this conference led to the adoption of engineering techniques for the software development process, one other concern associated with large systems remained – maintainability. This was difficult because most large programs had no apparent control structure: programs often appeared as a single block of code, the program and system logic were unpredictable, and poor or non-existent system and program documentation made the systems almost unmaintainable. Even if documentation did exist, it was generally out of date, thereby making it almost worthless.

At about this time, researchers were beginning to develop concepts and methods that were designed to reduce program complexity. They argued that the only way to deal with complex systems was to operate on the basis of functional decomposition – the division of the complete problem into a series of smaller units. As a result, new programming languages and techniques were developed, including structured programming. At this stage, the practitioner was still highly technical and paid little attention to the organization or the user. It was not until the user gained sufficient knowledge and insight into the capabilities of the technology that this would change. This

occurred during the boom at the end of the third generation of computing, especially in desktop technologies, which severely eroded the IT professional's monopoly on IT skills. Moreover, dissatisfaction with the information systems that were developed led the users to carry out the development process themselves. This resulted in a change of emphasis for the practitioner from one of analyst and designer, to one of adviser and supporter.

This process seemed to continue well into the early 1990s with the general commercialization of the internal IT department resulting from the emergence of outsourcing. There was a general recognition that to survive, software professionals had to become more user focused, and take a greater interest in the business. Indeed, developers even started to wear suits! However, more recently, the profession appears to have regressed into the technophile image once again, with more emphasis on the purity of language (for example, Java), and focus on technologies, such as enterprise resource planning (ERP), the Internet, intranets, extranets and so on. The gulf between the developers and users seems to be as big as ever.

THE BUSINESS USER

The end user of the 1950s was, as with the IT professional, an expert in computing. It was not only sufficient to understand the domain in which they were working, but they also had to understand the technology. With the development of new techniques, tools, programming and operating systems, together with the increasing power and improvements in the price–performance ratio, there was a greater use of computers within organizations by non-experts. As a result, end users were no longer required to understand the technology, as the packages they used removed them from the operating system by way of the interface.

The proliferation of computers and the perception that they could be used for almost any purpose led to increasing demands from the user community for more and more systems. The mushrooming of requirements overloaded the IT department, who were increasingly spending a larger proportion of their time maintaining existing systems. This, in turn, led to the end user becoming more and more dissatisfied with the lack of service and poor response.

Subsequently, there was an increasing backlog of systems development work that, when developed, often failed to meet the original user requirements, was delivered late, and was often substantially over budget. Furthermore, claims from the user community that the IT departments were incapable of developing systems to meet their business needs resulted in them taking the development into their own hands. These problems, coupled with the more favourable cost of computing power, led to the phenomenon of end-user computing. This term refers to the development or coding of information systems by the user or non-IT professional. End-user computing, which began in the mid-1980s, has increased substantially, so that it is now a significant proportion of an organization's information technology budget.

The perceived benefits of this shift to end-user computing were many-fold. For example, by developing their systems themselves, users were able to reduce the systems development backlog, thereby releasing the centralized IT department to take up other outstanding projects. Users also believed that better systems were ultimately produced because they, as users, were able to understand their requirements far better than anyone else – there was no gap in the business knowledge, so often encountered with the centralized IT department's approach. Users believed they could develop systems faster, although this was often achieved through the avoidance of the IT department's standards and procedures. They also believed that training improved, because they were training their fellow users with the same background and experience. However, users often cited these benefits without fully comprehending the wider issues that were equally important in meeting not only their needs, but more critically, the needs of the organization.

The proliferation of computers, software and systems within end-user communities soon became a major problem. Without an overall strategy within which new equipment could be procured and new systems developed, there was a duplication of hardware, software and data. Such duplication had serious implications for the organization, and not just in terms of cost. For example, it was possible to bombard the same customer with identical marketing and sales literature because similar data would be held in multiple – and often localized – databases. More importantly, this data was often out of date and inaccurate. Furthermore, the approach to development that avoided the IT department's standards and procedures often resulted in poorly engineered systems that were also difficult to maintain. This defeated the objective of bypassing the IT department in that these systems were often incapable of meeting their business objectives. No change there.

The information systems development backlog is unlikely to disappear in the short term, and if anything, it is likely to increase, because user departments lack the skills of the IT practitioner, especially when dealing with large and complex system implementation/ integration projects. With skill shortages increasing, and demand for IT growing, organizations need to become smarter in the way they invest in IT. But, with the continued advance of IT, there are two opposing forces that will make this difficult to achieve. On the one hand, the increasing sophistication of information systems means the end user is gradually removed from the minutiae of the business in which they work. This makes it much harder for them to articulate their business requirements, which in turn adds an additional overhead to the already problematical process of requirements gathering and specification. On the other hand, with the availability of an increasing number of packaged-based solutions, end users feel empowered and confident that they can manage their business using these desktop solutions without any help from IT. However, integrating these desktop solutions within the wider systems environment is something the end user cannot achieve alone, and with an increasing trend towards large enterprise-wide systems, they must still depend on IT to develop them.

This leads to additional tensions between business and IT, and makes the issue of value for money all the more pressing.

Before we leave the end-users' experience of the last 40 years, it is worth highlighting some recent research that has investigated the costs of end-user computing. Remembering that the case for end-user computing rested on, amongst others, the lower costs when compared to the expense of developing, rolling out and maintaining information systems by the centralized IT department, it should come as some surprise to discover just how expensive end-user computing is. Until recently, the true cost of end-user computing was difficult to ascertain, because, unlike the IT department, who operate under a specific technology budget, the end user does not, and is therefore able to hide the majority of their costs under their own non-IT budgets. This recent research suggests the true annual cost of personal computers – that is, end-user computing – when taking into consideration the hidden support provided by fellow users, is in the region of $23 500.[6]

SOME OBSERVATIONS AND CONCERNS

This historical perspective allows us to make some useful observations about how IT has evolved and, more importantly, draw out some key conclusions that underpin some, but not all, of the issues which are faced by the organization today.

HIGH AND INCREASING LEVELS OF IT DEPENDENCY

An organization's association with IT typically passes through four common and distinct stages (see Figure 1.2).[7] Initially, IT is restricted to limited, and potentially isolated parts of the organization. Once it has proved itself of value, other parts of the organization begin to realize its capabilities and start to invest heavily. It is this contagion phase that leads to a significant uplift in the application of IT across the organization, and, in particular, dependence upon it.

After contagion comes growth, which typically means the organization's dependence on IT is such that it cannot function effectively without it – what I term the 'dependency threshold'. The natural end point of an organization's experience with IT, is maturity. At this stage the organization has learnt to live with its IT dependency and has created the appropriate controls, processes and techniques to manage it. For those familiar with the Capability Maturity Model, which is usually aligned with software quality management, this could be considered Level Five of the five-step

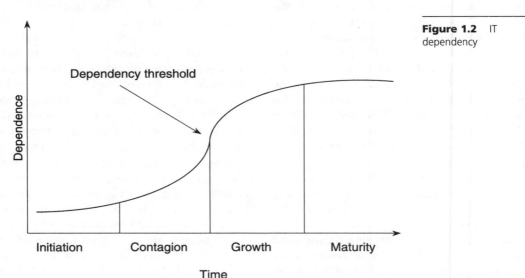

Figure 1.2　IT dependency

model. However, after forty years, many organizations remain at the contagion and growth phases, with very few reaching maturity. This reflects the experience of those organizations that have benchmarked themselves against the Capability Maturity Model: very few have reached Level Five, with most at Levels One and Two which represents an immature and inconsistent approach to software development.[8] Of course, for those organizations experiencing late growth in IT, there should be some advantage from being in a position to learn from the mistakes of others. Late growth also has the added advantage of allowing software development to be based upon the latest techniques. Whether this is true may be in some doubt given the general level of software problems, but countries such as India have been able to reach a degree of maturity not currently achieved in either the United States or the United Kingdom.[9]

The take-off and explosion of the application of IT within organizations was achieved through the miniaturization associated with the personal computer, during the third generation of computing. This facilitated the drive towards the widespread computerization of work commonly known as office automation, and to a major increase in both investment and dependence (see Figure 1.3). Moreover, with the standardization of operating environments through the efforts of companies such as Microsoft, software suppliers have been able to develop increasingly useful packages that can be run from the desktop.

THE BUSINESS–IT CULTURE GAP

Even at the outset, IT staff were treated differently from the rest of the business. There was a certain degree of mysticism that surrounded the technologists, who were able to tinker with the technology and craft it into something useful for the organization. As IT spread out from the finance division, this attitude of treating IT staff differently from others continued. Despite the introduction of the IT director/chief information officer, the problems of integrating the IT professional into the business remain. Euphemistically known as the 'culture gap', or 'disconnect', it is a major concern for most organizations who depend upon IT for their operational and competitive survival. Organizations have learnt to live with other professionals, such as lawyers, and accountants, but after forty years are still experiencing problems with integrating their IT brethren. There is, therefore, a tripartite problem between

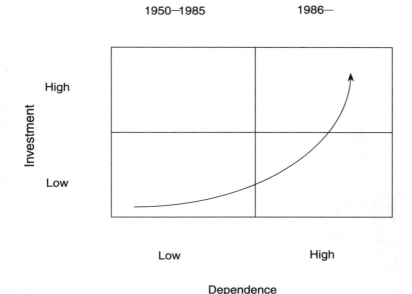

1950–1985   1986—

Figure 1.3 Take-off

the IT professional, the business user and the chief executive (see Figure 1.4).

THE BELIEF THAT PROBLEMS ARE ONLY SOLVED BY TECHNOLOGY

The problems associated with the application of IT, and in particular information systems projects, tend to manifest themselves within the technical domain. Therefore, it would seem reasonable that the resolution of these problems should also reside within the technical domain. Indeed, this is where the majority of the advice has been directed over the last forty years. However, it is a combination of technology, human behaviour and organizational factors that must be addressed if we are to truly resolve the problems with information systems projects (see Figure 1.5). This is so because of the need to recognize that IT is so ubiquitous and embedded within the modern enterprise that it impacts the behaviour of the staff, as well as the operation and management of the organization as a whole.

INFORMATION AS A SOURCE OF POWER

As the importance of the computer grew, and the appetite for more applications increased during the third and fourth generations of computing, organizations recognized the importance and value of information. As managers, and in particular middle managers, realized that information was a new source of power, problems of ownership and control of information started to materialize. Such problems have increased with the impacts of downsizing and the greater emphasis on knowledge, which is itself a major source of power in the modern-day corporation. As a result, a new phenomenon has started to appear known as information politics, where information is used for political advantage. Although somewhat innocuous, information politics can lead to significant problems within the organization, especially during the development of large information systems.

So what has history taught us? I believe the following:

- The failure of information systems projects cannot be attributed only to the general lack of project management disciplines.
- IT has, and will continue to dominate business agendas, especially in relation to the problems it seems to cause.
- The culture gap between business and IT professionals has deep historical roots, and hence cannot be resolved superficially.
- Organizations have been addressing the problems with IT and information systems projects from the wrong perspective.

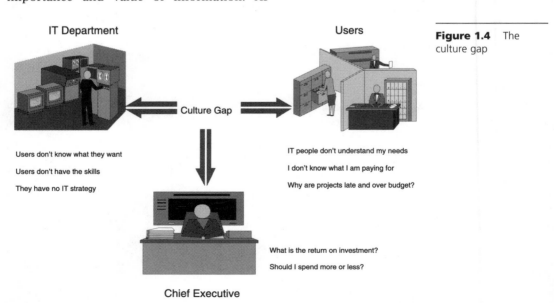

IT Department   Users

Figure 1.4 The culture gap

Culture Gap

Users don't know what they want

Users don't have the skills

They have no IT strategy

IT people don't understand my needs

I don't know what I am paying for

Why are projects late and over budget?

What is the return on investment?

Should I spend more or less?

Chief Executive

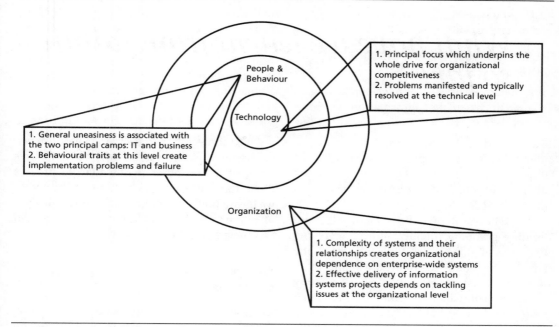

Figure 1.5 Problem domain

- Technology has enabled the adage 'information is power' to be taken to its logical extreme.

History can therefore provide organizations with an important insight into the problems we face today. But history on its own does not allow us to understand the full extent of why information system projects fail. We need one other perspective that will allow us to develop the complete understanding on which we can then develop the complete solution. We need to discover what we have learnt from failure thus far.

CHAPTER TWO

What have we learnt from failure so far?

As suggested at the end of the last chapter, in order to derive a complete understanding of failure we need to take one additional perspective: what we have learnt from the failures of the last forty years.

The failures depicted in Figure 2.1 are attention-grabbing, major failures, involving huge sums of money, and sufficiently traumatic to make the news. Yet there are many more information systems projects that fail, costing companies comparatively similar sums. Such failures tend to be hidden from view because organizations are naturally concerned about the effects that bad publicity generated by a major failure might have on their reputation and share price. It is a sad fact that very few organizations seem willing, or perhaps able, to understand why their project(s) fail, either blaming, sacking, ignoring, or hiding all evidence, thereby allowing them to repeat the same mistakes in the next project. It is in everyone's best interest to attempt to understand why such failures occur, if for no other reason than to prevent them from happening in the future. Fortunately, we have a pretty clear understanding of the level of failure from the many surveys that have been conducted over the last forty years.

FAILURE IS MORE FREQUENT THAN YOU THINK

In 1958, in the very first issue of *Computer Journal*, there was an article on information system project failure,[1] in which the author argued that the only viable way of tackling the problem was to automate the entire development process. Clearly, this was difficult to achieve then, and just as difficult now. A decade later there followed collective discussion on failure at the 1968 North Atlantic Treaty

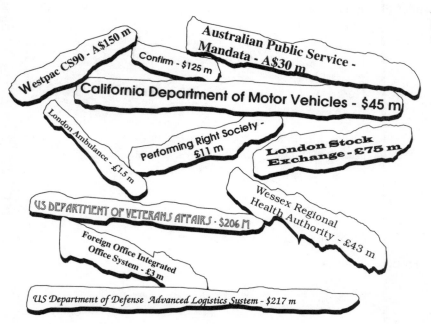

Figure 2.1 The price of failure

Westpac CS90 - A$150 m

Confirm - $125 m

Australian Public Service - Mandata - A$30 m

California Department of Motor Vehicles - $45 m

London Ambulance - £1.5 m

Performing Right Society - £11 m

London Stock Exchange - £75 m

US DEPARTMENT OF VETERANS AFFAIRS - $206 M

Wessex Regional Health Authority - £43 m

Foreign Office Integrated Office System - £3 m

US Department of Defense Advanced Logistics System - $217 m

Organization (NATO) conference on software engineering. Even then, system development projects were characterized by major delays, cost overruns and operational problems ranging from persistent bugs through to complete disasters.

But what of the last twenty years? The following surveys demonstrate that the commonality of failure continues:

- In 1982, Tom DeMarco suggested that only 15 per cent of information systems projects ever delivered anything useful and overruns of 200 per cent were typical.[2]
- In 1982, a United States survey discovered that 75 per cent of all systems development undertaken was either never completed, or never used if it was.[3]
- In 1988, a survey of its 600 largest clients by Peat Marwick Mitchell & Co. in the United States showed that 35 per cent admitted to their information systems projects spiralling out of control.[4]
- A 1994 report from Pagoda suggested that a 50 per cent failure rate was the norm within the European Union and 89 per cent was the norm in the United Kingdom.[5]
- In 1995, the Standish Group in the United States found that only 16 per cent of information systems projects were considered successful. Some 31 per cent were total failures and the remaining 53 per cent were late, significantly over budget and delivered much less than was originally expected. They concluded that in 1995 alone this level of failure equated to $81 billion in failed projects and $59 billion in cost overruns.[6]
- A 1996 survey conducted by Sheffield University in the United Kingdom found that 80–90 per cent of IT investments fail to meet their performance goals, and about 80 per cent are delivered late and over budget. Just 10–20 per cent meet all their success criteria.[7]
- A 1996 follow-up survey by the Standish Group found that Fortune 100 companies cancelled 33 out of every 100 software projects, and ran over budget or beyond the deadline on another 40. The failures alone equated to $45 billion in lost investment.[8]
- In 1998, Capers Jones stated that almost two-thirds of IT projects were delivered late and over budget.[9]

This collection of commentaries and surveys paints a worrying picture of a lack of success in delivering information systems projects. But how can this seemingly persistent problem be resolved?

WHAT HAVE WE BEEN TOLD SO FAR?

The key motivator for understanding why projects fail must be the increasing dependence on IT. One of the paradoxes with IT is that although designed to make the organization work and compete more effectively, to do so requires an increasingly complex web of technology. Such complexity means that it is harder to develop simple, stand-alone centralized systems, which were common in the 1950s, 1960s, and 1970s. Instead, the voracious appetite for information, the impacts of the globalization of business, and the need to react as quickly as possible to external and internal business events, necessitates complex information systems. Even if not complex in their own right, they are typically part of a complex web of feeder and receiver systems, making the introduction of new systems potentially more risky than they would otherwise be. Therefore, with the increasing reliance on IT to provide organizational longevity comes complexity, and with this, large corporate-wide information system projects with an increased likelihood of failure.

Clearly, with many project failures reaching the headlines, and chief executives concerned about their ability to control information systems projects, there has been a drive to understand why they are prone to failure. As well as the academic community, consultancies, professional bodies such as the United States Project Management Institute and the United Kingdom's British Computer Society, governments and IT service organizations have been actively involved in trying to improve the delivery of large-scale information systems projects.

The outcome of all this interest has been a plethora of surveys, books and papers, together with government and professionally sponsored advice describing the best way of tackling the problems.[10] Such data is of course invaluable, as it allows some of the common causes of project failure to be distilled into a series of actions and hot spots that must be attended to if the project is to be a success. Here are the most commonly cited reasons for project failure:

- insufficient user involvement
- lack of senior management/executive support
- ambiguous requirements – either poorly articulated, poorly captured, or just incomplete
- poor up-front planning
- planning to catch up
- unrealistic expectations
- no project ownership
- unclear, unambiguous objectives, vision and goals
- incompetent staff
- unrealistic project expectations
- inappropriate, or non-existent risk management
- severely compressed schedules – either imposed, or overly optimistic
- poor communication
- inappropriate productivity expectations
- generally poor project management
- concentration on the technological issues at the expense of the organizational.

In identifying these common factors, professional organizations, consultancies and government bodies have attempted to identify the actions required to correct them. Some have come up with statements that are nothing more than motherhoods – providing little in the way of practical advice, instead tending to merely reflect the particular problem back as an obvious statement. Typical of such statements include 'Ensure the users are involved' (one could ask how?), and 'Ensure the requirements are fully captured and signed off by the business community' (again, if they don't want to sign

them off, or feel they are inappropriate, what is one to do?). Others have developed methods, tools and models for managing a specific aspect of an information system project, such as requirements analysis. The danger here is that effort is directed at one small component of a much wider problem, and can lead to the silver bullet syndrome – the belief that the entire project's life cycle can be improved through the adoption of a single method, model or tool. Others still have developed and introduced new methods and tools, such as Computer Aided Software Engineering, Total Quality Management and Rapid Application Development to tackle the perceived, and actual, productivity and quality problems with IT. Then there are those that believe it is all about project management, and one cannot blame them: if you were to run down the list of common causes of failure above, it soon becomes apparent that most, if not all, fall under the umbrella of project management.

Further advice associated with critical success factors has been provided by other commentators. For example, the factors highlighted below are the result of one particular study and are considered fundamental to the successful delivery of any information system project:[11]

- Project mission – The mission (or objective) of the project should be clear, unambiguous, and regularly communicated to all project stakeholders.
- Top management support – The continuous support of senior executives during the life of the project is a vital ingredient if it is to succeed.
- Planning – Proper planning is always a prerequisite for successful project delivery. The military, with whom I used to work, favoured the phrase 'planning and preparation prevents piss poor performance' – how very true!
- Client consultation – It is essential to actively involve the users and all other key stakeholders throughout the project.
- Personnel – ensure the appropriate use of competent expert resources (both IT and business).

- Technical tasks – The correct functioning of the technology itself, together with the technical work required, makes it effective from a systems perspective.
- Client acceptance – The creation of the initial reception strategy for the project, as well as working with the ultimate users/client of the system ensures ultimate acceptance.
- Monitoring and feedback – Maintain a view of progress, and take the appropriate action when progress is at variance with the plan.
- Communication – Continuous communication with the principal stakeholders ensures that they are fully aligned with the project, and remain so as the project progresses.
- Troubleshooting – Expect to deal with the unexpected – after all, you cannot plan for everything.

Such advice is principally geared toward the management of a project, and would make sense to any professional project manager. Moreover, any chief executive would expect all of their project managers – or those employed externally – to perform these tasks, as a matter of course.

But why, with all this advice available, are information systems projects so prone to failure and slippage? Surely, if project managers followed all of the advice available they would be successful? Indeed, it is fair to say that if project managers followed all the advice showered on them then they would, without a doubt, have a significant impact on the outcome of the project. However, there are some additional elements to an information systems project that I believe cannot be fully managed by, or through, project management alone.

WHAT ELSE SHOULD WE CONSIDER?

What is it, therefore, that makes information systems projects so difficult to manage? Some of the difficulty lies within the information system project itself, in that there are significant differences between this and say, an engineering project (see Table 2.1).

From a simple comparison with engineering projects, it is possible to understand some of the problems with information system projects. But there is more. One of the results of the increasing complexity of IT and its ubiquitous presence in organizations is a trend towards large projects. It is no longer possible to tackle organizational change in a piecemeal fashion – the market is too unforgiving. Also, with increasing inter-system dependencies, changes within one part of the existing information systems infrastructure can lead to problems elsewhere. Thus organizations find that they must tackle change organizationally and holistically rather than functionally, and often with a critical IT component. This can create problems, as the following three examples illustrate.

THE LONDON AMBULANCE SERVICE

In the 1980s, the London Ambulance Service (LAS), like the rest of the National Health Service, was undergoing major change. The LAS decided that a radical and fast-moving agenda of change was necessary and key to this was to be a state-of-the-art computer-aided despatch system. A previous system, costing £7.5 million, was abandoned in 1990 after tests found that it could not cope with the demands that were likely to be made on it. Work on a new system began in the autumn of 1990, and it was recognized that this system would be a first, as no other emergency service in the United Kingdom had ever attempted such a major implementation. The LAS planned to make a quantum leap in the use of technology and it was clear from its dramatic failure on 4 November 1992 that this was a high-risk venture. Because of the public nature of the failure, a thorough analysis of the entire project was made by an inquiry team, which completed its investigations and published its report in February 1993.[12]

At the time of the procurement recommendation, references were sought for the third-party software supplier from their existing customers. These were very favourable as far as the technical quality of their work was concerned, but one reference expressed grave reservations regarding the company's ability to

Table 2.1   Comparisons between engineering and information systems projects

Aspect	Engineering Project	Information Systems Project
Physical intuition	Engineering projects by their very nature are physical, that is, they can be seen and touched, and most people have some basic knowledge of how they are executed. Therefore, if an engineer suggested it was a good idea to build a major road-bridge out of light wood, glass and plastic, they would be accused of stupidity because we know it would not be able to bear any significant load.	Software projects suffer from a lack of physical intuition. Software is typically hidden from view, cannot be touched, and most people do not have sufficient knowledge of how software projects are executed. Therefore, if a software engineer suggested it would be a great idea to build a new enterprise-wide system out of a mix of Java, client-server, UNIX, a tailored off-the-shelf package, with a touch of artificial intelligence and middleware, it might appear acceptable because, in general, we would not have any feel for its viability.
Stability of technology and techniques	Engineering has a long and stable past, partly because it exists in the physical world, and partly because it is designed to tackle physical problems. Such problems have remained constant over a long period of time. As a result, the technology required to execute an engineering project has changed little. With a stable technological base, the techniques used to execute engineering projects have also remained stable. They have also benefited from a gradual improvement and optimization. Engineering projects can also be considered to be consistent, as with a stable technology base and strong processes, most are executed using the same processes, tools and techniques.	Software is rooted in the intellectual and business domain, is very young compared to the engineering discipline, and is subject to a faster rate of change; the business world changes much faster than the physical. Therefore, rather than an incremental improvement in technology, software is subject to significant change. Moreover, in attempting to meet the requirements of a rapidly changing business environment, it has little choice but to change significantly. As a result, the underlying techniques have also changed substantially. Despite adopting engineering disciplines to develop software, techniques still must change with the advances in technology, but also in order to meet the demands of the business cycle they are designed to support. Software is unlikely to stabilize to a sufficient degree to allow the improvements and optimization commonly associated with engineering. Indeed, just as techniques begin to stabilize, a new technology, tool, or approach is introduced that unavoidably requires changes to how software is developed and controlled.
Progress monitoring	Monitoring of an engineering project is not always simple, but the one advantage it has is visibility. Not only is it possible to see the project unfold before your eyes, but it is also possible to monitor productivity. Therefore, if a labourer is lying down on the job, it is obvious they are not working. Other advantages which result from the degree of stability of the engineering discipline include the ability to spot defects and the usually obvious nature of poor workmanship.	Monitoring a software project is not simple. Due to the lack of end-product visibility, it is impossible to tell whether the software will work when completed, whether it is progressing according to plan, what the number and severity of defects are, or what the quality of the end product is likely to be. In addition, it is difficult to gauge the productivity of software engineers, as this work requires a significant degree of thinking time. Therefore if someone is sitting inactive at a workstation it may not necessarily mean that the person is doing nothing; they may in fact be thinking about how to solve a problem.
Failure	Apart from the occasional major structural failure, such as that of the Tacoma Narrows suspension bridge in 1940, the severity and frequency of failure is quite low. When failure does occur, every effort is made to understand why, and then feed this understanding into future engineering practice. Lessons are actively learnt. This may be due to the physical nature of engineering projects, and the more visible nature of defects; it is obvious to the wider population.	The failure of software systems and projects is high. But when failure occurs, organizations seem unwilling to investigate why. Moreover, the profession lacks the maturity of process and discipline to provide the necessary learning and feedback mechanisms required to improve the delivery of software projects. This is partly due to the high rates of change which the software industry is exposed to, but also the fact that lessons are not actively learnt.

deliver on time. Although this should have set alarm bells ringing, LAS management failed to act. The LAS Board also chose to ignore advice provided by many external sources regarding the tight schedule and the high-risk nature of the project. Furthermore, Systems Options, the company supplying the major software components of the despatch system, had no previous experience of this type of undertaking and, in order to secure the bid, had significantly undercut their nearest rival. The LAS Board were misled by the project team over the experience of Systems Options and an external report in late 1990 which called for more finance and longer timescales was suppressed by project managers.

In addition to this, the LAS had a history of severe industrial relations problems between management and ambulance crews. As a result, consultation with the ambulance crews during system validation was avoided. There was also a mismatch between the three main stakeholders – that is, the management, the ambulance crews and the control room staff – which was never appropriately managed or resolved. The system had been described as being introduced in an atmosphere of mistrust by staff, which was exacerbated by a lack of system ownership.

Furthermore, because the LAS director was desperate to redeem his promise to improve the performance of the LAS through computerization, the go-live decision had been set in stone very early on. As a result, the project team did not show or discuss with the LAS Board the independent references of Systems Options or their ability to handle such a major project. Both of these conspired to allow the system to be implemented, despite having 81 known bugs/performance problems.

Another important factor was almost certainly the LAS culture of 'fear of failure' – senior management were continually under pressure to succeed. This may have put undue pressure on those directly involved with the system to ensure that it was implemented on time and to budget, and blinded them to some of the fundamental flaws and difficulties with the system.

Thus, when the failure did occur, it had dramatic consequences. Not only were ambulance crews sent to the wrong addresses, but there were significant delays to the attendance of some crews to critically ill patients. In addition, calls were lost in the system. Therefore, although in monetary terms, this failure is dwarfed by many of the others highlighted in Figure 2.1, its consequences were more severe because of the life-critical nature of the service the system was expected to support.

THE CONFIRM PROJECT

In 1988, a consortium comprising Hilton National Hotels, Marriott Hotels and Budget Rent-A-Car subcontracted a large-scale project to AMR Information Services (AMRIS), a subsidiary of American Airlines, whose previous experience of airline reservation systems had been successful, having developed the highly acclaimed SABRE system. In this project they were to develop a leading-edge, comprehensive travel industry reservation system. But the system was never fully built and, after experiencing substantial problems in testing, it was abandoned after three-and-a-half years at a cost of $125 million.[13] Apparently, the clients were misled into continuing a project that was plagued with problems in databases, decision support and integration technologies.

The project was originally split into two distinct phases; design and development, with the option to withdraw from the project (with a $1 million penalty) when the development plan was presented. Although the cost of the project had risen from $55 million to $72.6 million by the time the development plan had been completed, the consortium decided to continue, based on the expected returns. Almost without exception, deadlines were missed and phases rescheduled, yet the software developers remained convinced they would be able to claw back time and implement as planned.

During the summer of 1990, two members of the consortium expressed severe concerns that the project would not be able to deliver. Employees at the project office also estimated that CONFIRM would not be ready in time. They were instructed by management to change the dates to reflect the original plan. To that end, they declared one part of the development phase complete but refused to show any of the deliverables to the consortium. In October 1990, the developers admitted to being over one year behind schedule, but insisted they would be able to meet the original deadline.

Later, after the project had been re-planned, Marriott Hotels, one of the consortium, claimed that AMRIS forced employees to artificially change their timetable to reflect this new project plan and those that refused were either assigned to a new project or sacked. The price for the system had now reached $92 million. In October 1991, the AMRIS president resigned. Eventually, the project was terminated and the consortium and AMRIS ended up in court.

I will come back to the CONFIRM project in Chapter 7, where I will use it to illustrate how irrational behaviour can cause organizations to continue with a project even though all indications suggest it will fail.

WESTPAC'S CS90

When the Australian banking system was deregulated in 1984, the existing banks were forced to take a hard look at the way they did business, because deregulation meant the invasion of foreign banks. Deregulation also meant increased opportunities to compete both locally and globally, and Westpac saw information technology, and lots of it, as the weapon that would allow them to do so. Its high-profile entry into the electronic financial services sector was called Core Systems 90 (CS90), and, when it was publicly launched in August 1987, expectations were high. CS90 had an initial cost of around $A100 million and a completion date in the late 1980s, but in 1992, still two years from completion and $A50 million over budget, the project was terminated and 500 employees sacked. At its height the CS90 project involved 300 IT staff with a salary and overheads bill approaching $A1 million a month.[14]

CS90 was always a very ambitious project which had at its core a suite of five applications and a set of development tools. The idea was that the applications and the development tools would be proved in-house and then sold world-wide. From a technical perspective, CS90 was always feasible. Westpac had problems,

however, in adapting its corporate culture to the demands of CS90, and although the initial marketing of CS90 to staff went well, it was not sustained. At first, staff were enthusiastic about the potential benefits, but once the development staff started to delve into the costs of individual bank products, the relationship broke down because of politics and the feeding of incorrect data to the development staff by the user communities. The IT staff also had major problems in trying to simultaneously create an in-house system as well as a commercially viable product for which there was an obvious global market.

Westpac went into partnership with IBM, who supplied the hardware and design expertise for the project. Problems immediately arose because of the major differences in culture between the two organizations. Much of the problem stemmed from IBM's use of staff who were more familiar with defence projects and dealing with United States government departments. An additional problem occurred when IBM attempted to graft extremely rigid and complex system development requirements and processes to the CS90 project. Although such discipline was necessary for the defence industry, it was far too detailed and restrictive for the bank. The Westpac corporate environment was also intolerant of mistakes, so when the project went late and over budget, CS90 management were forced to hype the project's benefits to keep funds flowing until its eventual failure in 1992.

There is a belief that the CS90 project made two quite fundamental mistakes. The first was that it went public, thereby putting itself under the scrutiny of its own users, as well as its competitors. The second was that it did not, or could not, control the project tightly enough: the bank had allowed changes to the original specifications to be accepted when development was underway, there was an ongoing disagreement with the users, and they were experimenting with new IT techniques.

SOME FURTHER OBSERVATIONS AND CONCERNS WITH INFORMATION SYSTEMS PROJECTS

In analysing these cases, and taking into account the nature of large information systems projects, it is possible to draw out some additional areas of concern on top of those already outlined in Chapter 1, which will help to define the full extent of the problems with information systems projects:

● There still remains a certain degree of magic and artistry to good software development. This tends to be reinforced by the continuous flow of new technologies and programming languages. Arguably, software cannot be engineered because it is too dependent on the intellectual creativity of those that produce it. Therefore, despite more than 40 years of IT, organizations remain in awe of the abilities of the software engineer, and still find it difficult to integrate the IT professional into the organization. The integration of the software engineer into the organization is made more difficult through the general skills shortage coupled with their tendency to job-hop. There is also a tendency for software engineers to identify with their profession, rather than the organization in which they work, thus helping to reinforce the culture gap.

● Most, if not all, large-scale projects are at risk from over-commitment, as each of the cases illustrate. Although not unique to software projects, there is a greater risk of over-commitment because of the increasing dependency on IT and the difficulties in monitoring and controlling information systems projects. In many instances, there also tends to be the belief that the project must succeed, no matter what the cost, especially if significant costs and benefits are involved. The danger of becoming blind to the reality of an impending failure is therefore very real. Once this happens, the risk increases to the point where the project's only outcome is failure.

● When large projects fail, there is always an attempt to find out who was responsible, in order to recover some, if not all, project costs. Increasingly, and especially in the United States, this involves legal action – itself very expensive, but considering the enormity of the sums involved, often the only way to recover the wasted investment. Where public money is involved, some form of inquiry is usually held to determine what went wrong – it is, however, rare to result in legal action. Even within those projects that are executed without third-party involvement, a similar pattern emerges. In this case, users blame IT, and IT blames the users. The result is an impasse and a reinforcement of the culture gap. Accountability within the software profession seems to be severely lacking.

● As projects have become more complex, organizations, and those that offer advice on the effective management of software projects, have generated silver bullet solutions: new tools, approaches, and methods designed to put to rest once and for all the problems with software projects. As with management theory, organizations have desperately grasped these single-shot solutions to their IT problems. Some have opted for new, leading-edge technologies, others for new tools, and others still for detailed and prescriptive methods, rules and assessments. Yet, none seem capable of guaranteeing project success time after time. Naturally, some of this elusive search is associated with the irrational belief that the problem can be cured by a single approach, itself often fuelled by the IT industry and a poor understanding of what the issues are. One of the key problems with these single-shot solutions is that they are self-defeating: a few months after their introduction, they are often discarded because they fail to live up to the lofty expectations, and the organization seeks out the next one. Clearly, there is a need to understand fully the scale and dimensions of the problem before seeking solutions.

● Very few projects seem capable of

determining, and ultimately managing, the benefits which result from the introduction of a new information system. Some of this may come from the general lack of any active benefits management process within the project – but certainly not all. For example, although it seems that the percentage of failed projects has remained fairly static over the last three decades, the investment in IT has not. Therefore, the scale of the problem can be considered to be growing, not decreasing. This points to an organizational issue associated with how information projects are appraised and how their benefits are realized. If the billions wasted on information systems on an annual basis is to be reduced, the rate at which failure is reduced would have to be faster than the speed at which IT investment is growing. A significant challenge!

This chapter, along with Chapter 1, has allowed us to complete the picture of information systems project failure. From the dual perspective of history and what we have learnt so far from failure we can see that attempting to resolve the issue is neither simple, nor associated with a single solution. Therefore, how can organizations piece together the complexities and tackle the problem of failed, late and over-budget information systems projects? The answer lies in:

1. developing a model within which the identified problems can be interpreted and pieced together;
2. coupling solutions with the identified problems; and
3. solving all the problems together so that it is possible to optimize the project delivery process, and in doing so, make project success the norm rather than the exception.

We have now created enough understanding to develop the failure model, and hence both explore the issues in greater detail and develop approaches to resolve them.

CHAPTER THREE

Introducing the failure model

Given the importance of IT to the modern corporation, and considering the amount of problems there have been in trying to use IT effectively, there has been very little by way of advice to help the chief executive navigate through the difficulties that present themselves. Where advice has been available, it either tends to be inaccessible and too wrapped up in specialist methods and tools, or too narrow in its analysis. This leads to the adoption of inappropriate solutions that are impenetrable to all but one or two people in the organization, or the acceptance of an approach that only ever deals with a small, and often superficial, component of the problem. In both cases, the problems are not fully resolved and at the very best only provide temporary respite.

To resolve information systems project failure requires a much broader understanding of the problems that cause it to happen, as it is only from such a broad base that a more comprehensive solution can be derived. The model in Figure 3.1 brings together the six concerns raised within Chapters 1 and 2:

● the issue of high investment but low return
● the problem of the culture gap between business and IT
● the difficulties presented by information politics
● the dangers of over-committing to information systems projects
● the lack of accountability for failure and poor software
● the acceptance of catch-all solutions to the problems of information systems projects.

For completeness, the model includes project management, because the success of any information systems project depends on having solid project management skills applied throughout its execution.

The model of Figure 3.1 is deliberately jumbled, in so far as each piece of the jigsaw is disconnected from the rest. This is because until

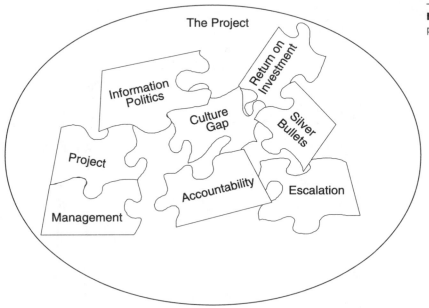

Figure 3.1 The project components

such time each piece is fully described and understood, it is impossible to piece them together to form the basis of their optimization.

Resolving information systems project failure is a three-step process: Step 1 involves understanding the problem, Step 2 requires individual solutions to the problems to be identified, and Step 3 involves bringing the individual problems together and solving them collectively to optimize the delivery of information systems projects. The remainder of Part I of this book is designed to address Step 1:

- Chapter 4 looks at the conundrum of high investment but low return from IT and in doing so draws out some of the current problems associated with the appraisal of information systems projects, the difficulties of achieving the expected benefit returns, and issues associated with the poor productivity gains from the introduction of new systems.
- Chapter 5 reviews in detail the issue of the business–IT culture gap at board and working level, and examines its consequences on the organization and information systems projects.
- Chapter 6 examines the changing nature of power and politics in organizations, and in particular, the emergence and implications of information politics.

- Chapter 7 introduces the issues associated with over-commitment in large information systems projects, describes the underlying behavioural components, and details the consequences of escalation on the organization.
- Chapter 8 highlights the problem of accountability – or lack of it – associated with the failure of internal and third-party information systems projects and software in general.
- Chapter 9 describes the propensity to accept silver bullet solutions to complex problems, and outlines the consequences.

At the end of Part I the organization will be able to:

1. describe the problems that currently cause information systems projects to fail;
2. assess the relative impact of these issues on their own organization; and
3. have the understanding necessary to begin to develop solutions to these problems.

The prize of eliminating information systems project failure can only be achieved once the solutions to the problems have been identified and brought together into an approach that is capable of optimizing the delivery of information systems projects.

High investment but low return

One of the areas where organizations feel the immediacy of the problems with information systems projects is in the relationship between their costs and benefits: they are continually frustrated by the imbalance between this relationship, experiencing high costs, but low return. To understand the dynamics of this conundrum, organizations must:

- place their own IT spending in the context of the wider business community;
- be aware of the consequences of getting the costs and benefits out of balance;
- recognize the pitfalls of justifying information systems projects, especially when trying to justify benefits that are intangible, and hence which cannot be described by financial measures alone; and
- realize that there are many factors that conspire to prevent the benefit returns and productivity improvements from materializing, particularly when no effort is applied to ensuring they are achieved.

Once organizations understand the problems in both assessing project costs, and in realizing the benefits, they will be in a much better position to develop a solution that is able to make high costs, and low benefits, a thing of the past.

RISING INVESTMENT

There can be no doubt that the modern corporation is becoming more dependent upon IT: in 1998, the top ten IT users in Europe spent in excess of $15 billion.[1] Spending by the one hundred European companies with the largest IT budgets grew by 7 per cent to $53.7 billion in 1998.[2] Such spending is reflected across the world's major economies, and is increasing every year. For example, in 1998, Western Europe saw a 9 per cent increase in IT spend to £271 billion, with a predicted growth of 8.2 per cent in 1999, and 7.5 per cent in 2000. Europe now represents 30 per cent of the world's IT market, the United States 36 per cent, Japan 11 per cent and the rest of the world 23 per cent.[3] Although it might be difficult to determine exactly the annual global spend on IT, estimates suggest something between $700 billion to in excess of $2 trillion, including headcount, hardware and ancillary services such as maintenance and training. Recent estimates also vary widely. For example, a 1999 European Information Technology Observatory report predicted the 1999 global spend would reach £1098 billion,[4] whilst a Gartner survey put this figure at $2.2 billion.[5]

Therefore, although from a revenue perspective IT may not be as significant as, say, the automobile industry, it is certainly more important, especially given the culture of dependency it generates. Furthermore, IT, and lots of it, appears to hold the key to success in the highly competitive global market. As the world is increasingly wired, the importance of IT and the money that is spent on it will grow. This, in many respects, is a self-fulfilling prophecy, as it is the constant torrent of technological change, fuelled by IT, that forces nations and corporations alike to seek out the newest technology in order to survive, and to maintain organizational prosperity and longevity. Moreover, organizations are also having to become more innovative in their use of IT to sustain revenues and steal the march on their competition – being first to market is increasingly vital and technology is the best way to get there.

In reality, for organizations that depend on IT, there is little choice but to continue to spend significant percentages of their annual turnover on it – US companies spent 43 per cent of their 1996 capital budgets on hardware alone, equating to approximately $213 billion.[6] But the rub is that despite such significant spend, returns cannot be guaranteed.

THE CONSEQUENCES OF GETTING THE COST–BENEFIT CASE WRONG

Any organization would be accused of crass stupidity if they were to invest in a product or service without first fully considering the return on their investment. But high investment in IT does not necessarily guarantee high return. If, for example, the more recent statistical evidence presented in Chapter 2 was to be taken at face value, and if we were to assume an annual global spend of $1 trillion and that all of this was spent on information systems projects, we would see that $310 billion is wasted on failed projects, $530 billion is spent on late and over-budget projects, and only $160 billion is spent on successful projects.

These figures do not tell the whole story, as they only relate to the outcome of the initial investment and do not take into account the benefits. Clearly, the return on any project that has failed is zero. Even in those cases where the money has been recovered through litigation, the loss is still evident because the problem or opportunity for which the system was intended either still remains, or may have been lost.

When considering projects that are late, over budget and typically de-scoped, the return on investment might also be negligible, not least because the full system capabilities may not have been delivered. Moreover, considering that when such projects are shoehorned into production, the full functionality will usually have to be developed as part of the new application's ongoing maintenance budget, additional costs will therefore be incurred. According to the Standish Group in the United States, the typical project overspend is in the region of 189 per cent.[7] This means that an organization may have to spend nearly twice the anticipated project budget to implement an incomplete system – somewhat different from the original business case. Furthermore, in those instances where, in order to meet the project's deadline, the scope is radically reduced, the benefits may also be severely undermined. The received wisdom, that if an information system is implemented with 80–90 per cent of its requirements it will yield an acceptable level of benefit, is wrong, as it is often the remaining 10–20 per cent that incurs the majority of the expenditure. Logic also suggests that it would be the complex parts of the system that would be dropped in favour of the simpler components, and therefore would support the argument that significant costs can be incurred once the system has been implemented.

Even in those small number of genuinely successful projects where everything hoped for is achieved, there can be problems. Naturally, the investment should return the anticipated benefits, but this cannot always be guaranteed because the benefits may have been poorly defined at the time of writing the business case, or, by virtue of the length of time required to develop the software, the business cycle may have changed, making the system obsolete. This is euphemistically known as 'shelfware'.

Therefore, getting the balance right between the costs and benefits of an information systems project can be very tricky, as the following examples illustrate:

- A 1979 United States Government Accounting Office (GAO) analysis of Federal software development projects found that out of a total of $6.8 million spent, less than 2 per cent was delivered and used as planned.[8]

- In 1997, the United States Internal Revenue Service (IRS) reviewed twelve of its projects to see if they should be terminated. The results of the review indicated that they had spent around $4 billion on computer systems that did not work in the real world. This review followed hot on the heels of a damning report of the IRS's modernization project by the United States General Accounting Office which criticized the IRS for spending $284 million on a project that failed to convert tax returns into electronic images.[9]

- In June 1989, the Bank of America abandoned a three-year, $20 million trust accounts system, having spent an additional $60 million trying to make it work. The bank no longer handles the processing of trusts, and the biggest accounts were given to a Boston bank. Top executives and an undisclosed number of employees lost their jobs.[10]

● The United Kingdom's Department of Social Security's Operational Strategy was designed to computerize all of its welfare offices at an estimated cost of £713 million. It was also expected that the total cost of this project would fall with the reduction in technology costs due to general improvements in the price–performance ratio. Instead the costs rose to some £2.6 billion, a 400 per cent increase.[11] Interestingly, a similar although much smaller-scale project in California also failed in the summer of 1999. This project was designed to allow the State's welfare offices to communicate and share information. It failed at a cost of somewhere between $18 and $52 million.[12]

● The US Department of War Veterans' Affairs expected a new computer system would cut the time required to process healthcare claims from an average of four months to six weeks. Two years into the project, the typical claim was taking eight months.[13]

● The UK Passport Agency hoped that computerizing its offices would reduce the time and unit costs associated with processing passport applications. However, software glitches, and a higher than expected demand for child passports, led to such a severe backlog during the summer of 1999 that the Deputy Prime Minister had to intervene to resolve the problem.[14] The cost of the additional measures taken by the Passport Agency to resolve the problems was around £12.6 million, and the unit cost of producing a passport for the year 1999–2000 was expected to be between £15 and £15.50, much higher than the £12 promised in the business case.[15]

● The UK £1 billion Horizon Project, designed to automate the Post Office and provide a fraud-resistant benefits payment card, was three years late by the time it was partially abandoned in May 1999. The government has been left with a bill of between £620 and £940 million, whilst the supplier had to write off £180 million.[16] As a result, the Post Office had to write off £571 million against its half-year earnings for 1999–2000, which in turn is expected to result in the Post Office making its first loss in its 23-year history (£386 million pre-tax).[17]

JUSTIFYING INFORMATION SYSTEM PROJECTS

The justification of information systems projects is a necessary activity for all organizations, especially as the dependency and associated expenditure on IT has risen significantly over the last two to three decades. Clearly, as organizations only have a finite budget and IT headcount, they are unable to undertake all the projects they would like. This is compounded by the need to maintain existing systems, which consume both headcount and budget. IT is, of course, not the only thing the organization wishes to invest in, so it is essential that the appraisal process furnishes the organization's decision makers with sufficient information on which to select the most appropriate projects – both IT and non-IT.

Although there are many different methods available to appraise information systems projects, organizations tend to favour just a handful (see Table 4.1). Because such measures tend to focus predominantly upon tangible costs and benefits, the intangibles are usually poorly treated, or are excluded from the business case altogether. But with many information systems presenting less opportunities for direct savings – especially in terms of headcount reduction – these methods are increasingly ill-suited to their appraisal.

This problem on its own is soluble through the appropriate application of appraisal techniques, but there are two other factors that compound the difficulty of getting the balance right in the investment appraisal process, and ensuring that the benefits outweigh the costs:

Table 4.1 Common justification techniques

Approach	Description
Return on Investment	This approach is based on the assumption that all projects will yield a positive return on the money invested in the project, and that money held now is worth more than the same amount at some time in the future (because of the effect of inflation). Therefore, in order to account for the changing value of money over time, a discount rate is usually applied. To allow comparisons between competing projects, a hurdle rate is usually set over which the projects must pass for them to be selected. Return on Investment approaches are normally supported by two investment appraisal techniques: Net Present Value and Internal Rate of Return (as described below), although they are sometimes applied in isolation.
Net Present Value	Net Present Value is the most commonly used method to justify projects. Essentially, the method takes a comparison between the costs of the project and the present value of the uncertain cash flows generated by the project at completion. The Net Present Value is a measure of how valuable the project will be to the organization, and thus the higher the Net Present Value, the more likely it is that the project will be accepted. Net Present Value is, however, limited by the accuracy of the predicted future cash flows and is usually biased toward short-term projects. It is also poor at handling non-financial benefits.
Internal Rate of Return	The Internal Rate of Return is calculated as being the rate at which the Net Present Value of the project is zero. This is a very common measure used in project selection, as it can be useful in providing insights into the cash flows of the project in terms of its costs and benefits. This technique assumes that all costs are committed at the beginning of the project, and the same interest rate is used throughout. Therefore, when dealing with a long-term project, the use of a single interest rate can be limiting (although this can be overcome through a more sophisticated, multi-interest rate model).

- The effect of the culture gap between business and IT which has led to some sharp practices when developing investment appraisals – This typically involves the overstating of project benefits and understating of project costs as a way of ensuring the project is approved.

- The mistake of confusing price with cost – All information systems have a useful lifespan often running into years, but most appraisal techniques fail to address the long-term costs of the systems they introduce. Instead, they tend to focus only on the short-term price of the development activity. This is a very useful way of ensuring the project's business case is accepted.

These, along with the issue of appraising intangible benefits, must be understood by the organization if it is going to develop an appraisal process that is capable of identifying those projects that will truly deliver benefit returns.

DEALING WITH THE INTANGIBLES

There are currently many types of project that deliver a significant degree of intangible benefit, but make it difficult for the organization to gauge the success, or otherwise, of their investment. Commonly quoted benefits include:

- delivery of competitive advantage over business rivals;
- improvements to the productivity of office staff;
- provision of enterprise-wide information management infrastructures or systems;
- diversification of the organization's business through the widening of business scope; and
- improvements to the marketing and image of an organization through better customer servicing, or the addition of new product functionality.[18]

Organizations frequently find that their evaluation practices cannot place a value on such intangible benefits and are thus unable to fully justify the investment on financial measures alone. Also, when conducting the appraisal, organizations tend to underestimate the human and organizational costs.

We can conclude that organizations are finding it increasingly difficult to appraise the feasibility of their IT investments because of the increasingly intangible nature of IT benefits. In the past, most, if not all, benefits came from the elimination of organizational headcount through the automation of manually intensive business processes. The case for the investment was simple and straightforward: a project costing £1 000 000 could more than pay for itself over five years, say, through the removal of twenty or so staff at an average cost of £20 000. Now, however, such simple approaches are few and far between for three reasons. First, the wholesale re-engineering of major corporations during the early 1990s has left the majority of organizations with little room for headcount reductions, as to do so would mean cutting muscle rather than fat. Second, it is more likely that only parts of a job can be computerized, which makes it difficult to replace whole jobs, and hence reduces the opportunity for significant headcount reductions. This also makes benefits more complex to identify, model and ultimately measure. And, finally, with an increased dependency on information systems, a significant number of projects are designed to replace existing legacy systems. Because such replacement projects cannot be easily justified, they are typically accepted on the basis of increased system performance and improved staff productivity. More often than not, however, such performance and productivity improvements fail to materialize. It is also worth noting that one of the reasons for such replacement projects is the need to maintain alignment with the latest hardware, operating systems and software packages. The in-built obsolescence of many of these products is designed to ensure ongoing revenue streams for the manufacturers, leaving the customers to play catch-up. In addition, such upgrades do not always run smoothly, and may require changes to connected systems to ensure full compatibility is retained.

In addition, not all information systems projects are about the introduction of radical change in organizations, as many focus on incremental improvements to existing processes and business activities that are often more intangible in nature. For example, providing better information to senior managers in order to improve their decision-making capability is a benefit that could be claimed through the introduction of a new management or executive information system. However, it is difficult, and perhaps impossible, to measure how an individual's decision making has improved as a result of the introduction of such a system without first developing a measurement system to collect 'before' and 'after' snapshots of decision-making ability – itself a difficult, and potentially expensive, exercise. In addition, as the need to tackle change across much larger parts of the organization increases, the information systems project becomes just one, albeit important, component of a much larger initiative. As a result, the tracking, measurement and claiming of benefits can become very difficult.

Identifying specific IT-related benefits also becomes more difficult because many are indirect, and cannot be classed as direct benefits themselves, but important enablers for others. Therefore, how can organizations compare competing projects, some of which purport to provide direct benefits, whilst others indirect? The commonly used investment appraisal techniques seem to be lacking in this respect, especially in their inability to model intangible benefits.

THE USE OF SHARP PRACTICES

When faced with such difficulties, organizations can be blackmailed into making leaps of faith into the unknown, because they see no alternative but to invest in the latest technological solution which they are led to believe will deliver them what they really need. This is often termed the 'bleeding edge' of technology, where IT bleeds money out of the organization. But such leaps of faith are fuelled by the general lack of technological awareness at senior levels within the organization. As a result, senior managers often push the justification of the projects to those that are expected to know, that is, the technologists. Unfortunately, these people tend to focus on the positive aspects of technology, and often tell the chief executive what he wants to hear, rather than providing an honest view of the realistic benefits attainable – which, of course, the chief executive does not always want to hear. With IT also failing to canvass opinion and support for their projects prior to preparing and presenting the business case, it tends to focus on the technological aspects without paying sufficient attention to the business benefits.

When it comes to the justification of information systems projects, the culture gap is often used to obfuscate the true costs and benefits to allow dubious, or difficult to justify, investments in IT to pass through the board.[19] The use of these 'hidden agendas', so called because the true purpose of the investment is hidden from the board, was identified in a survey in 1992 which found that almost 40 per cent of IT directors admitted to employing hidden agendas when putting forward proposals for investments in new information systems.[20] Although a number of sharp practices are used to ensure information systems projects receive the funding they need, there are two that are particularly damaging:

- Window dressing – Here, projects are justified on a combination of savings within the business, savings to the general IT infrastructure, and through the arbitrary association of financial benefits to intangible, or highly unlikely benefits. The project can therefore be made to look extremely attractive, but with so much vagueness around the benefits case, they usually end up being an expensive disappointment.

- Double vision – In this instance, the project is justified by emphasizing the short-term benefits the project can achieve, and, where required, expressing these in a way that disguises the true purpose of the project by playing to the known needs of the business. These projects provide a vision to the board

that is usually far removed from reality and certainly would not have been accepted had it been truthful. As a result, there tends to be a certain degree of post-project justification in which the benefits are reassessed as a fortunate outcome, or a side-effect of the original project.

Although the use of such hidden agendas is now out in the open, the problem of appraising information systems projects will not disappear overnight. Until such time the culture gap is comprehensively addressed, and more appropriate investment appraisal techniques used, IT directors will be forced to hide the real costs and benefits from the board. Unfortunately, such behaviour reinforces the culture gap and leads to further disappointment in IT's ability to deliver against their promises – a vicious circle of hype followed by disappointment or failure.

CONFUSING PRICE WITH COST

One of the fundamental aspects that seems to be overlooked with the majority of IT investments is the distinction between price and cost. When an organization embarks on a new information systems project, the primary focus is on the establishment of the business case, which typically involves making an assessment of the likely costs (or price) and benefits of the project.

As the project progresses, and the budget is consumed, management may lose sight of the purpose of the cost-benefit case and, if it is a large investment, become locked into an escalation of commitment (see Chapter 7). As a result, they can lose sight of the long-term costs of the new IT investment, especially if the project is running late and over budget. Indeed, if this is the case, the need to spend additional money is all the more likely.

Therefore, although a project may appear to look good at the time of the initial business case, it can soon turn out to be a very costly exercise, as, once implemented, it might require a string of people to maintain it, and if it also fails to meet the expected performance levels, limit the payback. For example, a number of years ago I inherited the maintenance of a system that had been implemented to develop and maintain a new product. By the time I inherited the system, it was some months after implementation, and the organization was spending something in the region of £200 000 per annum maintaining it (approximately four staff). I attended a product review meeting shortly after taking it on, and learnt that, having spent approximately £1 000 000 on the system and product development activity, only one customer had signed up to the product. Thus, for an initial investment of £1 000 000 and an ongoing maintenance bill of £200 000, the organization was only gaining some £40 000 in annual revenue. The business case may have looked sound, and the system and product development may have run smoothly, but the benefits case was significantly flawed. Needless to say, the organization did not kill the product line for fear of upsetting this one customer.

The problems of not considering the long-term costs of information systems, plus failing to consider fully the benefits side of the justification process, not only leads to cases described above, but also leads to the waste of valuable IT budget and headcount that could be better used elsewhere. But once locked into the system, organizations feel they have little choice but to continue to sink further money into these poorly constructed systems. Over time, this leads to a decrease in the organization's ability to develop new systems, because more and more staff are sucked into maintaining the operational systems. Therefore, the need to construct robust and near maintenance-free systems is a prize for which organizations are willing to pay. Indeed, one of the principal reasons for adopting the Capability Maturity Model as a way of improving software quality is to do just that: minimize the level of maintenance by developing first-class information systems first time round and hence reduce the variance between the price paid for the project, and its long-term cost. In essence, aiming for the highest quality should lead to a reduction in maintenance effort once implemented, and free up more of the IT headcount to develop other important applications for the organization. Investing in

the Capability Maturity Model can be very expensive, but the rewards can be significant. For example, three years after a software capability assessment, Hughes Aircraft's Software Engineering Division in the United States was making annual savings in the region of $2 million. The cost of achieving these savings was $450 000, clearly a price worth paying.[21] Of course, its successful introduction depends on the level of commitment from senior management, as well as the wider IT and business communities,[22] and because of this, it can be just as difficult to implement as any information system.

It is, of course, insufficient for organizations to consider just one side of the cost–benefit equation, as they also need to understand some of the problems associated with realizing the benefits from their information systems projects, something that is equally problematical.

WHY IS IT SO DIFFICULT TO REALIZE THE BENEFITS?

As we have seen, many of the decisions to invest in new technology have been made on the back of a reduction in headcount, and the improvements in productivity that come from the application of information systems in the workplace. Higher productivity has important consequences for both the organization and nation as a whole. If the introduction of a new information system allows the same or new products to be created faster, with fewer staff, the unit cost of these products should be reduced. Consequently, cheaper goods feed into the general economy, where individuals are able to buy more with their incomes, and ultimately the general standard of living should rise. When rolled up to the national level, such productivity increases are one of the vital ingredients in the achievement of global competitiveness. However, it appears that there are difficulties in assessing whether or not investments in IT have really delivered the productivity gains expected of them. Outlining some of the issues associated with the alleged poor return on IT investments is important because it serves to illustrate the difficulties and challenges of realizing returns on information systems projects – something with which all chief executives and IT directors/chief information officers should be concerned.

When considering the benefits side of the high investment, but low return, conundrum, organizations must understand:

- that without any active management of the benefits realization process, the achievement of project benefits will remain a lottery;
- there has been, and continues to be, a productivity paradox associated with IT investments, that is, designed to make significant productivity improvements, the majority of information systems projects have failed to deliver the productivity gains expected of them; and
- the reasons why the productivity gains from information systems have been negligible and appear to be so elusive.

ACCOUNTABILITY FOR REALIZING THE BENEFITS

The general issue of who should be held accountable for project benefits has always proved to be a problem for organizations. Historically, many have witnessed the over-the-wall approach to project delivery: the IT department would develop the new information system, implement it, wash their hands of it, and leave the users to figure out how best to use it. Although such an approach is less prevalent than it used to be, organizations still grapple with how to manage the benefits that are expected to come from the implementation of a new information system. With benefits often taking longer to come through than the original project appraisal suggested, organizations can lose sight of, and perhaps interest in, the benefits realization process, especially as they have been led to believe that the benefits realize themselves. Instead of maintaining a vigilant eye on benefit tracking, they often move on to the next project, rather than attempting to understand how effective the last one was at delivering its benefits. Without any measurement, benefits appear to be a fortunate outcome of a project,

not something that is actively managed. With neither the project manager, nor the end users attending to the benefits, who is? Thus, it is essential for organizations to take an active role in the delivery of project benefits, because if no one is held accountable, achieving them will remain a lottery.

Of course, the benefits realization process starts with the business case itself, and as we have seen, if this is badly presented, the benefits case is often doomed before the project has even started. It can be argued therefore that there should be some much-needed honesty about the likely returns a project is expected to achieve, particularly at the time of the business case. Such honesty is essential because the business case is a vital component in managing the expectations of the business. One of the main reasons for cost overruns is that full project costs are rarely identified, and often significantly underestimated if they are – often, it is said, so that the case can be accepted by the board. In particular, the failure to include non-IT costs is often singled out as a particular problem as these can account for a significant percentage of total project spend. Transparency of benefits is equally an issue, as illustrated in the case of an expensive system supporting a product that had only one customer. This highlights the trap of believing that 100 per cent of the stated benefits are achievable, and suggests that organizations do not consider the impact that a reduction in the benefits or an increase in costs may have on a project's viability. It can therefore be very easy for an investment to be squeezed both in terms of its inputs (costs) and outputs (benefits), leading to a very costly project, which delivers little or no benefit.

Even when someone has been appointed to monitor and control the realization of the benefits, and every effort has been made to develop a realistic business case, the benefits from information systems can still be elusive, as illustrated by one of the most contentious areas of debate over the last ten years – the productivity paradox. The sad fact is, that after forty years of investment, the productivity gains anticipated from IT have not materialized. With productivity often cited as one of the principal reasons for investing in information systems, the productivity paradox is worthy of some further discussion, because it alludes to some of the common problems experienced by organizations as they attempt to gain the benefits they seek from their information systems projects.

THE PRODUCTIVITY PARADOX

The rationale behind the computerization of the 1950s was to gain the increased productivity that had been established by the Industrial Revolution, when great tranches of manual labour were eradicated through the application of modern machinery. Therefore, it would be reasonable to assume that the growth of computerization and rising investment trends since the early automation projects of the 1950s and 1960s were the result of productivity payoffs from these investments. If coupled with the post-war boom, itself fuelled by computerization, it is easy to see why most organizations, especially those in the United States and Europe, were at that time unconcerned as to whether IT offered a good return on investment. It was not until the late 1970s, when the dominance of the US and European economies began to wane, that organizations started to question the high levels of IT investment.[23] But even then, the issue was clouded by Moore's Law, which stated that the number of transistors that can be housed on a microchip doubles every 18 months – a process which brings with it an increase in power and a corresponding reduction in price. This is also known as the price–performance ratio.

However, by the late 1980s, questions were being raised about the limited productivity payoffs from IT,[24] as assessments of the true economic impacts of IT revealed a far from rosy picture. For example:

- Since the introduction of office-based computer systems in the 1960s, US investment in information technology has been in the region of $4 trillion. By making comparisons of average Gross Domestic Product for the period 1973–83, it becomes

apparent that up to $30 billion per year has been lost in output as a result of the low productivity returns from information technology investments.

- Whilst manufacturing productivity in the United States grew by 4.1 per cent per year during the 1980s, white collar productivity rose by just 0.28 per cent a year, despite the massive expenditure in office technology.

- Buying computers and related technology appears to be a little more than 13 per cent less productive than other forms of capital investments.[25]

This analysis is borne out in reality, where it seems that, rather than reduce the amount of office-based work, IT appears to increase it. For example, in 1968, US hospitals employed around 440 000 administrators to serve approximately 2.4 million patients daily. By 1992, the number of administrative positions had increased to 2.2 million whilst the number of daily patients had dropped to approximately 840 000. This has, according to some commentators, been the direct result of the information explosion caused by the introduction of computer technology.[26]

If the productivity paradox exists, which I believe it does, it is important for organizations to understand the reasons why they cannot gain the expected productivity improvements they seek.

PRODUCTIVITY GAINS ARE RARELY IMMEDIATE

As we have seen, the majority of business cases predict healthy and immediate gains in productivity as soon as a new information system is implemented. This is usually far from the truth as there is usually a reduction in performance when they are introduced because of the need to retool and retrain staff. And, once implemented, there also tends to be a period of adjustment during which staff become familiar with the new system and the resulting subtle changes to the business process. It can therefore be some time before the existing level of performance is reached, let alone the predicted level (see Figure 4.1). Thus, the improved

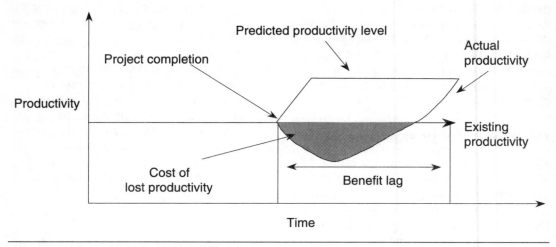

Figure 4.1   Performance and new investment

performance levels on which the investment was based may take a lot longer to materialize than anticipated. The grey area of the model reflects the additional costs associated with the initially reduced productivity that accompanies the introduction of a new system. This typically includes a performance dip prior to delivery when pre-implementation training and user-acceptance testing takes place. Once implemented, there is also an associated benefit lag during which additional costs are incurred and the predicted performance levels are finally reached. In this instance, this is associated with the time required for users to first familiarize themselves with the new system and, second, attain the competence levels necessary to improve productivity.

Ignoring the impacts on performance and failing to address these within the investment appraisal process can lead to information systems failing at, or very soon after, implementation. Users of these systems are frequently told they will be easy to use, when in fact there is a great deal to learn. Therefore, expecting users to learn on the job is likely to result in them having a poor perception of the system and an inability to use its full functionality.

The problem of lagging benefits can be further exacerbated through the rapid rates of change associated with IT. Therefore, just as the business

is getting used to the new system, and generating the expected productivity improvements, the system is typically upgraded or replaced.

TOO MANY, AND TOO DIVERSE, A RANGE OF TECHNOLOGY PLATFORMS

The large number of technology platforms, software systems, operating systems and packages available impacts productivity for two reasons. First, because each has its own language, syntax and unique make-up, it can be difficult to move from one system to another without an associated dip in productivity during familiarization, or refamiliarization. Second, despite notable attempts by the IT industry to provide genuinely compatible technology platforms and systems, there still remain significant problems in getting different systems and hardware platforms to communicate. This means that there can be more breakpoints between systems, and hence a greater opportunity for the introduction of data errors, especially where this involves the rekeying of data from one system to another.

SOFTWARE COMPLEXITY

As software is updated, it typically involves an increase in the number of features it provides. For example, the number of commands in Microsoft Word increased from 311 in the 1992 version, to 1033 in 1997.[27] If the user wished to master this later version, it would take a lot longer than it had with the earlier one. In addition, the power and memory required to run this later version is significantly higher than that required to run the former. As a result, any software upgrade – at least when associated with the desktop – can often require simultaneous hardware upgrades. This increasing sophistication of desktop software can have other impacts, especially in the levels of hidden support. For example, one study found that between 4 and 10 per cent of end-users' time was spent on helping their colleagues solve their software problems. This hidden time is believed to cost something in the region of $23 500 per personal computer per year.[28]

SOFTWARE FAILURE AND DOWNTIME

The unreliability of software is one of the greatest contributory factors to limited productivity growth. As software and systems have become more complex, it has become harder to test software thoroughly and as a result there is a greater opportunity for it to fail. Also, because of its complexity, software has a tendency to crash and fail when least expected. What is more worrying is that, because of the underlying complexity, it can be difficult to replicate the exact conditions that caused the failure in the first place. Indeed, the same software may crash at a different point the next time it is used. The loss of productive work when software crashes, or when a computer must be rebooted, can be very significant. For example, an extensive study of Fortune 1000 companies in 1991 by FIND-SVP estimated that computer downtime costs US businesses $4 billion a year.[29] This unreliability also extends into the network community, as highlighted in a recent survey by Black Box in the United Kingdom. The survey suggested that ten million man-days are lost each year due to network failures alone.[30] The cost of software bugs is also significant: recent reports suggest that poor software quality is costing the United Kingdom something in the region of £900 million per year.[31] In addition, if whole departments are dependent on the functioning of a particular software system, its failure can lead to unexpected downtime and productivity loss. A recent example of this is the ongoing debate in the United Kingdom around the reliability of the government's Contributions Agency National Insurance recording system (Nirs2). Since its implementation in July 1998, there have been a reported 1500 system problems, which have created a backlog of 17 million contribution records.[32] Finally, a recent IBM Consulting engagement at Hershey Foods in the United States resulted in their supply chain being tied up in knots, the company losing shelf space at retailers, and their share price dropping 22 per cent over 1999.[33]

THE OPPORTUNITY TO DO LESS WORK

With so much software on the desktop, the opportunity for employees to avoid productive work in favour of tinkering with their software packages is very seductive. Employees with access to the average desktop's software can send personal e-mails, write personal letters, and play with their electronic diaries, all of which serve to reduce productivity. Increasingly, with access to the Internet, or their company's intranet, the opportunity to surf for information is appealing, but again serves to distract them from their day-to-day activity. The phenomenon of the information junkie is also a worrying trend, as employees become obsessed with finding as much information as possible about a particular task before they take action. In extreme cases, this generates bottlenecks within the decision-making process. A desktop software environment also allows the employee to revise their documents and rework them many times over, and probably more than would have been acceptable in the days of the typing pool. Creating a document becomes a work of art, rather than something that should be considered in the context of fitness for purpose. Yet again, productivity can dip. Finally, the rapid move to electronic commerce is a double-edged sword: although it can provide the organization with new opportunities in the way it conducts its business, staff are only too happy to take advantage of the new technology for personal use. A recent survey by Black Box in the United Kingdom estimated that this abuse was losing some eight million man-hours per annum.[34]

POORLY EXECUTED SOFTWARE UPGRADES

Where, for example, an organization has standardized its office automation on a single suite of software (for example, Lotus or Microsoft), productivity issues can arise when the upgrade of this standardized environment is poorly executed. This is a particular headache for global organizations that depend on their ability to operate effectively, efficiently, and seamlessly, using a standardized environment. The lack of compatibility between software versions means that significant time can be wasted in trying to open documents that have been created with a later version, which has yet to be implemented locally. This also works in the opposite direction, where in order to ensure compatibility, the document, spreadsheet, or presentation has been saved in the updated desktop environment but using the previous version of the software package. Here, the advantages of the newer version are lost and in many cases some of the information or formatting contained within the document or spreadsheet can be lost. This ensures the document either has to be reworked or altered to fit the constraints of the older version of the package. All of this additional activity leads to reductions in productivity. This also ensures that the advantages of standardization are lost, albeit temporarily, whilst the rest of the organization catches up with the software.

TECHNO-STRESS

We have all been led to believe that the computerization of work would release the average employee from the trials and tribulations of boring and repetitive work in order to perform higher-order activities. Although this has occurred in many organizations, it seems that the use of computers in the office has resulted in increased stress associated with the work employees now perform.[35] Studies in the United States and the United Kingdom point to the increasing stress levels associated with computer-based work, and the costs of stress-related illness. For example, this is believed to cost the United States something between $50 billion and $75 billion per annum.[36] According to some, computers are transforming the modern corporation into an electronic sweatshop.[37]

Looking down this list of potential productivity blockers, it is no wonder that organizations find it so difficult to realize the benefits they expect from their investments in information systems – the list highlights the importance of managing the process.

BEWARE A WOLF IN SHEEP'S CLOTHING

Naturally, the software industry would like us to believe that all of their products can produce the benefits they quote. Of course, there are plenty of examples where there have been spectacular improvements in productivity and business performance, but there are plenty more where the reverse is true. Organizations would do well to familiarize themselves with the contents of Table 4.2, as they must realize that they are not in themselves conclusive evidence that software produces a significant upward lift in productivity.[38]

The academic community have also been embroiled within the debate, but just as with the business community, they cannot provide conclusive evidence of its non-existence. Whatever the evidence and counter-evidence, it is clear that productivity gains from IT investments are not easy to identify or measure. Moreover, the intensity of the debate surrounding the productivity paradox tends to support this view – if they were obvious, studies would not be necessary. There is therefore some advantage to adopting a conservative stance when it comes to defining benefits.

TURNING THE BENEFITS CORNER?

If organizations are going to resolve the high investment but low return conundrum they must:

● Be more business-like in the way they manage the investment appraisal process by taking more time and care in identifying both the costs and benefits of the project.

Table 4.2   Don't believe what you hear

The argument	The truth
Faster ways of working cannot be easily measured by standard economic measures. Therefore, the effects of technology do not appear in these measures.	People are not necessarily working faster, but they are working longer, most of which goes unrecorded. Moreover, the mismeasurement this argument suggests would have to have been going on for many decades for it to be substantiated.
Organizations have not purchased enough hardware for them to fully exploit the productivity benefits available from IT.	Hardware alone does not constitute a useful information system. Without software, hardware would provide no function at all. Thus if the additional components are considered, including software, telecommunications and other related office equipment, there would be enough technology and software to exploit the benefits the argument suggests.
There is usually a many-decade lag from the initial investment and take-up of a new technology to the realization of significant economic gain (for example, the electric motor did not boost productivity until forty years after its introduction).	Computers have been around for at least forty years now, and their significance within the majority of organizations should be sufficient to generate the productivity gains put forward by the lag argument.

- Be willing to exploit the potential benefits derived from the introduction of a new information system by taking the care to reorganize work to complement it.
- Introduce the necessary structures, processes and accountabilities to aid in the process of managing the benefits.
- Be willing to admit that without the active management of the benefits realization process, the lack of benefits will continue to dog the organization.

In discussing the problems with the investment appraisal process, we have tackled the start and end points of the information systems project. Even if these are well defined, there are a number of other issues that have to be understood before we can move on to the solutions. Key within this is the culture gap between the business and IT communities – itself a major problem, and one which can lead to major disruptions as the project is executed.

CHAPTER FIVE

Business and IT: they just can't communicate

One of the most persistent problems with IT over the last forty years has been the apparent disconnect between it and the rest of the business community. This culture gap, so called because IT appears to operate on a different agenda to the rest of the business, continues to cause major problems in all but the smallest of development projects. Although organizations have attempted to resolve the problem, it still remains, and suggests they have approached it from a position of limited understanding. Therefore, before organizations can comprehensively tackle the problem of the IT–business disconnect they must understand:

1. *why* it exists
2. *how* it is manifested
3. *where* it is manifested
4. *what* has been done to resolve it, and whether these attempts have been as successful as hoped.

Realizing that the culture gap is not a simple problem between the business and IT communities, but something more complex and involved, will help organizations generate more comprehensive solutions to eliminate its worst excesses, especially failure.

WHY DOES THE CULTURE GAP EXIST?

As we saw in Chapter 1, back in the 1950s, organizations were not really sure how to handle the new technology that had started to impact their operations. And, because they did not fully understand how it worked, they decided to leave it, and those who understood it, alone to make their own way in the organization. In doing so, however, they allowed it to develop its own unique culture disconnected from the rest of the organization – focused on technology rather than business imperatives, and developing ways

of working that, even now, appear to be quite alien from the rest of the organization.

Clearly, this historical perspective is important, but it is insufficient on its own to allow organizations to develop the necessary awareness to resolve the problems the culture gap currently presents. To do so means placing the IT culture in the context of the other functional cultures that exist within the organization and understanding what motivates and drives the IT professional.

THE NATURE OF THE IT CULTURE

Although an organization may appear to have an outwardly homogenous culture, it is in fact far more heterogeneous in nature. Any organization consists of various departments and functions established to provide a particular internal, or external, service. And, although all are geared toward the stated ambitions, goals and objectives of the organization, each has its own set of values which, along with its activities, help to define its own unique culture – the way we do things around here. For example, the Finance Department has a fundamentally different culture to the Marketing Department because Finance focuses on the financial health of the organization, whilst Marketing focuses on the development and marketing of the organization's products, as well as establishing and promoting its brand. Although such differences in culture can create friction from time to time, they rarely develop into psychosis. Then, there is IT.

There seems to be a fundamental problem with how IT is viewed within organizations, and here's why:

● Unlike other organizational functions, IT is omnipresent in that most, if not all, other departments, depend on the IT function for their own operational efficiency. Such dependency on a single function is not replicated anywhere else in the organization. This brings IT's particular strain of culture into constant and sharp relief – it cannot be ignored. Other functions may clash from time to time, but because of the infrequent nature of these clashes, they are able to coexist in relative harmony. With IT, however, such clashes are generally more frustrating because they are far more frequent.

- Whereas the general concepts and processes of, say, marketing and finance can be understood by the layperson, those of IT are less accessible. This is partly due to the speed at which IT changes against the relative stability of other organizational departments, but it is also due to the language they use, which tends to have a much higher percentage of jargon when compared to other functions.

- IT is essentially about change, whereas other units are usually about operational efficiency and stability. The introduction of any new information system invokes change that creates turbulence within these generally stable environments. When this fails to deliver, something needs to be blamed – IT is the obvious candidate.

- The typical IT professional is more likely to associate with their profession than the company they work for; ask anyone what they do, and whereas the average employee will respond with 'I work for company x', the typical response from the IT professional is 'I work in IT', or 'I'm a database administrator', and so on. This view is supported by research from the UK's Cranfield School of Management which found IT professionals were more loyal to IT than their employer.[1] They also suggested that this was exacerbated by the predominantly technical training they received compared to the more general and wider-ranging training had by their business colleagues. More recently, the UK's government Labour Force Survey showed

that IT professionals change jobs more frequently than people in any other industry, with more than 40 per cent spending less than two years in a job.[2] This can create problems for organizations: when the experience walks out of the door, the continuity required to both develop and maintain systems is lost. Couple this with the generally poor level of documentation, and you have a recipe for disaster. The important thing to remember here is that, unlike finance and marketing, developing and maintaining an effective system requires a blend of technical, business and systems knowledge. As a result, only one or perhaps two people know the system in enough detail to be able to keep it running, make enhancements to it, and troubleshoot when there are problems. Thus, when IT staff leave, the organization can find itself without the support it needs to maintain business continuity.

- Those that seek a career in IT do so because they find the allure of technology irresistible. They feel more comfortable communicating with their machine than their colleagues. This is a significant problem and one that has major implications for the organization, not least in the problem of IT and business being unable to communicate on the same wavelength.

- Studies have found that the attractive forces of the IT culture are extremely difficult to resist, especially in how they relate to the end-user community.[3] On entering the profession, someone with limited IT experience tends to have a natural affinity toward the business end of the spectrum, and maintains a good working relationship with the end-user community. However, after a period of months, the attraction of the IT culture shifts the individual's attitude toward the technological end of the spectrum, and the person assumes the mantle of the techie.

MOTIVATION AND THE IT PROFESSIONAL

Research into the psychological profile of IT professionals has concluded that there are major differences between their motivational needs and those of their business compatriots.[4] IT professionals have been found to have a higher growth need – a need for greater responsibility for their own work and tasks – and lower social interaction need. Similar studies seem to corroborate this finding, in that programmers have been found to have high achievement, cognitive structure and endurance needs, but low affiliation and social recognition needs.[5] These analyses are borne out by personal observation by a project manager, managing teams of programmers and analysts. On the whole, the majority were unassuming, technical geniuses – place them in front of a computer with a problem to solve, and they were fantastic; they were dedicated and would do whatever was necessary to develop a piece of usable code. Place them in front of a senior manager, or user, and it was a different matter. In some instances, they would be eaten alive. On the whole, programmers are believed to prefer non-management roles, do not possess good management skills, often lack good communication skills, are rather introverted, and have a narrow view of the business context.[6]

Unfortunately, organizations have pandered to this isolation by providing them with a very narrowly defined career path. Careers in IT have traditionally followed a fairly standard route. Beginning as a programmer, and having mastered the craft, the IT professional's next obvious step is the opportunity to move into analysis and design. From analysis, it might be possible to move into either a business analysis role, or perhaps team leading. From team leader the natural step is to project manager, and, if the individual is able to demonstrate the necessary managerial capability, to IT management, and ultimately to IT director/chief information officer. There is, unfortunately, a fundamental problem with this career ladder.

Despite accepting the need to provide a career route for the IT specialist, organizations have failed to broaden it beyond technology. And, whereas many other organizational disciplines such as finance, marketing, and general operational management are seen as necessary strings to the professional manager's bow, IT still regards specialism as more important than generalism or hybridism.

Furthermore, the seductive nature of technology means that many in IT do not have the desire to ascend the IT career ladder for fear of losing their technical expertise. For example, there is a generally held belief that IT project management is a non-value adding task. Indeed, many programmers and analysts feel that moving into project management is a retrograde step, but are often forced into it because of salary and status implications. This can create problems down the line for the management of information systems projects, because those charged with running them feel more at home with the technology than the business problem they are trying to solve. For example, I have personally known senior IT managers who would rather roll up their sleeves and tend to some technical difficulty than run their department. I have also known business analysts who would rather remain at their relatively junior level than move into the higher-order activities, such as project management, for fear of losing the value-added content of their work. This is clearly at odds with most other functions, where employees are keen to move between departments as a way of gaining broad business acumen and organizational experience. It is this breadth of experience that provides the ticket to the career progression they seek. With a narrowly focused career route and aspirations, it is no wonder that so few IT professionals reach the board of directors: they lack the general all-round business exposure required to perform effectively at these levels. It is also no surprise that those that do, find it an alien and hostile place, and the transition from specialist to generalist very painful.

Perhaps the rise of IT contracting, in which IT professionals branch out on their own to provide a specific service, such as testing, business analysis, or programming expertise, is an indication that the average IT professional would rather remain in a technical role than follow the usual career path and lose the skills they covet so highly. Contracting provides the IT professional with what they seek: high levels of remuneration, and the opportunity to remain an expert in their discipline, be it database administration, programming in Java, or testing. The other advantage often cited by contracting colleagues of mine, is that they do not have to get involved with organizational politics – they can just beaver away, pretty much undisturbed, and more worryingly, often unsupervised. I believe this lack of faith in the IT career path is reflected in the current level of contracting, which in the United Kingdom represents approximately 22 per cent of the IT workforce.[7]

HOW DOES THE CULTURE GAP MANIFEST ITSELF?

Although the culture gap manifests itself in a variety of ways, it depends to a great extent upon the individual relationship people have with technology in general, but, more specifically, with the IT professional. The following are typical:

- The non-specialist either has a deep-seated mistrust of computers, or believes that anything is possible at the press of a button.
- The quasi-specialist is typically adept at developing end-user applications, such as spreadsheets and databases, and, by virtue of their own limited experiences in IT, believes the creation of information systems is a straightforward task.
- Senior management increasingly find it difficult to justify the escalating costs of computerization, particularly when it is so hard to see any significant return on investment. They are tiring of the hype and many believe IT has been oversold.
- Directors do not, or will not, understand IT, believing it is someone else's problem. As a result, they fail to keep up with the trends in technology and therefore fail to recognize the significance it may have on their organization.

Each of these creates problems within information systems projects by creating disconnects in the use of language, in the management of expectations and so on. It is easy to see how the culture gap can affect the outcome of an information systems project. Typical problems include:

- Difficulties in eliciting, capturing and agreeing the requirements – Very often, the inability to articulate the business problem to which IT is being applied leads to problems during the remainder of the project. Instability of requirements is symptomatic of a poor or incomplete requirements specification.

- The limited use of business experts during the main development activity – This often means a disconnect develops between what is expected and what is delivered. This lack of involvement is often the result of the deliberate non-usage of business personnel during development, as it is perceived by IT that they can't add value to the process. Further problems arise from the inability to engage the wider business community in the project, which is especially problematical at implementation when, because of this limited involvement, the system fails to live up to the expectations set at the start of the project.

- Blame, buck-passing and finger-pointing when the system fails to deliver to expectations – This is a frequent occurrence, and usually involves conflict between IT, who believe they delivered everything that was expected of them, and the business, who feel cheated. The inability of the business and IT professionals to reconcile these problems by working more closely together is symptomatic of the gulf that has been created by the culture gap, but also of the differing operational imperatives. IT is projectized, and works through projects. The business is operational, and is generally disrupted by project work.

- Failure to learn – One of the greatest tragedies created by the culture gap is the inability to learn from past mistakes. Organizations are very poor at picking up the pieces from a failed information systems project and learning from it. The animosity that results from poor implementations leads to some of the irrational behaviours to be discussed in Chapter 7. But, more importantly, the perception that IT cannot deliver, or that the business cannot articulate their requirements, becomes embedded in the attitudes of both IT and the business, making it harder to limit the ongoing tensions between them. Clearly some form of accountability is required in those instances where IT has been negligent, but in the majority of cases, the failure is the result of both IT and the operational line failing to work together. Without change, organizations are destined to repeat the same errors, and experience the same degree of conflict, time and time again. And, it has to be said, the same level of failure.

TECHNO-SPEAK AND TECHNO-ILLITERACY

One of the most obvious ways in which the culture gap manifests itself is through the purist technical stance of the IT professional, and the general superficial understanding of technology by the business. This leads to claims by the business that the IT professional speaks in an incomprehensible stream of buzzwords and technical jargon, and counterclaims from the technologists that business fails to understand technology to any degree.

It should, of course, come as no surprise that subtle differences in language and jargon exist across the organization, as this reflects the specialisms that are needed to execute its business. Indeed, commonality of language at the functional level provides some of the glue that binds people to their function, and ultimately the organization in which they work. Although it is important to recognize that technical language and jargon will be present in any function, it is much higher within IT. With a continuous stream of new technology, the techno-speak of the IT expert is quite often meaningless to the average employee, and here's why:

... computer scientists deal with artefacts created by man and not existing independently in nature. Because of this arbitrariness, computer professionals have considerable latitude in formulating new terms and assigning new names. This provides a seemingly interminable stream of idiosyncratic nomenclature, which descends all too easily into jargon.[8]

Although the use of techno-speak is designed to provide a common language for the IT professional, it can be used to confuse the layperson to the point of blind acceptance. Some commentators call this 'silicon snake oil'[9] – people take the benefits of adopting a new technology at face value, only to be disappointed with the finished product. This techno-speak occurs at all levels in IT, from the programmer through to the IT director/chief information officer, and also includes the technology vendors and computing press. Charles Wang, chief executive officer of Computer Associates, terms the use of such techno-speak the 'ignorance lobby', because there are numerous consultants, analysts, associations and journalists who want to reinforce the high levels of technical ignorance within the general populace. All, he suggests, have a stake in the continued ignorance of information technology, as this allows each to cultivate their business by peddling the latest technology, designed to solve the latest business problem.[10] Admittedly, it is difficult to keep track of the rapid advances, numerous product launches and technical literature associated with IT, so it would be unfair to accuse the average IT professional of acting in such a manner deliberately. Indeed, there is anecdotal evidence to suggest that even those in IT have difficulty in keeping up.[11] If this is true, what hope has the general business user?

Focusing on the IT professional is, of course, not the whole story because some of the reasons why the culture gap persists is associated with the general techno-illiteracy within many parts of the organization, but especially within the board. In the past, it might have been acceptable to plead ignorance of the advances in information technology – IT was less important then. But now, as IT takes centre stage, the 'ignorance is bliss' stance is no longer a viable position to adopt. The ability to understand what the latest advances in information technology mean for the organization is a vital competency. Furthermore, the business often fails to question the efficacy of applying the latest technology before making significant investments in systems development projects. This blind acceptance is often created by what is read in the press, or what is fed to them at sales presentations and demonstrations. It is clear from experience that lofty claims rarely materialize into significant benefits. Clearly more realism and challenge is needed from the business community, but this can only come through a greater understanding of IT and how it can benefit the organization. And the business community can no longer blame the IT industry for all the woes that beset it when IT fails to impress.

WHERE DOES THE CULTURE GAP MANIFEST ITSELF?

The culture gap between business and IT manifests itself at two distinct levels: the working level between the developers and users of the applications, and the strategic level between the IT director/chief information officer and their fellow board members. Both serve to perpetuate the ongoing battle between IT and the rest of the organization, and create significant barriers to the learning required to prevent further project failures.

THE WORKING LEVEL

The working-level culture gap exists between those people directly involved with the development and delivery of information systems and those that use them. As we have already seen, at least some of the problem at this working level stem from the differences between the two groups in terms of the language they use, the level of technical sophistication and business understanding they possess, and the

different career aspirations and psychological make-up they have. Although this creates intense pain for both parties, it is the business users who seem to suffer the most, as the following suggests:

> An IT system starts out for its users as an entity, created, in its details by an alien people – techies – and posing the problem of whether it really will be workable, cost effective, adequate, secure, upgradeable, compatible, etc. Techies are always moving the technology goal posts, increased penetration of IT continually increases an organization's exposure to risks of disruption. Thus for users, an IT system is always a problem.[12]

It is at this working level, because of its direct link to project failure, that the culture gap creates the most turbulence and angst within organizations. If the business users and IT professionals cannot get on and work together to deliver the information systems project, then failure is likely. In order to understand how the culture gap can develop, it is worth modelling it as this provides an insight into the various factors that impact its severity. It also allows particular factors to be identified that are unique to an organization. The model in Figure 5.1 shows a subset of factors derived from observation by a project manager, and is loosely based on systems dynamics, a technique that allows the natural feedback loops of any system to be modelled.[13] The example illustrates how a number of seemingly independent factors can impact the culture gap, and hence suggests that it is more than just an 'us and them' problem. Each loop, labelled 1–3, on Figure 5.1 is discussed in more detail.

LOOP 1 – DEVELOPMENT METHOD

In general, the culture of the organization is likely to exert a strong influence over the development method adopted and deployed within their information systems projects. For example, bureaucratic organizations tend to favour structured methods for both developing their software and managing their software

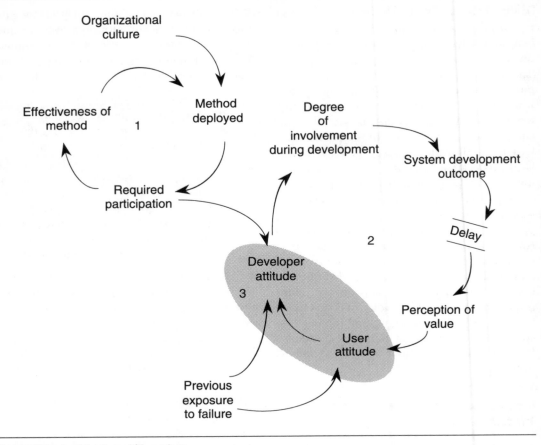

Figure 5.1 Participation within projects

projects. Typical of this is the use of the Structured Systems Analysis and Design Method (SSADM) and the associated Projects In a Controlled Environment (Prince 2) by the United Kingdom's Civil Service. Highly participative organizations, which tend to focus on the human element of working life, favour the people-centred approaches, such as Soft Systems, or the Effective Technical and Human Implementation of Computer-based Systems (ETHICS).[14] Whatever the method deployed, it will influence the level of participation required of the IT development staff which itself can have major implications for the system that is ultimately delivered. The use of the method will, particularly if new, be closely monitored and its effectiveness assessed against the outcome of the project. Depending on the outcome, the method may be retained, replaced or tailored.

LOOP 2 – LEVEL OF PARTICIPATION

The degree of involvement during the software development process will be influenced by the attitude of the software developer. This is influenced by both the expected level of involvement required by the development method deployed, and the relationship that exists between the IT and business communities. The level of involvement will impact the outcome of the development activity, in that the end user will have been able to influence – to a greater or lesser extent – how closely the system will fit their requirements. This is a rarely an instant affair, as it is only through a period of operational use that the value of the participation can be assessed, mainly because of the time it takes to familiarize oneself with a new system. This perception of value will ultimately impact the end-users' desire to participate in future projects.

DEVELOPER–USER ATTITUDES

The attitudes of both the user and developer, indicated in the shaded area in Figure 5.1, will be affected by their previous exposure to project failure. Clearly, if the user has been involved with a failed information systems project, they will retain a degree of scepticism as to the viability of any future project with which they might be involved. Conversely, if their experience is positive, they will probably have a positive attitude toward future projects and IT staff in general. The developer will be equally tainted by their experience of failure, but also by the users' attitude towards them. For example, if the user was considered to be antagonistic by the developer they are more likely to exclude them from future developments. If more supportive, the developer will probably be more receptive to their active involvement. It is this relationship that is the cornerstone to the culture gap's severity, and it should be clear that there are many influences that can affect it.

In extreme cases, culture gaps can develop within the IT function itself and this is often the result of a disjointed and semi-focused approach to IT integration. Organizations that make a clear distinction between IT development and maintenance activities can allow IT itself to become disconnected. In such cases, the two cultures that develop neither trust nor respect each other. IT maintenance typically see themselves to be 'on the fag end of development', and view development as slip-shod and lacking process. IT development, on the other hand, view maintenance as unresponsive and staffed by unskilled people. This uneasy relationship results in finger-pointing and blame when misunderstandings and errors occur and serves to reinforce this cultural difference, and more importantly, the general culture gap with the business.

THE BOARD-LEVEL CULTURE GAP

The second area where the culture gap manifests itself is at board level. As we saw in Chapter 1, when we reviewed the last fifty years of IT, the principal reason for bringing a senior IT professional on to the board was to give IT an appropriate voice in the governance and direction of the organization. However, this has clearly not worked because of the disconnect that has developed between the technologist and the rest of the board. As with the working level, some of the reasons for this disconnect are the same, including the technical focus, narrow experience and use of vast amounts of jargon. However, I believe there are other factors that have helped to make the board-level culture gap as problematic as that at the working level. Such factors include:

- The recognition that IT is now a significant factor in organizations has disrupted the existing balance of power between the functions, and they don't like it.

- The board feel uncomfortable with IT because they don't or won't understand it – it exposes a weakness which they do not wish to confront.

- The board still sees IT as a support function, rather than one that provides direction. As a result, they tend to treat the IT director/chief information officer accordingly by focusing on the operational problems with IT rather than its strategic value.

- Although the IT director/chief information officer may believe that IT is adding value to the organization, the rest of the business does not believe this to be the case. For example, a survey conducted for Novell found that although 85 per cent of IT managers believed they had a role in convincing senior management of the importance and benefits of new technology, only 48 per cent of board-level directors viewed IT as either advisers, or strategists.[15]

- IT people feel uncomfortable sitting on the board because they lack the general business acumen required to govern the organization. As a result, their contribution becomes narrowly focused on technology which reinforces the disconnect and the board's preference for the IT director/chief information officer to discuss operational rather than strategic issues.

Although the board identifies the problem to be fundamentally one existing between the users and developers, it is clear that there are just as many problems on the board itself. The irony is that, according to a recent survey, 47 per cent of IT directors/chief information officers believed their main problem was the culture gap between IT and business professionals, and 56 per cent believed it was damaging the organization's ability to gain the competitive edge.[16] What they fail to see, of course, is that they are contributing to it, and that the disconnect at board level influences the working level, and indeed, how the rest of the organization relates to IT. The need to address this board-level problem is, in my opinion, just as important as addressing the working-level problems, as it is through bottom-up and top-down effort that the culture gap can be eliminated.

WHAT HAS BEEN DONE TO RESOLVE IT?

In attempting to resolve the problems that the culture gap presents to the success of information systems projects, organizations have used a variety of structural approaches, including:

- centralized information system development and rollout in which the responsibility for the IT infrastructure and information systems rests with the IT department;
- decentralized information systems development in which the end-user departments develop and maintain their own information systems without input from a centralized IT department; and
- outsourced information system development in which the development and maintenance of information systems is transferred to a third-party supplier.

Each approach attempts to balance the need to retain control over the organization's IT infrastructure, in terms of its costs, resources and so on, whilst trying to ensure it is best positioned to serve the needs of the business. Not surprisingly, each of these has failed on its own to resolve the problems of the culture gap.

However, this is not to say that each is not applicable under certain conditions. But organizations have tended to go for the 'all or nothing' approach rather than mixing them to provide an optimum balance.

The relative pros and cons of each of these approaches is summarized in Table 5.1 together with their typical impacts on information systems projects.

It should be clear from Table 5.1 that whatever approach is adopted, it will not, on its own, resolve the problems with the culture gap. Nor will it address the performance issues associated with information systems project failure. The sooner organizations recognize that they cannot solve these problems using structural approaches alone, the better. As we will see in the rest of Part I, there are a number of other issues that must be tackled before organizations will achieve the success they are looking for.

If organizations are going to resolve the problems that the culture gap presents to them, they must:

- recognize and understand that the culture gap is not a straightforward 'us and them' problem, but one which touches on, and involves the whole organization, the wider IT profession, and those that serve it including professional bodies, recruitment agencies, and the education and training establishments;
- create ways of breaking through the 'us and them' mindset which persists throughout organizations, and in particular at the board and working levels;
- reframe the relationship between IT and the business into something that is energizing as opposed to debilitating; and
- provide the IT community with fulfilling careers that are capable of meeting all of their expectations.

Finally, with the increasing emphasis on information, and the emergence of information politics, the culture gap can be exploited by those with political intentions. Hijacking an information systems project as a means of gaining power through information ownership is another problem which can lead to failure, as

Table 5.1 Structural attempts at resolving the culture gap

Approach	Pros	Cons	Effect on information systems projects
Centralized	• economies of scale • simpler to implement organization's strategic direction • reduces duplication of effort • reduces costs • balances resource needs • allows consistent approaches to be applied to the development process	• harder to implement local requirements • slower development times • increases systems development backlog • powerful functions' needs met before those with less influence • increases the disconnect between business and technology • reduces flexibility	• projects can stall as functions argue over functionality • large projects, which involve significant cross-functional collaboration, are prone to both escalation and failure • sniping between business and IT leads to poor cooperation, and usually badly designed systems • difficult to realize the benefits from projects, as IT do not see it to be their problem and the business is not sufficiently involved to understand how to do it
Decentralized	• allows lower-level empowerment and decision making • improved focus on local IT needs • better fit between business and technology needs • better working relationship between business and IT • improved system design	• limited or no development standards • proliferation of systems to support individual needs • IT spend invisible • local systems not aligned with the rest of the organization • harder to cope with complex intersystem relationships • leads to islands of information, and data integrity problems • increases overall (organization) IT spend	• systems developed without any standards, and this lack of consistency can lead to the failure of local projects • cross-functional collaboration is lost, which makes the resulting systems isolated from the rest of the business • no opportunity for learning from project failures because they will be hidden from the view of the rest of the business
Outsourced	• reduces IT infrastructure costs • increases speed of information systems development • improves service quality and productivity • allows access to leading-edge technology • reduces technological risk • increases technological flexibility • eases the overall management activity associated with IT	• increased costs (over the long term) • increased risk • loss of internal technical knowledge • loss of flexibility (especially if locked into a long-term contract) • access to technical talent within the vendor is often limited • increased information management complexity through having to manage a third-party vendor relationship over which there is limited control	• problems surface late in the project, as progress is typically hidden from view • large projects are particularly prone to over-commitment and escalation • with no control over workloads, supplier can shift resources and delay projects without the consent of the organization • loss of internal expertise required to challenge the supplier on efficacy of solution and on implementation issues

the London Stock Exchange found to its detriment in the Taurus project. The next chapter draws out such political issues in greater detail.

CHAPTER SIX

Information politics: the new organizational battleground

The concept of power, and understanding its implications within organizations, has long been of interest to the academic, consultancy and business communities. Understanding how power can be gained, applied, and retained, together with its impacts, is critical knowledge for the aspiring chief executive. Clearly the application – use and abuse – of power within organizations is rarely a straightforward affair and not only restricted to the higher echelons of the board. It manifests itself at all levels of the organization, both within and between functions, by individuals, and within and between groups. Therefore, anything that disrupts the balance of power should expect a turbulent ride. In addition, with the shift to the Information Age, employees are recognizing that information can provide them with a source of power and, if manipulated carefully enough, can be used to get their own way. Given that the success of an information systems project depends on having the correct information on which to base the requirements, it soon becomes clear that if people manipulate information for their own ends, the project can end up producing little of any value for the organization.

In understanding the impacts of information politics on their information systems projects, organizations must:

- recognize how power and politics in general are manifested within projects;
- accept that any project, but in particular information systems projects, will disrupt the balance of power in the organization, and hence, may be resisted;
- realize that the nature of power is changing, with it shifting away from the traditional sources associated with position and status, and towards those associated with information and knowledge; and

- understand that information politics is increasingly a factor in major information systems projects, and that this can contribute to failure.

POWER AND POLITICS IN ORGANIZATIONS

Power in its simplest form is the influence one person has over another to get something done. Power is partly about inequalities, ownership of resources in its various forms, and control. It reflects the ability of individuals to exploit the inequalities that exist within organizations to gain advantage, and hence power, over their rivals. This perspective mirrors Machiavelli's in his book *The Prince*[1] – in writing about sixteenth-century court life, Machiavelli observed that the locus of power at any one time reflected the contingent nature of the situation, the people and their interaction. Power was continuously produced and reproduced; the retention of power, once gained, required immense effort and constant vigilance. Maintaining one's power within the modern corporation is not as violent as it was in the sixteenth century, but it certainly requires some of the many subtleties described by Machiavelli. For example, whilst people may compete for position and power within a single department, they, as members of the same department, are also involved within a wider power game with other departments. Resource scarcities and turbulent business environments create the same shifting of power observed by Machiavelli, in which organizational functions jockey for organizational dominance by aligning themselves with the key issues facing the board of directors. Over time, the relative power of functions will ebb and flow as the key issues facing the board change.

Power is accepted because it is legitimized through social and organizational norms, structures, and their implicit and explicit rules. The principal source of power within an organization is that associated with position. An individual typically has little or no power without position, and positional power provides the individual with the ability to control organizational resources. Furthermore, power is as much about perception as reality, because it affects the way other members of the organization behave towards those that have it. For example, the majority of employees live in fear of the chief executive, as though he is some kind of demigod – all seeing, all powerful. The fact that the chief executive is a normal person who has a position that is held in high esteem means, in reality, very little. It is only the power created by the legitimization of position that creates this behaviour. Of course, organizations would not function in the way they do without the power created through position – it establishes the basis for decision making, and control.

Politics, on the other hand, is perceived to be the illegitimate use of power for personal means. Politics circumvents the legitimate power that resides in organizations, and is a way of gaining power through means other than those prescribed by the organization. For example, the use of hidden agendas by managers is a common manifestation of political behaviour, and is seen as a way of manipulating those who are able to provide access to the power these managers seek. Because politics is seen in such a negative light, the majority of employees try to ignore it. Yet, with the heterogeneous nature of organizations, politics is a common, and natural, behaviour. Acting in a purely rational way is unrealistic, and those who ignore politics within organizations do so at their peril.

In Table 6.1, I have included some of the most commonly used political behaviours used within organizations.[2] It should be remembered of course that these political behaviours are essentially about power, either its acquisition or retention. These are especially important within the context of an information systems project because of the damage they can cause. For example, dealing with these behaviours can result in valuable time being wasted on trying to gain buy-in from reluctant functional units, seeking out vital information on which the project depends, or gaining access to senior managers. All of these sap the project's energy, and, of course, are usually deliberate moves to limit the project's impacts.

PROJECTS AND THE BALANCE OF POWER

Incremental change associated with ongoing process improvements typical of most operational activity is insufficient to maintain business viability. Rapid business change and responsiveness are the order of the day. Organizations have realized that projects are the most effective means of introducing radical, and rapid change. But such radical change can result in major upheavals in the balance of power across the organization, and as such, the projects used to introduce the change are rarely perceived as being neutral. For any project to succeed, there are often major political battles to be fought during its execution. Such battles can occur at all stages of a project, from inception right through to implementation, and the nearer to implementation the higher the stakes. Information systems projects are no exception, and indeed are probably a significant cause of political and power plays within the modern corporation. There are four reasons for this:

- The ubiquitous nature of information systems means that any new system is likely to disturb multiple organizational functions and hence disrupt the existing power, and political status quo.

- The culture gap between business and IT allows the information systems project to become a convenient battleground and ultimate scapegoat for the political battles that occur as the project progresses. IT's focus on the technological aspects of the project, together with the often naïve belief that the project is acceptable to all stakeholders, results in a lack of sensitivity to the political problems that can occur.

Table 6.1   Common political behaviours

Political behaviour	Description
Ownership	An individual or group owns a project, product line, department, process and benefits from the status and rights of ownership. Occupation is all about control by being there first. Within projects, it is the ownership of resources that typically creates the greatest amount of political turbulence.
Information manipulation	Knowledge is power. More information generates more filters through which the information must pass. And each filter provides ample opportunity for information distortion. Typical tactics include withholding information, and manipulating it to change the message (for example, distorting bad news to appear good, or not divulging it). Information manipulation is increasingly linked to ownership.
Alliances	Political battles within organizations usually involve taking sides, and an information system project is no different. Types of behaviour include those associated with sycophants, sleepers (waiting to join the winning side), shoulder rubbers (face-to-face contacts), and those that monopolize others' time.
Invisible walls	This is especially applicable to projects where rules, procedures and information access are placed in the path of the project to slow it down, de-rail it and generally prevent it from achieving its objectives. The invisible wall game is best played by those who can maintain the appearance of sincere effort, but without actually achieving anything.
Strategic non-compliance	Agreeing up front to cooperate, and default on the agreement at the last minute, leaves little or no opportunity for the other party to do anything about it.
Discrediting	It is said that reputation is one of the cornerstones of power, and once lost is almost impossible to regain.[3] Therefore, discrediting individuals is one of the surest ways to gain power.
Camouflage	The purpose of camouflage is to distract or confuse people long enough to defuse or deflect a course of action. This type of behaviour within projects would usually result in the project team hunting down needless information, at the project's expense. Camouflage can sometimes be associated with discrediting.

This can result in the project becoming a pawn in a wider political battle.

- The ability to eradicate headcount is often one of the principal benefits arising from the introduction of a new information system. However, removal of headcount has a direct impact on a department's power, as it is often directly associated with the very headcount it is about to lose. If an organizational function perceives the introduction of a new information system will negatively impact their status, they will do everything in their power to ensure the

project fails, even though it might be of benefit to the organization as a whole.

- The lack of physical intuition associated with an information systems project as outlined in Chapter 2 can expose the project to political manoeuvring. For example, difficulties in defining business requirements during the requirements elicitation and specification stage can result in incomplete, and possibly incorrect, requirements to be specified, ensuring the project will fail to deliver that which is expected of it.

In order to combat the many political and power-based problems that can beset even the best information systems project, the usual advice is to engage a powerful sponsor. This is quite natural as, without a powerful backer, the project may fall at the first hurdle. But depending on a single source of power may be insufficient to guarantee the continued support of the wider stakeholder community, especially if it is a large enterprise-wide project. Therefore, understanding how projects impact the balance of power is vital.

RESISTANCE TO CHANGE

Many information systems projects seem to fail at the very last hurdle of implementation. The project appeared to have all the support necessary to allow it to succeed, and yet, just as it was about to complete, it was rejected, and terminated. The reasons for its rejection are usually associated with it failing to deliver what was expected of it. While clearly frustrating, much of this final rejection can be put down to the political manoeuvring related to the realization of the impacts the system will have on, amongst others, the balance of power. It may also be due to the strategic non-compliance game in which the project appears to be in a healthy position, with all the signs indicating that the end users are going to accept and use the new system, until, at the very last minute, rejection at implementation. At this point in the project, there is very little one can do.

Not all change will be resisted, as most organizations are able to absorb the ongoing incremental improvements and changes to their operations. For example, the activity of maintaining an information system falls into this category because it involves making general improvements to existing functionality with which the end users are familiar. It is usually major or radical change that leads to resistance from those impacted by it.

A number of factors are present within any organization that make change either less or more readily acceptable:[4]

● Structure – Most organizations have a well-defined structure with established rules and procedures. These are designed to maintain the status quo and, depending on the flexibility of such structures, the ability to change will vary significantly. Very rigid hierarchical structures are more likely to resist change than those which are more fluid and loosely structured.

● Culture – Some organizations have very rigid cultures, themselves partly created and reinforced through structure. Such organizations tend to be very adept at resisting change, or providing the illusion of change when in reality they have not changed at all. They are like a piece of rubber that snaps back to its original form once stretched. This is especially true for bureaucratic organizational forms, such as government bodies. Equally, there are those cultures that exist which are sufficiently fluid and flexible to cope with continuous, radical change. This is typical of the high-technology sector, for example, Silicon Valley in the United States, where because of the rapid pace of change, organizations who are not able to respond, die.

● Individual habit – Individuals and groups within organizations prefer routine – it provides comfort and allows personal competence to develop. Routine also creates a sense of community within the local working environment, something that can benefit the function, and organization as a whole. When this environment changes, the comfort provided by habit, routine and familiarity are disturbed, and this often leads to resistance.

● Security – It is paradoxical that, despite record levels of employment in the United States and United Kingdom, people feel very insecure. This insecurity, it is believed, stems from the general economic turbulence, the throw-back from the downsizing experience of the early 1990s, and continuous advances in computer technology. Insecurity can breed resistance, as the fear of being downsized is a great motivator for entrenchment. It also limits organizations' creativity as employees believe that taking risks exposes them to personal failure, and probable dismissal from the firm, which is regarded as being more brutish and unforgiving than it was prior to downsizing.[5] Downsizing has also diminished the trust between employees and their employers, thereby reinforcing the view that it is better to commit to oneself than to an employer who will eliminate headcount at the slightest hint of a market downturn.

- Power, status and esteem – As suggested earlier, by their very nature, projects will upset the balance of power within an organization. Therefore, where a change is perceived to detrimentally affect a person's power base they will do all they can to protect what they have. Of course, there will be those who see the project as an ideal opportunity to gain power, and so will do all they can to ensure it succeeds. This tension is always present within a project, and must be carefully managed.

Resistance to change in relation to IT is not, therefore, a simple rejection of a proposed, or newly implemented, information system. It is a complex combination of factors that can be organizational or individual, but primarily situational in nature. The strongly held belief that resistance to change is a phenomenon that needs to be eliminated by the information systems professional is indicative of a technocentric mentality that puts technology before people in organizations. Resistance to change ought to be recognized as action – rather than reaction – conveying important messages for systems professionals. It should also be recognized as being a normal course of events for organizations, particularly successful ones.

Finally, it should be stated that rapid technical change associated with computer technology can lead to resistance through technology fatigue because of the need to continually learn new techniques, systems and ways of working. Information systems professionals also have their fair share of problems with rapid technological change, as

organizations expect them to be able to apply the latest techniques, tools and technologies, often without any formal training. This leads to the following types of problem:[6]

- Ignorance of prevailing knowledge – Information systems professionals may not be aware of the full extent of the new technologies and techniques available, even though the organization expects them to understand all aspects of IT. This can place them in a difficult position when expected to implement a new technology which they know little about. With faster cycle times, and shortening project horizons, there is often no time to gain the necessary understanding prior to attempting its implementation; as a result, the project becomes the training ground.

- Failure to use prevailing knowledge – Although aware of current tools, techniques and technologies, organizational pressure for rapid implementation often means there is no time to use them. Such time pressure results in little time to train staff, which in turn reduces the chances of delivering the project successfully. Indeed, a recent report from Kennedy Research Group suggests that, as organizations clamber for more and more IT, they, along with consultancies, are fielding second-rate staff.[7] The same report goes on to cite a civil suit that has been filed by W. L. Gore Associates against Deloitte Consulting, who, according to Gore, had assigned unskilled and inexperienced consultants to install PeopleSoft human resources software to integrate payroll automation. According to the suit, the resulting chaos led to payroll accounts that did not balance, employees not getting paid, and vacation and health benefits that could not be tracked.

- Conditions beyond prevailing knowledge – This is the classic leading-edge project that typically involves pioneering activity and trailblazing by the IT expert, using hitherto untried and untested technologies, tools or techniques. This can be a significant problem if this occurs on a business-critical project, such as with the Westpac CS90, London Ambulance and CONFIRM projects described earlier in Chapter 2.

These conditions can pose a significant risk to the information systems project and, ultimately, the organization; unfortunately, they can also serve to reinforce the culture gap because of the strong likelihood of failure that accompanies them.

THE CHANGING NATURE OF POWER

Apart from the general manifestation of power and its associated political activity within organizations, there is a further and newer form of power associated with information. As organizations hurtle through the Information Age, in which information and knowledge are becoming fundamental building-blocks to survival, they see IT, and lots of it, as the key to achieving success. Individuals within these same organizations are also waking up to the need to harness their own intellectual capital. Books and articles abound which describe apocalyptic tales of the information-intensive company, in which only those who are able to acquire, manipulate and apply knowledge will succeed. These 'symbolic analysts', as they are sometimes called, are expected to become a smaller and smaller elite as technology takes over the majority of organizational activity. This does not necessarily mean massive unemployment, but what it does mean is that the majority of work is likely to become low paid and mundane. With knowledge becoming a valued organizational asset, the adage 'knowledge is power' is a watchword for not only the ambitious employee, but also for those who wish to stay in reasonably well-paid employment.

Therefore, the ability to control information that is important to the organization has become a basic form of power that can be harnessed and wielded by managers and subordinates alike. This emphasis on information has been reinforced by the blood-letting associated with the business process re-

engineering projects of the early to mid 1990s. Although not intended to become a euphemism for downsizing, such projects led to corporations removing great tranches of their middle management and employees – the former through the reduction in management layers by delayering, and the latter through removal of staff by the re-engineering and automation of business process. In many respects, the business process re-engineering fad was, at least in part, designed to improve the level of payback from IT, which at that time was in question[8] (see also Chapter 4, and the productivity paradox). Unfortunately, the success rate of these projects was as poor as that experienced with information systems, with only 16 per cent providing the benefits expected of them, and 68 per cent experiencing problems of one sort or another.[9]

As well as the problems that delayering subsequently brought to the organization – such as increased costs, removal of the wrong staff, and difficulties in meeting client demands with a reduced and demoralized workforce – downsizing has had another side-effect: the removal of some of the traditional sources of power within the once deeply layered organization, typically status and position. This absence of power was soon replaced by another: information. If an organization is dependent on its information infrastructure, then what better way to gain power than through the control of information? This shift toward information-based power was probably going to occur anyway, but the downsizing of the 1990s accelerated it significantly. This is supported by a recent survey of the United Kingdom's Times Top 1000 companies, which in 1998 revealed that critical decisions were being taken without access to vital facts because of the 'information is power' attitude prevalent in corporate culture.[10] Islands of information jealously guarded by the managers that possess them are leading to decisions being made in the absence of the right information. The survey also revealed that these same organizations typically had a computer on every manager's desktop, and yet they often complained of not having access to the information they really needed.

Clearly, the power that information gives is like any other form of power, that is, to be retained and jealously guarded, rather than freely shared. For example, one study found that 20 per cent of employees believe that it is not in their best interests to share knowledge, preferring to hoard it to win promotion, or to take with them when they move to another employer.[11]

INFORMATION POLITICS

Clearly, if information and knowledge are to become fundamental organizational assets, they must be universally accessible. This means a technical infrastructure and organizational culture must be in place that allows information to be freely shared. However, change, and increasingly change that impacts the information infrastructure in its widest sense, leads to a greater degree of information politics. This is because a larger number of jobs and roles have become defined by the unique information they hold, and they may be less likely to share this with other parts of the organization – it is possibly their only source of power. It should come as no surprise, therefore, that a truly information-sharing organization is largely fantasy, as most information is produced and consumed at the sub-unit level of the organization. For example, of the 25 organizations studied by Davenport in 1992, all attempts at creating an information-based culture failed, for the most part, due to the failure to manage the politics associated with information.[12] One reason why the stakes are so high in information politics is that there is more than just information at stake, as information encapsulates the methods, processes and systems used to produce and consume it.

Such problems in trying to create an information-sharing culture are in many respects a legacy of the way in which organizations traditionally collected and stored data prior to the introduction of IT. The concept of personal ownership was acceptable, because if someone had worked hard to get the information they needed, they could legitimately class it as their own personal property. The introduction of IT challenged this view. Initially, there was good reason to retain data locally, because of the inaccuracies of the data held in the computer together with the unreliable nature of software. Although the computer is more reliable now, the attitude of data as property dies hard. In the modern corporate environment, information is possibly the greatest asset to have, but it is one that is not openly shared. For example, ICI in the United Kingdom has witnessed three major knowledge-management efforts to establish company-wide yellow pages through its intranet. Each attempt failed. As the vice-president of IT stated in 1999, 'the mere fact that we have a technical facility does not necessarily make it right to use in the business.'[13]

The vacuum created by the absence of an information-sharing culture is filled by a variety of typically dysfunctional behaviours.[14] These behaviours can be defined by the level of control exerted over the information and its sources (which can be either strong or weak), and the perceived information needs of the organization or function (which can be either narrow or wide). These behaviours manifest themselves within the organization as a whole, as well as within individual functions, and as a consequence can create a confusing mix of political behaviour around information.

At the more general, organizational level, there are four dysfunctional behaviours, as illustrated in Figure 6.1.

Organizations that have a reactive stance tend to have a limited level of control over what information is created and consumed, whilst having the perception that they require lots of it. As a result, there is a tendency to focus on immediate information requirements without thinking of what is actually required from a strategic standpoint. Therefore, immense effort can be used to collect information which is not useful. The opposite behaviour is the regressive stance, in which information needs are considered to be wide-ranging, and the level of control strong. Here there is a tendency to focus on greater control and detail, at the expense of viewing information strategically. Therefore, organizations will explore known information to the extent that it can result in information

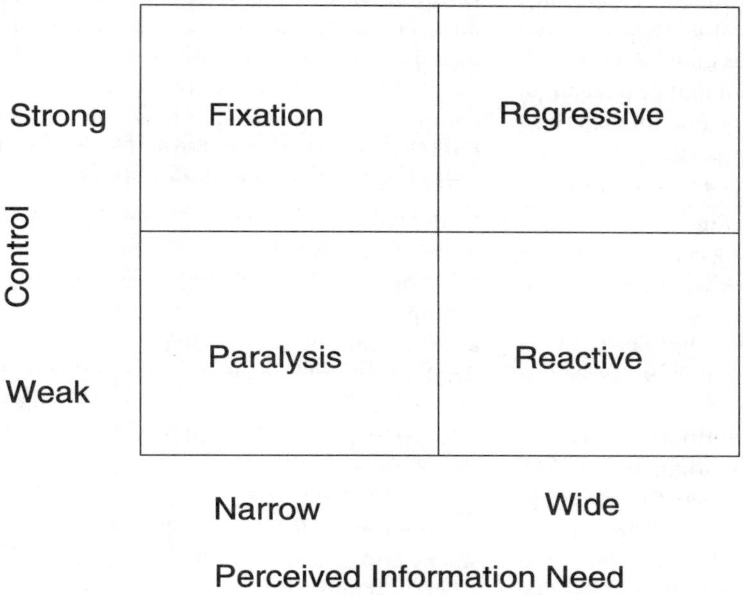

	Narrow	Wide
Strong	Fixation	Regressive
Weak	Paralysis	Reactive

Control

Narrow   Wide

Perceived Information Need

Figure 6.1
Dysfunctional
information behaviours
(organizational)

overload. For those organizations that have a narrow perception of their information needs, there are two types of dysfunctional behaviour. Where the level of control is weak, the organization suffers from information paralysis in which there is a tendency to focus on existing information and associated processes to the detriment of the new. Where there is strong control, fixation results in which there is an even greater concentration on a narrow band of information.

The types of dysfunctional behaviour that manifest themselves at the functional level can vary significantly from the organizational level because of the influence of functional cultures (see Figure 6.2).

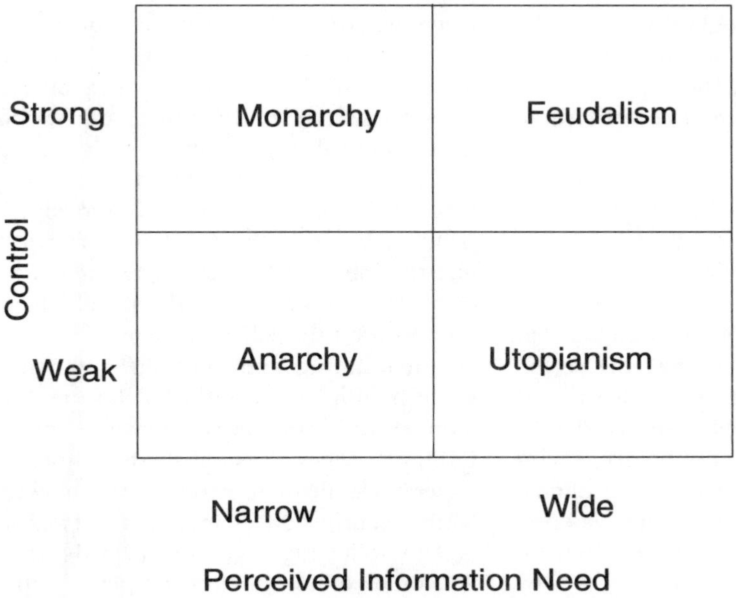

Figure 6.2
Dysfunctional
information behaviours
(functional)

	Narrow	Wide
Strong	Monarchy	Feudalism
Weak	Anarchy	Utopianism

Control

Narrow   Wide

Perceived Information Need

Functions that display the utopian behaviour typically have the belief that, through the application of leading-edge technologies, it is possible to have all the information needed by the function at the touch of a button. This utopian view often fails to consider the wider political circumstances, and plays into the hands of the pure technologists. For those functions that exhibit a strong control over their information resource, and a wide information need, the management of information is usually focused on their own particular needs. As a result, little, if any, information is passed out to other functions, and each function acts like a small kingdom in which information becomes one of the cultural glues holding it together. Hence the term 'feudalism'. Where the perceived information needs are narrow, and the level of control weak, anarchy results, in which the absence of any information management policy allows the function, and individuals within it, to determine their own information needs. This leads to the creation of islands of information, duplication, and the proliferation of systems to support personal information needs. Where information needs are considered to be narrow, but control is strong, monarchy results, in which ownership of information resides with those who collect it, and at best is shared on a need-to-know basis, or more typically, not at all. This classic form of dysfunctional behaviour can be particularly damaging, as it ensures that a fully information-sharing organization can never be achieved, and is arguably a more severe form of feudalism.

These functional behaviours can manifest themselves within any one of the four organizational information cultures previously identified, and will themselves vary between each one (see Figure 6.3).

The variety of information behaviours that can occur represents a major challenge to the information systems project, especially where it cuts across the entire organization. Having to satisfy top-down, organizational needs and those of individual functions can be almost impossible, and often leads to the watering down of requirements, compromising on functionality, or the hijacking of a project by those with the most power. The following example provides a short insight into the problems that can occur.

POWER, POLITICS AND INFORMATION POLITICS – THE TAURUS PROJECT[15]

In 1979, the London Stock Exchange automated share dealings between stockbrokers through the introduction of Talisman. Its success prompted a proposal in 1981 to extend this automation by introducing a centralized database system to enable paperless trading. This proposal was rejected by share registrars, who were paid to hold the paper records of shareholders for listed companies.

The 1986 Big Bang in the City of London represented a fundamental shift in the way stocks and shares were traded on the London Stock Exchange. But the Big Bang was not only associated with the shift to electronic trading, as it also replaced the cosy gentlemen's club with the hard-nosed, hard-working US style of stockbroking.

Initially, the early introduction of electronic trading was restricted to the front office, with the back office functions such as settlement retaining their existing processes and focus on paper. With an electronic front office, and a paper-based back office, backlogs between when the deal was made and completion of the sale were not uncommon. This came to a head during the stock market crash of October 1987, when banks and security firms found it difficult to determine their positions – that is, identifying how much and to whom they owed money, and how much and by whom was owed to them – required to settle the £13.4 billion's worth of unsettled shares. The crash highlighted the risks of having a slow and burdensome settlement process. After the collapse of a previous attempt at streamlining and centralizing share and share-holding information – Taurus 1 – an industry-wide committee, known as the Siscot Committee, was established to design a paperless settlement process acceptable to the banks, security houses, investors and registrars.

The following vignettes provide a short illustration of how politics and power impacted

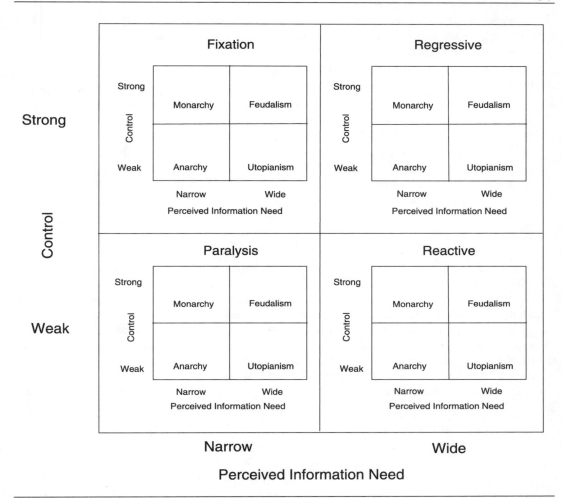

Figure 6.3 Combining organizational and functional information behaviours

the project. And, although a major factor in the failure of Taurus was associated with the technological problems related to the tailoring of an American package originally designed for the US stock market, many of the underlying causes stemmed from the power, politics and information politics of the key participants:

● Power and politics came into the project very early on, as each of the major stakeholder groups – brokers, market makers, registrars, banks and the Stock Exchange – had different objectives, with many wanting to retain the status quo of their operations. Each member of the committee fought their own corner, regardless of the common good.

● The initial design of Taurus met considerable opposition, and had to be changed substantially because the focus on a centralized database ignored the established interests of the market. In essence, the design reflected the utopian view of information management, and ignored the wider business requirements. It therefore had to be redesigned.

● This redesign benefited the most vocal groups within the committee, which included the stockbrokers, listed companies and registrars. For example, the registrars wanted to retain their role within the stock market that was at risk with the possible elimination of share certificates, listed companies wanted to be able to track share ownership, and brokers wished to minimize the costs of maintaining records unnecessarily.

● The adoption of a design-by-committee approach reflected the lack of power the Stock Exchange had over the market, and, rather than impose a system upon it, had to engage all the main stakeholders during the design stage. Because no one party held the balance of power, the entire process dragged on and was beset by change after change. The resultant design was more complex than it would otherwise have been, and reflected the existing imperfections within the paper-based system and a significant degree of compromise.

● The design-by-committee, consensus approach to the development of Taurus led to so many changes, that by the time the project was abandoned in March 1993, a full design had never been completed, and the core part of the system never built.

● The United Kingdom's Department of Trade and Industry's insistence on sophisticated encryption techniques resulted in increased costs and complexity and led to another layer of politics around information.

● The market, who was one of the principal stakeholders, knew the least about the project – as it became more dissatisfied with Taurus it quietly moved resources onto other projects and spread rumours to the press suggesting the project was in trouble.

The success of any information systems project is clearly dependent on the information it receives throughout its life cycle, but especially during the early stages. When, as with the Taurus project, this proves to be confused and open to political manoeuvring, the result can be disastrous, and very expensive – Taurus cost the finance industry in excess of £300 million.

To address the problems that information politics presents to information systems projects, organizations and the project managers they employ must:

● embrace the new political landscape that exists around information;

● avoid shying away from managing the political dimensions of the project;

● recognize that technology on its own will not provide the basis for project success; and

● develop ways to eliminate information politics by promoting information sharing, and implementing a technical infrastructure that is able to support it.

Finally, it should be remembered that information politics at the project level can be used to ensure a continuous flow of funds and support when the project is running late, over budget and, in extreme situations, failing. Such irrational behaviour is the topic of the next chapter.

Over-commitment in information systems projects: when failure is the only option

Escalation refers to a predicament where decision makers find themselves trapped in a losing course of action as a result of previous decisions. Costs are incurred; there is an opportunity to withdraw or to persist; and the consequences of withdrawal or persistence are uncertain. Typically, the response of such dilemmas is irrational persistence.[1]

It has long been believed that in order to deliver an information systems project successfully there must be a sustained level of commitment. Commitment provides the necessary level of energy and enthusiasm to make the project a success. However, no matter how vital, organizations can sometimes become over-committed to a project, to the point where they ignore some of the basic warning signs that the project is failing. Such excessive commitment, termed 'escalation', also prevents the decision to terminate a project from being made early enough. In such circumstances, organizations continue to sink additional money and resources into the project, and in doing so increase their commitment to it. This creates a vicious circle of increasing commitment, costs and probability of failure.

When it comes to understanding how escalation can lead to information systems project failure, organizations must understand:

- the basic project and organizational components of escalation, including its irrational underpinning;
- where irrational behaviour, and hence escalation, is likely to occur within the project's life cycle; and
- what the consequences of escalating are on an information systems project.

THE PROJECT-RELATED COMPONENTS OF ESCALATION

Why should projects continue when the warning signs seem clear to both internal and external observers? The reason why such persistence in the face of failure exists has a lot to do with the basic human condition. It also has to do with the increasing investment trends in IT, and the need to tackle organizational change on a much wider footing. When large amounts of money have been invested in an information systems project there is a lot at stake, including reputation. For example the director of the London Ambulance Service ignored repeated warnings that the Automated Despatch System would not cope with the demands that were to be placed on it. Also, despite the strong evidence that the project would fail, the senior managers of California Department of Motor Vehicles project continued to invest in the initiative. The project eventually failed at a cost of $44 million.[2]

Key to understanding why organizations continue with what turn out to be lemon projects involves recognizing some of the basic behavioural traits of those working on, and committed to, the project, and how these behaviours can extend beyond the project team into the wider organization. Although the visible evidence of a failing project is usually restricted to increasing costs and slipping schedules, there are hidden behavioural factors that create an environment in which commitment to the project can be escalated to the point of no return.

The model depicted in Figure 7.1 is designed to illustrate how the commitment to an information systems project can escalate to the point of failure. Initially, commitment is focused within the project team itself, which is a

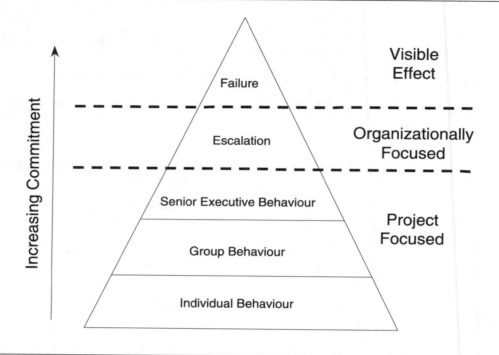

Figure 7.1   The escalation model

necessary and sufficient condition to allow the project work to progress at the pace required. Equally, it is in the project's best interests to ensure the project's stakeholders are fully engaged and also committed to the project. When the project starts to falter, however, over-commitment can result. And where the organizational conditions permit, this over-commitment can extend beyond the immediate project team into the wider stakeholder community. This is usually accompanied by action from the project team to ensure continuous flow of funds into the project despite its problems. Once this over-commitment is widened, the likelihood of the project continuing to the point of failure is greatly increased.

This model, and indeed escalation, of commitment has its foundations in the irrational behaviour of those involved with the project. At the lowest level, this is associated with the individuals within the project team, the organizational groups involved with the project, and the senior executives who are committed to the project through their sponsorship. As commitment extends beyond the project team into the wider organization, the level of commitment is increased because the number of people involved with or dependent upon the project increases. This too has its foundations in the irrational behaviour of the people involved, but at this level some wider organizational factors come into play. It is at this stage that the commitment to a project can reach the point of no return.

The following sections describe the model in more detail.

IRRATIONALITY – UNDERPINNING OVER-COMMITMENT

The foundation of escalation lies in the irrational behaviours of people. When irrational behaviour is restricted to individuals its effects are generally isolated. However, where this manifests itself within groups – and especially project teams – the results can be far more severe. Furthermore, as irrational behaviour extends from individuals into groups and ultimately senior executives, the likelihood of a project escalating out of control is more likely.

This irrational foundation to escalation can be viewed at three distinct levels – the individual, the group, and, as a special case of the individual, the senior executive. This extra level has been included because the positional power of the senior executive allows the intensity of the irrational behaviours to be amplified. Although it can be argued that the behaviours identified at this level are equally applicable to the individual level, it is power that makes these behaviours more damaging. To begin with, the irrational behaviours are usually project focused, but as the influence of these extends beyond the project team itself, there is an enhanced risk of commitment escalating out of control. I would, however, argue that a project must have a certain degree of organizational commitment for this to happen. Therefore, a project that has strong and powerful champions and supporters across the organization is more likely to suffer from escalation than one that has weak sponsors and little organizational commitment.

The generic irrational behaviours, together with their manifestation within the information systems project, are summarized in the following paragraphs and tables. Each level of the model is dealt with in turn, starting with a description of the generic behaviour followed by a more detailed review of how this manifests within an information systems project. From the summary that follows, it should become clear that many of the problems associated with the culture gap, unwise investment decisions and the general failure of information systems projects stem from these irrational behaviours,[3] and not, as is often stated, in the technological elements of the project.

INDIVIDUAL BEHAVIOUR

Availability error
The most recent material is 'available'. Previous knowledge and data is lost in the immediacy of the event. Not surprisingly, this type of irrational behaviour is often stimulated by dramatic events.

Halo effect
The tendency is to see all personal attributes consistently, for example, a good sportsman is expected to be a good businessman, father, indeed good at everything. This can equally work in the reverse, where someone is classed as being a general all-round poor performer.

Primacy error
Beliefs are formed by first impressions, with later evidence interpreted in light of this initial impression. The adage, 'first impressions count' is applicable here. If powerful, primacy error can generate positive or negative halo effects very early on in a relationship.

Conformity error
Individuals conform to the behaviour of others whether they know they are making a mistake by doing so, or whether they are unaware both of their mistake and of the social pressure that has induced them to make it. (See Table 7.1.)

GROUP BEHAVIOUR

Groups
Where group members' attitudes are biased in one direction, the interaction of the group will tend to increase this bias because of the need to be valued and suppress criticism. Engaging in a common task only decreases hostility between groups if the outcome is successful. Where it is not, blame is passed from one group to the other, with any existing divisions widening.

Stereotypes
Stereotypes are convenient tools for assessing an individual who belongs to a group. As a result, rather than expected to act individually, a member of a group is expected to conform to the stereotypical behaviour of the entire group. Therefore, no attempt is made at assessing an individual's behaviour in isolation from the rest of the group. Stereotypes tend to be self-fulfilling because of both primacy and availability errors.

The following describes the attitudes of a group of aristocratic Jews towards the fascists in Italy at the outbreak of World War II, and neatly sums up the problems that group behaviour can present (see Table 7.2):

> 'We've been here for a long time,' they said. 'We are one of the most distinguished families in Italy.'

Table 7.1   Individual irrational behaviours in information systems projects

Behaviour	Manifestation within information systems projects
Availability error	The most recent project outcome can be considered available to the users, IT staff and senior executives alike. If, for example, the most available experience is that of failure, it is likely to taint any future information systems project, and probably make the organization more cautious about their IT investments. Conversely, if previous project outcomes have been successful, the organization may become more risk-seeking in its projects and risk the danger of over-extending its capability. It should also be recognized that the external environment may influence decision makers, as information about successful implementations at rival organizations may lead to the inappropriate adoption of similar projects in their own organization.
Halo effect	This can manifest itself in all project stakeholders, although it tends to be particularly prevalent between software developers and end users. For example, end users may believe that, based on their experiences to date, and a certain degree of stereotyping, the software developers with whom they are working are consistent in all their attributes. Thus if considered poor at gathering requirements they would also be considered poor at documentation, testing and so on. The opposite is also true and can lead to the end users only ever dealing with one or two trusted IT staff. Equally, developers may consider the end users who are involved with the project to be consistently poor because they are ineffective at communicating their requirements, or using information systems in general.
Primacy error	First impressions formed at the beginning of the project must be as positive as possible. If poor, the effect of the primacy error can be quite damaging. Therefore the image of an introverted uncommunicative software developer can lead to all events being interpreted under this first impression. Equally, disinterested users who appear to have little concern about their involvement in the start-up phase of the project will be treated as though they are disinterested throughout the whole project, and probably not involved at all. The persistent nature of the culture gap makes the likelihood of this type of behaviour much more likely because of the stereotypes that already exist.
Conformity error	This is particularly evident with project champions and counter-champions (who seek to undermine and limit the likelihood of project success). Generally champions are chosen for their charismatic style and ability to get people to follow a particular course of action. This powerful style can lead other staff/stakeholders to conform to their view without question, or in fear for not following consensus. Strong cultures and sub-cultures can also lead to the manifestation of this type of irrational behaviour, particularly those associated with the fear of failure.

And so they continued to play tennis behind the high walls of their castle and they ate at their chandeliered dining rooms, and continued business as usual. While each person in the family was deeply worried individually, as a group they would not express their worries. As a group enchanted with their past, they were paralyzed to deal with their future. The group dynamics were stronger than the individual fears.[4]

SENIOR EXECUTIVE BEHAVIOUR

Public decisions

Public decisions are more likely to be executed than those taken privately. In general, people do not want to lose face, especially in public.

Misplaced consistency

Someone who has embarked on a course of action may feel they must continue to justify their initial decision. People who have made a sacrifice – time, effort or money – in order to do

Table 7.2   Group irrational behaviours in information systems projects

Behaviour	Manifestation within information systems projects
Groups	Projects are about groups, and group behaviour exerts a strong influence over the outcome of a project. Projects usually involve opposing camps both for and against the proposed change; information systems projects are no different. Clearly, the existence of the culture gap immediately creates two groups between which conflict can arise. When this situation is made more complex by the addition of other groups for and against the wider change, a potent mix of conflicting needs can result. Some of the problems that helped to destroy the London Stock Exchange Taurus project were clearly group related.
	When information systems projects are successful, the culture gap is often slightly reduced, but when failure occurs it only serves to reinforce the culture gap and often extends it. In some instances, when the culture gap is particularly severe, even successful projects can be dismissed as a one-off, and as a result the severity of the culture gap can remain unchanged.
Stereotypes	The culture gap provides a concrete foundation to the application of stereotypes within information systems projects, particularly between the IT developers and the end users.

something, tend to go on doing it even when they stand to lose more than they could gain by continuing. There is always the hope that the situation can be retrieved.

Ignoring the evidence

People tend to seek confirmation of their current hypothesis whereas they should be trying to dis-confirm it. In general, there is a refusal to look for contradictory evidence or, indeed, believe or act upon it if it is brought to one's attention.

Distorting the evidence

Evidence favouring a belief will strengthen the belief whilst contradictory evidence is ignored. As a result the belief remains intact. Therefore, when faced with evidence that is contrary to a particular viewpoint, it will be distorted and dismissed as being irrelevant or inapplicable. Where the evidence is partially correct, it will be distorted to emphasize the positive aspects over the negative. (See Table 7.3.)

THE ORGANIZATIONAL COMPONENTS OF ESCALATION

As the basis for escalation lies within the underlying irrational behaviours of the project team, it should come as no surprise that a higher form of irrationality manifests itself within the organization. The severity of this escalation depends on three sets of factors – project,

psychological and social. Clearly, the project will have a significant bearing on the degree of this severity, and this must therefore lie at the heart of any escalation.

Project factors are typically concerned with the perceived benefits of the project and the organizational costs of withdrawal. There is also a tendency to hype project benefits when they start to go wrong. Such a tactic is designed to ensure the continual flow of funds. Escalation may also be perpetuated by political pressure, corporate pride, entrenchment and administrative inertia.[5]

The psychological component reflects the wider manifestation of irrational behaviour within the organization. The difference between this and the project factors previously described, lies in the number of people conforming to the four behaviours described below. When this happens it is as though a psychosis grips the entire organization:[6]

● Self-justification theory – Suggests that the organization escalates its commitment to a course of action – and undergoes the risk of additional negative outcomes – in order to justify prior behaviour.
● Prospect theory – Suggests that organizations exhibit risk-seeking behaviour when a problem is framed as a choice between two losses; this helps to explains the sunk-cost effect in which

Table 7.3   Senior executive irrational behaviours in information systems projects

Behaviour	Manifestation within information systems projects
Public decisions	Many information systems fail because of public decisions; the London Ambulance failure is but one example. Although this type of irrational behaviour is especially frequent in public sector projects, it also occurs in private sector projects, and is not always restricted to just those that are very large. Even on a limited scale, public decisions made within the confines of an organization can have similar effects.
Misplaced consistency	It is typical to find major information systems projects suffering from this type of irrational behaviour, especially those based on public decisions. Many projects continue despite information and data pointing to a failure in the making. For obvious reasons, this misplaced consistency is usually displayed within the project team; the team have invested significant time and effort, and are unwilling to give up the project that easily. With powerful organizational backing, the board itself may suffer from misplaced consistency. I have heard an apocryphal tale of one organization in which an independent review was conducted on a multi-million dollar project. The review concluded the project would fail. 'Wrong answer' said the board. The reviewers went away, and after a few days came back with 'the project will succeed if a further x million is spent on it'. Misplaced consistency within senior management can be extremely damaging to the balance sheet.
Ignoring the evidence	As the influence, and hence commitment, to a project extends beyond the immediate project team, the danger of both ignoring and distorting the evidence is greatly increased because a lack of independence from the project can cloud judgement. In such instances, a project that is running late and over budget is unlikely to be terminated because of the wider organizational investment and commitment to it. Therefore, any information that points to an impending failure will be ignored, overlooked and generally avoided. The adage 'Don't give me problems, give me solutions' is applicable here.
Distorting the evidence	Distorting the evidence is a more virulent form of ignoring the evidence, as this involves the active distortion of any information that points to failure. Political behaviour is fundamental to this form of irrationality within projects, as it allows the evidence to be reinterpreted as sniping, deliberate spoiling tactics, or gaming, as opposed to being used to good effect within the project.

decision makers exhibit a tendency to throw good money after bad.

- Agency theory – Suggests that individuals will hide negative information from their superiors if it is likely to have a detrimental effect on their career.
- Completion effect – Suggests that, as the project nears completion, there is less likelihood that the organization will terminate it, a case of 'we have come this far, so we might as well finish.' Finish in this instance could mean failure.

The social factors are associated with the wider group interactions of the organization and indicate that escalation may be motivated by the desire not to lose face. Other social factors include competition, job security, imitating the behaviour of apparently successful colleagues, and the cultural norms of consistency.

The combination of irrational behaviours within the immediate project team and wider social and psychological behaviours of the organization can create a potent mix in which a project can take on a life of its own and become a runaway train. The general lack of sensitivity to the warning signs of an impending failure means the project can continue almost unchallenged until failure is just too obvious to ignore. By then, of course, millions might have already been wasted and the damage already done. In such cases there is very little that can be salvaged.

THE PROJECT LIFE CYCLE AND IRRATIONALITY

It is important for organizations to understand how the basic irrational behaviours described above manifest themselves within an information systems project, and where these typically occur within the project's life cycle. Irrational behaviour can manifest itself at any time during the project, and it is important to recognize when it is likely to occur. Figure 7.2 highlights where each behaviour typically occurs along a standard project's life cycle of initiation, execution and implementation.

In general, it should be expected that only those immediacy-type behaviours such as availability error, primacy error, halo effect and public decisions will appear at the start of the project. This is because there are usually relatively few people involved with the project at this stage. The behaviour with the most impact is that of public decisions, as it is this that can do the most damage. Public decisions early on within a project can set it on the path to failure and it was this that led to the Westpac CS90 project being such a public disaster. This problem is particularly true of government-sponsored projects, because these are very often politically driven and usually disregard the application of common sense when it comes to setting achievable project time scales.

As the project moves from initiation into execution, a greater number of the irrational behaviours are likely to materialize as the numbers involved with the initiative increase. The likelihood of escalating commitment is also enhanced at this stage. With increasing numbers comes a general increase in the severity of irrational behaviour. However, the group and senior executive behaviours are likely to dominate because of the influence of positional power. Finally, as the project nears completion – implementation – the number of behaviours that manifest tend to reduce; depending on the outcome (that is, success or failure), the severity of the behaviours will vary. For example, if the project is successful, or partially successful, the severity of ignoring and distorting the evidence will be restricted to the limited number of things that may have not gone to plan, or where functionality and system performance fail to meet expectations. When the outcome is failure, these behaviours are likely to be more extreme and directed to the distortion of the facts and apportioning of blame.

It is important to note that the common behaviour across all three phases of the project is that of public decisions. This is

Behaviour	Initiation	Execution	Implementation
Availability error	✓		
Halo effect	✓	✓	
Primacy error	✓	✓	
Conformity error		✓	
Public decisions	✓	✓	✓
Groups		✓	✓
Stereotypes		✓	✓
Misplaced consistency		✓	
Ignoring the evidence		✓	✓
Distorting the evidence		✓	✓

Figure 7.2 Irrational behaviour and the life cycle

because of the influence that public decisions can have on people's behaviour in general, but especially the strong motivational and conformity effects it can have. Indeed, the majority of the major failures that have come to public attention usually have involved an early and continuing public commitment to the project, thereby setting major external expectations and focus on the project as it progresses.

THE CONSEQUENCES OF ESCALATION

Escalation occurs where the commitment to a project is fuelled and maintained to the point of over-commitment. When the behaviour of the project team, and principal stakeholders, reaches this stage of commitment, it is likely that the project will be unstoppable. But for this to escalate to the wider organizational commitment necessary to maintain support and hence provide an environment for a major disaster, the following conditions must apply:

- There must be an organization-wide commitment to the project, extending well beyond the project team itself.
- The project must involve significant organizational investment either in terms of money, non-financial resources or reputation.
- The project team and principal stakeholders must exhibit the irrational behaviours that underpin escalation.

When these three conditions are present, they serve to minimize the opportunities for early, and in some cases, even late, project termination. The nature of escalation is that once started, it is very difficult to stop, and it soon becomes a Catch-22 situation.

Escalation of commitment is not just restricted to major investments in information systems. All projects are susceptible to escalating commitment as long as they satisfy the three conditions identified above. The following example of a non-IT project shows that significant money can be wasted on a project that ought to have been terminated a long time before it actually was:

The construction of the nuclear facility at Shoreham, New York, which began in 1969 with a projected cost of $75 million and an expected completion date sometime in 1973, continued for 23 years before it was finally closed without ever being commissioned. During this time it suffered from a massive increase in both cost and schedule – the final cost of $5.5 billion was over 73 times its original budgeted cost, and 16 years later than planned.[7]

Escalation does not always result in total failure, as there are many examples of projects that may have suffered from escalation, but have still delivered something, albeit less than originally planned. This may help to explain the 53 per cent of projects that are delivered late and over budget which were identified by the Standish Group survey of 1995.[8] The following example illustrates how a technology component of a major civil engineering project almost led to the failure of the entire project. The example below also demonstrates how increasingly critical the technological components are to a non-technology project:

The completion of the Denver International Airport in 1994 depended on the installation of an automated baggage-handling system that would transport baggage seamlessly around the airport, using 22 miles of track and 4000 cars. Although this aspect of the $5 billion project was only $230 million, it proved to be problematical, because of technical problems with the software, physical problems with constructing the tracks within the constraints of a partially completed airport, and intense media interest. In addition, the time allocated to develop the system was severely constrained – two years, against an estimate of four. The airport was due to be opened in December 1993, but was continuously delayed so that by May 1994, four opening dates had come and gone. At this stage, the project was costing $2.1 million a day in interest and operating costs alone, and there was no end in sight, and no one could predict when the baggage system would be completed. Termination was not an option as the project was publicly sponsored, and suffered from the commitment generated by public decisions, and intense media interest. Eventually, to allow the airport to be opened in February 1995, only one-half of the baggage system was completed – to cope without outward baggage movement – with the other system components being completed at the end of 1995.[9] Interestingly, the work took four years to complete, similar to the original estimate. There was, therefore, little point in setting the unrealistic time-frame of two years. Also, had the original estimates been accepted, the public embarrassment of the late opening of the airport would have been avoided.

ESCALATION IN ACTION – THE CONFIRM PROJECT

The following example provides a powerful illustration of how irrational behaviours within individuals, groups and senior executives can lead to the escalation of a project to the point of failure. To aid interpretation, the relevant irrational behaviours have been highlighted in brackets.

In 1988, a consortium comprising Hilton National Hotels, Marriott Hotels and Budget Rent-A-Car initiated a large-scale project to develop a state-of-the-art travel reservation system combining airline, car rental and hotel information. The project was to be run by AMR information services (AMRIS), a subsidiary of American Airlines, whose previous experience of developing the SABRE airline reservation system had been highly successful *(halo effect, primacy error, availability error)*.

The project was originally split into two distinct phases – design and development – with the option to withdraw from the project (with a $1 million penalty) when the development plan was presented. The design phase was to last seven months, and the development phase a further 37 months. The project was due to complete in June 1992, and the cost was not expected to exceed $55 million. In March 1989, the development plan, which followed the completion of the design in December 1988, was presented by AMRIS. This was considered to be unacceptable by the consortium, and was subsequently reworked by AMRIS over a period of six months. During this time, AMRIS senior executives were at pains to reassure the consortium that all was well with the project. Although by this stage, the project's costs had risen from $55 million to $72.6 million, and implementation had slipped to July 1992, the consortium decided to continue, based on the expected returns *(misplaced consistency)*. The project benefits went without challenge and were later found to be significantly at variance with those presented by AMRIS *(halo effect, primacy error)*.

Almost without exception, deadlines were missed and phases rescheduled, yet the software developers remained convinced they would be able to claw back the lost time and implement as planned *(ignoring the evidence)*. Despite continued assurances from AMRIS that the project would meet its time and budgetary targets, it consistently missed major milestones in January and February 1990. At this time, AMRIS admitted to being 13 weeks behind schedule, but still remained confident of meeting the deadlines.

During the summer of 1990, two members of the consortium expressed severe concerns that the project would not be able to deliver within the remaining schedule. And, although this was ratified by the project, they were instructed by management to change the dates to reflect the original plan, which they duly did *(distorting the evidence, misplaced consistency, conformity error)*. To that end they declared one part of the development phase complete in August 1990, but refused to show any of the deliverables to the consortium.

In October 1990, the developers admitted to being over one year behind schedule, but insisted that they would be able to meet the original deadline *(misplaced consistency, ignoring the evidence, completion effect)*. In February 1991, AMRIS replanned the project which resulted in further slippage and a phased implementation of system functionality. So although Hilton would receive all the functionality relevant to their requirements by June 1992, Marriott would not receive theirs until March 1993. Later, after the project was replanned, Marriott claimed that AMRIS forced employees to artificially change their timetable to reflect this new project plan and those that refused were either reassigned to a new project or sacked *(distorting the evidence, groups, conformity error)*. By this time, the price for the system had reached $92 million, significantly above the maximum of $55 million.

In October 1991, the president of AMRIS, along with a number of other AMRIS employees, resigned. A report by an external consultant was buried by the vice-president of AMRIS and the consultant dismissed because of dissatisfaction with the findings *(ignoring the evidence, agency theory)*. Despite all that had happened, and all evidence pointing to the non-delivery of the system, Marriott and Hilton were still willing to give AMRIS one last chance *(misplaced consistency, completion effect)*. AMRIS assured both that it was still able to meet the project's deadline *(ignoring the evidence)*. Finally, in April 1992, AMRIS admitted it was between two and six months behind schedule, but it was not until major problems materialized during testing that they admitted the system would not be fully complete for at least another 18 months. This announcement was shortly followed by AMRIS sacking a number of top executives and employees. It was also acknowledged that members of the project team had not raised their concerns early enough, instead preferring to allow them to remain hidden *(conformity error, groups, agency theory)*.

As with many other major project failures, AMRIS and the consortium ended in court, where the accountability for the failure could be decided. Suits and counter-suits followed in which each party blamed the other for the failure. Eventually AMRIS made an out-of-court settlement of around $160 million.

If organizations are going to avoid the trap of escalating commitment, they must:

- become sensitive to the irrational behaviours that can lead to escalation;
- create an objective assessment mechanism that is able to capture the warning signs of escalation early enough to do something about it; and
- address the tendency to hide and cover up bad news, which only serves to reinforce the irrational behaviours leading to escalation and failure.

Finally, when information systems projects fail, little if any real effort is spent dissecting the failure, and feeding the results into the management of future projects. Instead, energy is usually directed to apportioning blame for the failure to one party or another, wasting further effort and time. Accountability for a failed project is clearly important, particularly where there has been negligence or dereliction of duty. But where every effort has been made, and due process followed, effort would be better directed toward learning, rather than finger-pointing. It is to this general lack of accountability that we now turn.

CHAPTER EIGHT

Where is the accountability when information systems projects fail?

As software takes on an increasingly dominant role within the business community and society in general, the implications of poor software design ought to be considered within the wider legal framework. Therefore where software gives rise to harm or financial loss when it has been negligently constructed, those who developed it should be held accountable. Equally, where a contractual agreement has been entered into for the design, development and implementation of a software system, accountability for its failure, should it occur, must also be considered. Finally, there ought to be more responsibility placed on the creators of packaged software if their software malfunctions, or turns out to have fatal flaws.

Accountability across each of these areas is, at present, severely lacking within the IT industry and the professional bodies that promote it. Of the many examples to support this, here are just three:

- The Therac-25 radiation treatment system managed to kill or overdose a significant minority of cancer patients due to the subtle flaws that existed within the system's software.[1]
- Recent Airbus, fly-by-wire aircraft disasters – in which the pilot's controls are controlled by software rather than cables and hydraulics – have been strangely classed as software-induced pilot error, rather than the result of software malfunction.[2]
- The loss of telephony across major geographical regions has been due to the failure of switching software, such as that which occurred in June 1991 in Washington, DC.[3]

There are other instances of software malfunction that cause financial loss, organizational disruption, personal stress, and so on. The increasing computerization of personal records, for example, can often lead to the mistaken identify of individuals, which can, in extreme circumstances, lead to their wrongful arrest. Who answers for these disruptions? The answer often appears to be nobody.

Accountability is, of course, not solely restricted to the external provision of software services, as it is equally a problem with internally developed software. Unravelling internal projects that have failed can be just as acrimonious as those which end up in court. Internal finger-pointing is no way to establish the accountability for a failed project.

If organizations are going to be able to deliver their information systems projects more effectively in the future, they must be willing to learn from the past and, more importantly, be able to objectively assess who should be held accountable when they fail. Equally, the software profession must be more willing to take ownership for some of the problems that are caused by poorly implemented information systems and defective software. Before this step can be taken, however, organizations and software suppliers must understand:

- that it can be very difficult to establish exact accountabilities when software fails;
- that the way in which they react to failure can create barriers which prevent the effective introduction of accountability. They should also understand that this leads to escalation, the late surfacing of project problems, and failure.
- why some form of accountability is necessary;
- what barriers to accountability currently exist; and
- what the implications are of this accountability deficit.

WHY SOFTWARE PRODUCTS APPEAR TO DEFY ACCOUNTABILITY

Software, it seems, has escaped some of the basic laws governing consumer rights, quality assurance and negligence commonly associated with other products and services. For example, if a major construction company used substandard concrete during the construction of a building or bridge that later collapsed, there would be a case of negligence to be heard. Yet, if software fails, it is usually seen as an unfortunate side effect of the brave new world of technology, rather than the result of its negligent construction. In this case, it is usual that no case for negligence is heard.

There seems to be a number of reasons for this:

● The lack of physical intuition with software means that it can be very difficult to demonstrate exactly where the fault arose within the construction process, and who was responsible.

● The received wisdom is that the perfect system can never be guaranteed. Every piece of software can be assumed to contain errors, even after a long period of operational use. This permits the delivery of bug-infested software and, more importantly, the acceptance of what can be considered a substandard software product.

● The belief that software systems produce believable and consistently accurate results is surprising when the collective experience suggests the opposite. For example, the main mirror of the $4 billion Hubble space telescope was never physically tested prior to its launch. Instead, its acceptance for operational use was based upon a computer simulation, which at the time was considered more cost effective. Poor data used for the simulation meant that the results could not be appropriately interpreted prior to its launch into space. The mirror failed to operate as expected, and the only way to rectify the problem was to adjust the mirror's optics *in situ*. The space shuttle mission sent to repair the

telescope was considerably more expensive than the thorough testing that should have occurred prior to its launch.[4] A particularly insidious example is that of Therac-25, in which the operator of the system insisted to a patient, who had just been administered an unusually high dose of radiation, that the equipment could not have given an overdose because it was computer controlled.

● It is difficult to keep pace with changing technology not only from a learning and competency perspective, but also a legal one. The legal framework finds it difficult to keep up with the implications of a changing technological environment. Naturally some degree of lag should be expected, but the rapidity of change makes the catch-up process increasingly difficult. Contrast this with the changing legislation and institutionalization of controls that followed the Industrial Revolution. These checks and balances managed to catch up within approximately fifty years, and allowed the excesses and negative consequences of industrialization to be tempered and controlled. Many of these controls and institutions are still present today and attempt to control the latest form of technological revolution. However, in the majority of cases, these controls and institutions are outdated and cannot hope to manage the excesses associated with IT. New institutions and legal frameworks are necessary.

● With the general ignorance of technology, it is almost impossible for organizations to question and challenge a software product sufficiently to make an informed judgement about its acceptability.

These factors help to create an environment in which the acceptance of poorly constructed software products is the norm, and which, as a result, institutionalizes the avoidance of establishing true accountability when software and projects fail. However, this is not the whole story, as the suppression of accountability lies in the way organizations respond to the failure of an information systems project.

ORGANIZATIONAL RESPONSES TO FAILURE

It is common for organizations to react in a number of ways when an information system project fails. The form the response takes depends on the degree to which a fear of failure exists within the organization and the strength of the underlying culture. Figure 8.1 is particularly relevant to the failure of an internally funded and executed project, as it is here that the full set of organizational responses tends to be exhibited. However, the model, and especially the top right-hand quadrant – blame – is equally relevant to third-party projects. Because such projects tend to be expensive, large scale and often long term, the desire not to lose face can be a strong motivator to blame when things start to go wrong. This type of behaviour is displayed in many of the major failures outlined in the earlier chapters (for example the CONFIRM, London Ambulance Service and Westpac CS90 projects). Such behaviour, as we have seen, promotes escalation.

Focusing on the internally funded and executed projects, it can be seen that there are four basic ways in which an organization can respond to a failed project. Where the fear of failure is high and the culture hard – that is, brutish and unforgiving – there is a tendency to blame and sack staff rather than learn from the failure. In such instances, the blame and associated removal of staff is normally misdirected and is rarely the result of a full and thorough analysis both of where the project went wrong, and where true accountability lay. The problem with this type of reaction is that it creates a culture in which the fear of failure is reinforced. It also tends to increase the likelihood of irrational behaviour and project escalation within the project team. Software developers also fear that they can become tarnished by association when the project on which they have been working fails. As a result, and as a means of protecting themselves, the behaviour of software developers shifts toward the non-disclosure of problems, and creates an environment in which the early resolution of project issues becomes almost impossible. In organizations where the fear of failure is equally high, but the culture more forgiving, there is a bias toward brushing the failure under the

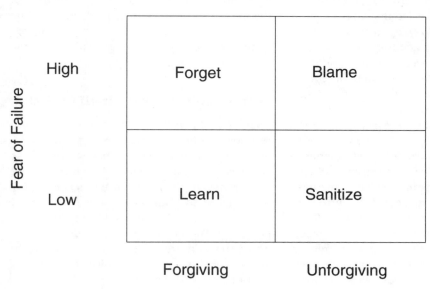

Figure 8.1
Organizational responses to failure

carpet and trying to forget that it had ever happened. In both cases, the opportunity for learning is typically lost and the organization is destined to repeat the same errors of judgement in future projects.

It is where the fear of failure is low that the ability to learn from past project experiences is maximized, although not always carried through. For example, where the fear of failure is low and the culture unforgiving, the usual response to failure is a 'going through the motions' post-failure analysis in which the reasons for the failure are analysed, reviewed, sanitized and stored without ever reaching those people that could truly benefit. It is as though there is a need for the organization to wring their hands as a means of exorcising the failure. Learning is therefore restricted to a limited number of people, and the experience adds no intrinsic value to the future management of information systems projects. Finally, where the culture is more forgiving and the fear of failure low, the organization is able to genuinely learn from the experience of failure and feed this into the management of future projects. Needless to say, such organizations appear to be very rare.

Research from the United States tends to support the view that very few organizations seem able or willing to learn from their project failures. The survey revealed that 70 per cent of organizations failed to keep records of their abandoned projects. In addition, 60 per cent of the organizations surveyed indicated that more than one project had failed for more or less the same reasons.[5] As a result, these organizations are cursed to repeat the same errors of judgement and mistakes on every information systems project. This type of behaviour tends to be exacerbated in organizations that experience high staff turnover, since in the absence of data relating to why projects have failed in the past, new staff will often make similar errors of judgement. Little or no institutionalized learning of project experience takes place. Failure to keep and disseminate records on project experience, both positive and negative, also robs the organization of valuable inputs into the development processes. It was also apparent from the survey that many organizations treat project failures as embarrassing experiences which they wish to forget as quickly as possible. Even in the limited number of organizations that maintain records of failed projects, these are rarely used to improve the general project management processes. It is clear from this analysis that the majority of organizations, when faced with a failure, fall into the forget, blame or sanitize quadrants of Figure 8.1.

Some commentators suggest that the reason why only four out of every one hundred failures get to court is because organizations do not see any merit in making their failures public, especially if they can gain a suitable out-of-court settlement.[6] This has important consequences, since without sufficient public examples and legal judgements, it is unlikely that there will be the much-needed collective experience of failure required to mobilize the IT profession and associated professional bodies into making improvements in the general level of accountability. It has been suggested that to facilitate more litigation, there must be greater opportunity for evidence to stand up in a court of law. However, it is clear from those project failures that end up in court that there is immense difficulty in assessing the evidence and demonstrating negligence in the delivery of the software product. It is also difficult to define exactly what constitutes an effective software system in the first place, especially when the requirements might be considered vague.

WHY ACCOUNTABILITY IS NECESSARY

There can be little doubt that information technology is bringing major changes within the business and social environments. With these changes comes an associated increase in the level of risk to which organizations and society are exposed to. This makes the need for an acceptable level of accountability all the more necessary. The insistence on accountability, in which the software professional is expected to answer for their work, recognizes the value of high-quality work and directly encourages the adoption of diligent approaches to software development. By contrast, no accountability means that no one answers for the risks to which businesses are exposed to; instead, they are seen as an unfortunate accident or the consequence of a brave new technology.

Accountability means that there will be someone to answer for failed projects, defective software and any harm or business loss that results. This also extends into the ethical domain of business management. If the information technology profession and the professional bodies that purport to support them are serious about the value they can add to business and society, they must consider the ethical nature of their work. This would suggest an underlying concern about the consequences of computerization, which would not only feed into the practices and behaviours of information systems professionals, but also mean that the software professional accepts an appropriate level of accountability for poor software design and implementation. All the evidence to date suggests there is a professional and ethical deficit within the IT profession.

BARRIERS TO ACCOUNTABILITY

Establishing accountability within the software profession would mean creating the type of recognized qualifications, standard methods and tools commonly associated with other professions including medicine, law, engineering and accountancy. Each require entry-level qualifications, such as a relevant degree as well as significant post-graduate training, and further qualifications to gain the requisite competency levels necessary for professional status. Ongoing professional development is also needed, to ensure that professionalism and competency are maintained during the individual's working life. All of this is supported by a professional body providing the necessary infrastructure to ensure that individuals follow an appropriate code of conduct, with sanctions when they do not. Being a professional means being accountable for negligent behaviour, but it also means that clients expect a level of competency and professionalism that goes with it. Contrast this with the IT profession that is increasingly

amateur in nature – anyone with a personal computer and an idea can develop and market a new software product. It is also clear that a significant number of people drift into IT, rather than seek it out as a profession. Repeated attempts by the British Computer Society, for example, to instil professionalism within the IT community have failed because the sanction of the withdrawal of professional status is not a particularly meaningful threat within a commercial environment that allows anyone to develop software. This lack of professional status is the result of the way in which IT has shifted from organizational insignificance to one of primary importance. As IT has become more important, its complexity and consequences of failure have led to a realization that some form of professional accountability is probably required. There are, however, a number of reasons why such accountability is difficult to introduce:[7]

- Too many hands – Most information systems are the result of collective action. Consequently, when a system gives rise to harm, the identification of who is responsible is obscured. Moreover, how and where the problems or errors within the system were introduced is often very difficult to identify. This barrier is clearly the result of the power of computing which is permitting teams of software developers to create systems that no single person can fully comprehend. This makes it very difficult to determine the accountability for flawed systems, especially when these are poorly documented.

- Software error – There can be no denying that software bugs constitute a major reason for failure, but it is not so obvious how they are related to accountability. Software bugs are considered to be an unavoidable side effect of systems development: it seems that they remain in systems however rigorous the testing may be. Consequently, the prevailing view is that it is unreasonable to hold programmers, systems engineers or systems designers accountable when the system fails. Clearly, if rigorous development practices have been applied and thorough testing has taken place prior to the software's release, there would be a strong argument for not holding the software engineer accountable. However, where software has been developed in the absence of due process, and in instances where testing can be classed as insufficient, some degree of accountability must prevail. Most software developers are aware that it is always the testing window that gets compressed when projects start to run late. Failure to test software proficiently can have major consequences. For example, in June 1991, DSC Communications made some late changes to its call-routing software that only affected three lines of code – out of several million. With such a small change, it was decided to ship the software without the usual 14-week testing cycle. The result was a series of failures within the call-routing software that led to the loss of telephony in a number of major cities in the United States.

- 'It's the computer's fault' – It is quite common to blame the system for anything that goes wrong with it or the processes around it. How many times during the course of a working day can people be heard cursing their computer, or blaming the system for something that has gone wrong? Such claims may in some circumstances be hiding an individual's inability to carry out their job: the computer is always a convenient scapegoat. Naturally, some of the problems may be genuinely associated with the way in which the information system has been designed, but there are many related to the inability of staff to use the system in the way it was intended. Blaming the computer allows people to hide their incompetence or other underlying problems within the organization in which they work. Such a tactic serves to obscure the accountability issue even further, and allows both the information systems developer and the end-user staff to blame each other for software problems when they arise.

- Ownership without liability – The majority of packaged software comes with warranties that are practically useless, and provide little by way of protection against malfunction. Compare this with most other products that usually have some form of guarantee that provides an indication of expected quality and protection against poor craftsmanship. If the product should malfunction within, say, a twelve-month period, it would either be repaired or replaced at no cost to the consumer. If a software product should malfunction, it is unlikely the package will be replaced immediately, and it is the consumer who usually must pay when the upgrade arrives. Sometimes this is too late. For example, a software bug in the tracking software within the Patriot missile defence system meant that, after continuous operation, it was unable to identify incoming Scud missiles. The bug, which was noticed very early on in the Gulf War, was finally installed within the Patriot batteries shortly before the end of the war. In the meantime, the bug was linked to the death of 28 US servicemen in Dhahran, Saudi Arabia the day before the upgrade arrived.[8] Therefore, not only can the consumer of packaged software purchase a substandard product, they also have to pay for any upgrades designed to fix problems. I am aware that some software companies wait until a significant majority of customers have notified them of a bug in their software before doing anything about it. Clearly, the software industry is setting a worrying trend in demanding maximum property protection for commercially available software, whilst denying accountability for any problems caused by its use. This, of course, also happens with in-house software projects, where organizations allow an incomplete, poorly constructed software system to enter production, and then continue to pay for its development under the guise of maintenance. This costs the organization dear because valuable resources are used up trying to make the software useable, and the productivity gains expected of the system do not materialize.

- Dishonesty – Typically, when failure occurs, there is rarely self-examination, but instead systematic dishonesty about the nature of the failure. Effort is generally directed towards the punishing of whistle-blowers within the organization who have identified the people and procedures responsible for the failure. This links back to the organizational responses to failure identified in Figure 8.1, especially those which have a high fear of failure.

- The unwillingness of the software professional to recognize the need for social responsibility and accountability – For many IT professionals, there is an important aspect missing from their discipline, and one that lies beyond the technical skills gained through education, training and experience. But with software taking on an ever-dominant role, such a one-dimensional technical focus prevents them from taking the full responsibility now expected of them.

Rehabilitating accountability within the IT profession is unlikely to be achieved over the short term, because it will require a concerted effort from the profession, governments – in the form of legislation – and professional bodies. Despite the barriers and effort required, accountability must be introduced if the general effectiveness of information systems projects is to be improved, and an open environment created in which projects can be executed.

WHAT ARE THE IMPACTS OF THE ACCOUNTABILITY DEFICIT?

The impacts of having no accountability are clear from the increasing level of court action over failed system implementation projects. For example, despite so few cases ever coming to court in the United Kingdom, the scale of courtroom conflicts has grown significantly, with claims for damages extending well into hundreds of thousands and even millions of pounds.[9] This increase not only reflects the apparent lack of accountability, but also the increasing scale of computerization and the

shift toward larger information systems projects. The barriers to accountability identified above can mean that the legal machinations associated with a failed project can last many months, and sometimes years. It can also be made all the more difficult through the limited number of legal precedents available to guide the potential litigant. With the majority of cases being settled out of court, there are very few rulings on which to base precedents. Furthermore, the cost of pursuing the software vendor through the courts is also increasing as the complexity of the systems being developed increases. Arguments tend to revolve around the issue of quality, performance and misrepresentation by the sales team, rather than the cost of the hardware, which is where the focus was ten years ago.

Without accountability, the many problems associated with the information systems profession will continue to dog organizations well into the future. The lack of accountability, and, in many cases, professional pride, means that problems with projects will rarely surface until too late; shortcuts will be taken, and the necessary due care and attention required to develop a complex information system neglected. Clearly, accountability is not about persecuting the information systems professional, but rather the establishment of an appropriate framework within which it is possible to analyse a failed information systems project and, more importantly, as a means of establishing professional ground rules for executing projects competently. Projects are rarely simple, and trying to understand who is responsible for a failed project is a difficult process, as the following example illustrates.

ESTABLISHING ACCOUNTABILITY: THE STATE OF FLORIDA'S BENEFIT SYSTEM[10]

In May 1989, the State of Florida signed a contract with EDS (Electronic Data Systems) to develop a welfare payment system. This system was designed to integrate six software modules that were used to manage the various functions required to administer state benefits. The system was expected to cope with a minimum of a 120 per cent increase in benefit cases per year, which at the time were running at approximately 2.3 million per annum, essentially meaning an increase to 5.1 million records per annum. The project did not go according to plan, and in June 1992 the contract was terminated, with Florida claiming that EDS had delivered a system based on an unproven configuration. It was also claimed that because of this, old systems had to be retained and supplemented to cope with the increased workloads. This, they claimed, led to financial loss. In addition, the system failed to perform against its performance targets, such as response times. As usually happens in these cases, there was a counter-claim from EDS. In this case EDS sued the State of Florida for $40 million for non-payment of fees. Florida immediately counter-sued for $65 million in damages associated with breach of contract and warranty. The court case lasted over two years and illustrates the difficulty in establishing responsibility and accountability for a major project failure. It also highlights the general complexities associated with major system implementation projects.

The key to unravelling the issue of accountability, and hence establishing the amount of compensation in the EDS vs. State of Florida case, was the original contract. For example, although the State of Florida claimed that EDS stated that its solution (CRIS-E) would have handled the caseload required at 80 per cent of hardware capacity – whilst at the same time meeting or exceeding response times – it admitted that it had relied on the EDS proposal in which it stated that the system would be designed to cope with a peak loading of 20 per cent above the average transaction volume. It is not sure the degree to which this was tested during the proposal stage, if at all. As the project progressed, there were changes to the underlying technical architecture that proved

incapable of meeting the performance targets set out in the original contract. This, together with the capacity problems that resulted, were heavily disputed in the courts as both claimed it was the other's fault. In this case, EDS won the claim for the non-payment of fees. And, some six years after initiating the project, the State of Florida was ordered to pay EDS $50 million.

Clearly, when a failure such as the EDS vs. State of Florida case comes to court, the aim of both parties is total victory. Neither are willing to settle for less. It would be far better to resolve problems before they come to court, but the effects of escalating commitment can prevent such problems from being tackled early enough to prevent disaster and litigation. If there was a stronger sense of accountability and professionalism within the IT community, and a shared sense of responsibility with the business community, such court cases might not be necessary.

If organizations are to address the issue of accountability successfully, they must:

- become more willing to learn from their past project failures, and rather than blame, sack, hide or sanitize, take the time and effort to understand why the project failed; and
- develop an objective approach to assessing accountability.

In addition, the IT profession must be more willing to:

- surface problems sooner, rather than later;
- accept accountability for poor software design and badly implemented information systems; and
- embrace true professionalism and all that this entails.

Finally, the legal profession must consider how it can help in eliminating the problems associated with software accountability, and develop ways to address it.

The silver bullet syndrome: expecting the problems with information systems projects to be solved by a single-shot solution

There is no single development, in either technology or management technique, which by itself promises even one order of magnitude improvement within a decade in productivity, in reliability, in simplicity.[1]

The silver bullet syndrome is the term applied to the search for and acceptance of a single-shot solution to a complex business problem. Silver bullet solutions are, by their very nature, inherently seductive because they provide senior business managers with a straightforward method of resolving a challenging business problem. Under intense pressure to improve operational efficiencies and increase competitive advantage, these managers will grab at anything that, according to those who peddle them, is capable of solving their business problems – often without too much difficulty. This focus on a 'one size fits all' approach to management is nothing new. Originating within the discipline of management theory, it has more recently spilled over into IT, with similar results.

Organizations must understand that in order to avoid the knee-jerk reaction to the problems they face with IT, they must recognize that:

- Just like management fads, such short-term solutions to the problems of information systems project failure will not yield long-term benefits.
- Technology on its own will not solve organizational and managerial problems.
- Repeated attempts at trying to solve the problems of IT and information systems project failure have failed because of the naïve belief that a single-shot solution will result in its resolution.

- There is the danger of falling into the vendor-induced trap of believing that massive increases in software development productivity and quality are possible overnight.
- Adopting these productivity and quality tools in a scatter-gun fashion only adds to the problem of information systems project failure.

MANAGEMENT FADS

Management fads have descended on the business community with such ferocity over the last two to three decades, that it's no wonder senior executives just do not know which way to turn. Management theory, be it of the 'In search of excellence' genre, total quality management, business process re-engineering, Japanese management, empowerment, human resource management, self-managed teams or, latterly, knowledge management, is pervasive. Each new theory professes to provide the organization with the tools and wherewithal to achieve competitive advantage. Experience suggests that this is not the case. There may be some short-term gain in adopting the latest management technique, but rarely the long-term advantage or organizational longevity that is hoped for. Adopt Japanese management, and it will be possible to replicate the success of the post-war Japanese economy: but who wants to emulate the Japanese given their recent economic difficulties? 'Don't automate, obliterate' came the war cry from the business process re-engineering gurus: downsizing, misery and a subsequent fear of failure was the response from corporate America. The history of management theory is littered with the failed implementations of catch-all solutions to organizational effectiveness. The gurus will say that these are the result of failing to implement these solutions properly (maybe), but failure is also due to the way in which the gurus distil a complex problem into a simple, single model, and then peddle this to the desperate business community, who are made all the more desperate by what they read in the press, academic journals and books, often, it has to be said, written by the gurus.[2]

Perhaps managers should be forgiven for making the mistake of believing that each new management theory will be the one that provides them with the success they are seeking. But in believing there is a one best way, they feed the theorists and peddlers of such approaches. Moreover, when a particular theory fails to live up to its expectations it is secretly buried, or rejected as being unsuitable. The organization will typically seek out the next silver bullet, with equal fervour and, it should be said, with equally patchy results. Unfortunately this cycle of adoption, failure and rejection is repeated many times over without ever finding the success they seek. This also subjects the organization to a constant tirade of change and innovation, the majority of which is pointless and possibly self-defeating; no one is really bought in to the change beyond the superficial compliance expected by management, often termed as 'going through the motions'. There is never any long-term commitment required to make the innovation a success.[3] The belief that an organization and its internal and external environments can be distilled into a few simple models is missing the point by a very wide margin. The business environment is complex, and a complex organization is required to be able to respond to it.

IT'S SILVER BULLET

This obsession with finding the most applicable management approach has spilled over into the technological arena and tends to fall into two distinct areas:

1. With the failure of many of the approaches focused on the motivation and organization of human capital, chief executives have looked to IT to provide the performance improvements they seek. This technological focus, however, has often been interpreted by the organization as needing to concentrate exclusively on the technology at the expense of the human dimension.

2. There is the need to improve the general effectiveness of information systems projects. This stemmed from the 1968 NATO Conference on the Software Crisis, and stimulated great advances in the adoption of engineering approaches to the development of information systems. It also started the silver bullet syndrome, in which entire organizations and individual projects adopted new tools, languages and methodologies in the belief these would provide the immediate improvements in team productivity and software quality they were looking for. The naivety of this approach beggars belief, because the collective experience since the NATO conference clearly demonstrates that there is no single silver bullet capable of curing the software productivity and quality problem. One only needs to consider the statistical evidence of Chapter 2 to reinforce this.

Both issues are worthy of a little more exploration.

ASSUMING TECHNOLOGY CAN SOLVE ALL THE PROBLEMS

The allure of technology, and especially of what computer technology can do for organizations can seduce them into assuming that technology is able to solve all of their business problems. To a large extent, this widely held belief is fed by books which focus on the power of technology without discussing some of the problems it brings. This belief in the technological silver bullet can lead organizations to make decisions around major change, or move into new markets based on technology alone. This is corroborated by research conducted by the University of

Sheffield in the United Kingdom in 1996.[4] This extensive survey into the performance of IT and the role of human and organizational factors found that:

- Most IT investments are technology led.
- Most projects address too narrow an agenda which itself reflects too technical an emphasis.
- The majority of the organizations surveyed were not successful at managing the human and organizational aspects of a changing technological infrastructure.
- Organizations are poor at considering the impacts of technology on jobs and work organization, and at getting the most out of their IT investments.
- Technology is perceived to be the most important part of a major IT project.

There is, therefore, an inherent danger of assuming a business problem can be tackled with a suitable million-dollar investment in IT. Indeed, research highlights a general inability of managing directors to handle rapid change: only half of chief executive officers consider themselves capable of planning for change.[5] This suggests an attitude of 'throwing money and technology at problems', rather than tackling them from an holistic standpoint, and considering the non-technology dimensions of change. This is superbly illustrated by General Motors who, in the early 1980s, embarked upon an enormous investment in automation in its automotive production plants.[6] In 1985, it opened its showcase factory that boasted 50 automatic guided vehicles and 260 robots. Almost a year later, however, performance of the plant was significantly lower than expected: it was only capable of producing half the number of cars per day it was expected to. The production lines ground to a halt with regular frequency, whilst the technicians tried frantically to debug the software. Even when the robots did work, they tended to smash cars, fit the wrong equipment and even dismantle each other. It later transpired that General Motors' problems lay not with its production processes, but with the way the company treated its employees – it had implemented a solution to the wrong problem. This meant that they had to revisit their approach to managing their human resources – which they had assumed, quite wrongly, was not the problem – at an equally enormous expense.

Occasionally, an outspoken business leader is prepared to state publicly what is known privately to be true. Speaking at a debate on the impact of IT and the Internet on users in 1999, ICI's vice-president of IT stated: 'Technology drives absolutely nothing. People drive change. I have never seen an industry like IT where there is a total lack of quality and which produces products that do not work.'[7]

This problem of focusing on technology is also reflected in the way in which software products are marketed by the IT industry. There have been many instances of a software company desperately looking for a problem to which their IT solution can be applied. Solutions looking for problems usually means an overstating of benefits, and a superficial analysis of the problem. This fuels the catch-all, silver bullet view so common with IT products. For example, an article in one of the UK's computer magazines in the spring of 1999 had the headline 'Office 2000 promises real productivity gains'. Office 2000, according to Microsoft, is essential for employees to work together more effectively and improve the competitiveness of the business. It can also have a dramatic effect on a company's IT infrastructure.[8] Does this sound familiar? One has to wonder on what basis these benefits are going to materialize, especially given the problems of information sharing due to information politics. Organizations, of course, will tend to accept such claims at face value and make the necessary upgrades in the hope of achieving the productivity gains the product professes to provide. But beware the productivity paradox: with more powerful and functionally rich software, the opportunity to tinker, and do less productive work, is all the more seductive to the average employee.

IMPROVING PRODUCTIVITY AND QUALITY

The second and equally problematic focus for the single-shot solution has been within the productivity and quality of software projects. This search has been fuelled by three drivers: the general problem of failures and overruns within information systems projects, rapidly changing technology, and organizations' voracious appetite for more IT. This has created an environment in which the organization is unable to give as much time as is necessary to allow new methods and tools to be fully bedded in and productive before their rejection. The IT industry, in trying to meet the needs of the single-shot, silver bullet solution, has developed numerous approaches, methods and tools, some of which have undoubtedly provided some relief to the problems associated with software development. However, what the industry has failed to deliver is the elusive solution to the issue: 'You can dismiss any claim of an ability to improve productivity by more than 25 per cent out of hand as a silver bullet claim.'[9] This, of course, does not prevent either the industry from peddling such silver bullets, or organizations from seeking and accepting them at face value.

There have been three areas that have had more than their fair share of silver bullets over the last twenty years:

- Software languages – Significant efforts have been directed at creating an efficient coding language that is able to improve the productivity of the software developer and the general quality of the code that is created. For example, the Ada language was heralded in the late 1980s and early 1990s as being a major breakthrough in programming quality and productivity. This was particularly evident within the defence industry. As the reality dawned that Ada might not prove to be the silver bullet it was held up to be, organizations looked elsewhere – fourth-generation languages, object orientation and latterly Java have all been heralded as the languages to provide the fillip the industry and organizations seek.

What they turn out to be is another way of developing software and merely serve to fragment the industry. This also means that, for the software professional to be genuinely useful to the wider business community, he must be capable of programming in any of these languages to a highly competent level, something that is increasingly difficult.

- Development methods – Just as with the low-level focus on programming languages, there has been a great deal of interest in development methods to improve the management of the software construction process. Such approaches have reflected the frustration caused by the inability to marry up requirements with the end result – the information system. Development life cycles such as the waterfall, evolutionary, incremental, and spiral approaches have all been recommended as the solution. And, as with the language camp, each one has their supporters and dissenters. In addition, there have been various methods that follow the basic management theory schools of thought. For example, structured approaches, such as the UK's Structured Systems Analysis and Design Method (SSADM), reflect the scientific management school of thought and focus heavily on the functional decomposition of a problem into a well-defined series of steps. Equally, methods such as Soft Systems and the Effective Technical and Human Implementation of Computer-based Systems (ETHICS) reflect the human relations and socio-technical schools of management thought. Just as with programming languages, these require experience, training and expertise, and also lead to the fragmentation of expertise across the industry.[10]

- Tools – The majority of tools have been directed at improving the productivity of the software developer, and in turn the software construction process. Some, including tools that facilitate the prototyping of requirements, have been introduced as a means of driving out the ambiguities associated with understanding the business requirements of a new information system. Others, such as Computer Aided Software Engineering (CASE) tools, have been geared toward improving the productivity and completeness of the design and build of software systems. Although all tools are capable of providing benefits to those that are willing to commit to them over the long term, it seems that many organizations are taken in by the predicted short-term productivity gains, only to be disappointed later. According to Capers Jones there have been false productivity claims in 75 per cent of the marketing materials published by software vendors over the last few years.[11] For example, some of the reasons for the failure of CASE to make the productivity impacts expected of them include:

* The failure to recognize the long learning curve, which can take up to three years;
* The typically unstructured approach to their introduction;
* The under-estimation of the ongoing operational costs;
* Difficulties in measuring the productivity gains from the tools;
* Ignoring the economies of scale, and not rolling out the tools as widely as possible; and
* The inability of CASE tools to be fully integrated into the various forms of development life cycles used within organizations.[12]

More recently, there has been a lot of interest in the area of quality management, especially in the institutionalization of best practice within the software development process. Therefore, approaches such as the US Capability Maturity Model (CMM) in the US and the International Standards Organizations' (ISO) 9001 – commonly known as 'TickIT' in the United Kingdom – have made significant headway in many organizations. Furthermore, many organizations, and especially those on the supply side, have chosen, or have been forced, to adopt ISO 9001, the CMM or TickIT as a way of demonstrating the maturity of their IT

capability. In many instances, this is the only way for them to be able to bid for contracts, and is especially true for suppliers to government organizations. Each of these quality models provides two essential elements: the ability to measure, and hence assess the general capability of the information systems development processes, and more importantly, provide a set of objective measures and route maps to improve these processes. However, designing, implementing, tailoring and maintaining these within an organization can be time-consuming, costly and, it should be said, does not guarantee a successful project. Having implemented ISO 9001 within a UK government organization, there can be significant problems to overcome to make it truly valuable, not least the buy-in from the IT staff who are usually more or less unconcerned with documentation and following due process.

FALLING INTO THE SILVER BULLET TRAP

Why, therefore do organizations fall into the silver bullet trap? Clearly, at least some of the problem lies in the historic separation of IT from the business, which evolved into the culture gap. This disconnect has meant that senior executives have had to rely on and trust both their internal IT experts and external vendors for the provision of appropriate advice where IT is concerned. Without having the necessary level of understanding with which to challenge the IT expert, the senior executives have had little choice but to accept the advice at face value. Falling into the silver bullet trap has been easy. Tools that purport to provide double-digit growth in productivity or quality are therefore snapped up. CASE tools are a prime example.

In falling into the silver bullet trap, organizations usually base their decision to roll out new tools, languages and methods on a pilot. Although such pilots are designed to provide an objective assessment, they often fail to do so because the organization adopts an approach that immediately biases the results towards success by adopting one of two approaches:

- Repeating a completed project – This involves repeating a project that has already been completed, but in this case using the new tool, method or language. The two projects can then be compared in terms of their costs, productivity and quality of outputs. When this comparison is made, the second project normally looks far better than the first and, as a result, the new tool, method or language is adopted. Unfortunately, the project cannot be considered to be an accurate test of the tool's, method's or language's capability because, in repeating an already completed project, most, if not all of the usual project problems would have been encountered and resolved. As a result, the pilot takes on all the qualities of a laboratory experiment and it should come as no surprise therefore that the second project comes out on top. It is also common for the organization to use its most talented staff when conducting the pilot, which itself tends to bias the results toward success. This makes the decision to adopt the new method, tool or language a relatively easy, although possibly flawed task, mainly because any productivity gains are unlikely to be reflected in future projects – at least not immediately. For example, studies have found that there is significant variation between the productivity and effectiveness of individual software developers: one found a 25:1 variation between the best and worst performing programmers,[13] whilst another suggested that the top 1 per cent of programmers outperformed the average by 1272 per cent.[14]

- Engaging the external supplier – The second approach normally involves the use of an external supplier, who has a vested interest in the successful outcome of the pilot. If the pilot involves a large project, the supplier will typically provide support either free of charge or at significantly reduced rates to ensure the organization accepts the results. This in turn allows the supplier to publicize the results, thereby giving them further sales, and additional market share.

Assuming a successful outcome, both the supplier and organization get what they are looking for. But again, a true understanding of the tool's, method's or language's capability is never really achieved. For example, the full cost and time required to undertake a similar project with in-house staff cannot be fully gauged, because the pilot may have included external experts charged out at either minimal rates, or not at all. And, as with the repeated project approach, the organization tends to use its best staff.

Even though the pilot may have been successful, the projects that follow are unlikely to be quite as effective. This can lead not only to disappointment with the new tool, method or language, but also its possible rejection. This, of course, provides no real value to the organization and serves to compound the problems with information systems projects.

HOW SILVER BULLETS IMPACT PROJECTS

The silver bullet syndrome can impact information projects severely, especially where the organization expects the silver bullet to have the instantaneous impact the suppliers suggest. Therefore, timescales may be reduced based upon the assumption that the particular tool will increase productivity by, say, 25 per cent. Compressed timescales often translate into cutting corners and taking shortcuts in order to meet the almost impossible time constraints. As a result, functionality, quality, or both, may suffer and the project, if it doesn't fail, may deliver a poor-quality product at the end of it. The reaction of the organization is usually one of dismay and can in many cases lead to the rejection of the new tool, language or method. There is little merit in this, as it is clear that when this happens insufficient time has been allowed for the tool, language or method to bed in and hence achieve the expected productivity gains. Research has shown that the introduction of a new tool is usually associated with a reduction in productivity, for quite obvious reasons, not least because of the time required to familiarize oneself with the tool and become competent in its use. Therefore, it may take two or three projects before the expected productivity improvements are achieved. By then, of course, the organization will have rejected the tool and moved on to the next one, only to repeat the same mistakes.

The silver bullet syndrome has a number of other side effects. First, it can lead to the strengthening of the cultural differences between business and IT. This is principally because of the inability of these new tools fail to live up to their often publicly stated benefits. Failure to deliver the productivity or quality gains provides further ammunition to the business community. Second, it can increase the fear of failure prevalent in many organizations, and hence limit the learning that can result, even from a failed pilot. And, third, it ensures an increased desperation on the organization's part to find the genuine article, and hence the next silver bullet.

The silver bullet syndrome is not necessarily a straightforward problem to resolve, as it is wrapped up in the general issues outlined within Part I of this book. Equally, it requires more than just a little bit of care and attention when considering and accepting a new tool, language or method.

Before leaving this subject, it is worth noting that during the late nineteenth century, a German by the name of Paul Ehrlich had a vision of being able to shoot (and eliminate) deadly microbes with a single magic bullet. Mocked by his fellow scientists, Ehrlich worked ceaselessly for ten years before finally achieving his aim. During these ten years, he held on to the vision of being able to develop this magic bullet and, more importantly, never rejected his initial approach. The IT community could learn something from Ehrlich.

If organizations are going to avoid future silver bullets, they must:

- ensure they are aware of the impacts of adding new tools or technologies to the software development process;
- understand that if they want to be

successful in the execution of their software projects, they have to be predictable in the way they apply their methods and tools; and
- assess each new tool in a way that is able to determine exactly what benefit it provides.

It is hoped that Part I of this book has allowed the scale and underlying factors of information systems project failure to be fully elucidated. It is also hoped that the reader now recognizes that the failure of an information system project is the result of a complex interaction of a number of organizational and behavioural factors. He should also recognize that reducing, or eliminating, the failure of information systems projects is not a simple task, nor one of short duration – history has, in my opinion, clearly shown this.

I believe there are a number of key themes that can be drawn out from Part I:

1. The dependence on, and level of investment in, information technology will continue to dominate organizational expenditure well beyond the twenty-first century. IT is here to stay.

2. The majority of information systems projects are poorly appraised from both a cost and benefit perspective.

3. Information systems projects concentrate too heavily on the technological components, at the expense of the organizational and behavioural elements.

4. The culture gap between business and technology professionals is both highly damaging and unlikely to narrow for some considerable time to come.

5. The shift to the Information Age has resulted in a new dimension to the failure associated with the politics of information. This can make an information systems project more prone to failure.

6. Irrational and escalatory behaviour features heavily in many failed projects, and especially those which involve significant investment.

7. There is currently little or no accountability for poorly developed software, nor is there a will within the profession to establish such accountability.

8. The increasing pace of change, itself fed by the increasing use of technology, is leading organizations to seek out the latest technological advance without first fully considering its impacts.

Part I of this book has therefore been designed to raise the level of awareness and understanding of the fundamental problems that can occur in any information systems project. For some, it will have provided a reflection and augmentation of what they already know. For others, it will have advanced their understanding beyond the narrow definition they may currently have. For others still, it may have been a complete re-evaluation. In all cases, it is hoped that this part of the book has created a sense of concern in the reader's mind and equally a desire to address the problem from a more sophisticated standpoint. Simple or isolated solutions will not provide the answer, and should be avoided.

Focusing on the problems of failure, of course, is no use by itself, as it fails to provide those charged with unravelling problem projects, and improving the performance of IT in general, with answers on how to tackle this seemingly impossible task. Part II starts to piece the jigsaw together, providing approaches and ideas of how these individual issues can be tackled. Part III will take these pieces and outline how information systems projects can be made more successful, maybe even failsafe – but that would be falling into the silver bullet syndrome, wouldn't it?

BREAKTHROUGH TO PROJECT SUCCESS

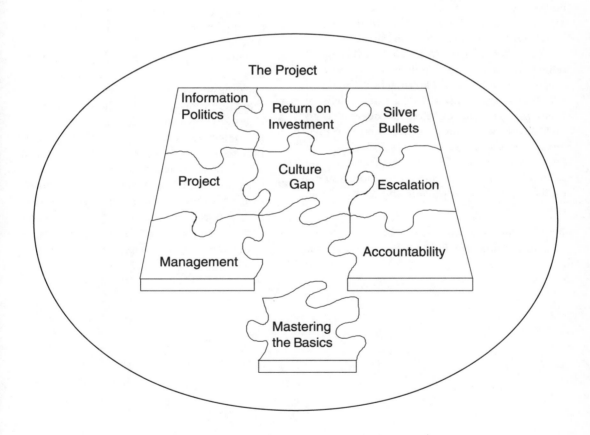

Awareness, it is said, is an important ingredient in realizing one's potential. Clearly, awareness brings an understanding of one's strengths and weaknesses, and therefore allows these to be maximized and minimized respectively. It should also be said that becoming self-aware is not always a pleasant experience, because it exposes facets of behaviour that are difficult to come to terms with, and correct. However, breaking through these barriers creates the opportunity for real improvement and growth. The purpose of Part I has been to lay bare the problems and difficulties associated with information systems projects. Exposing these issues has, I believe, provided sufficient awareness on which to base the improvements necessary to execute information systems projects successfully. Highlighting these improvements is the purpose of Part II.

To facilitate this, the format of Part II is one of reflection; each issue highlighted in Part I is mirrored with ideas and approaches which can serve to reduce their severity. In order to achieve breakthrough, however, it is necessary to include one additional piece that I have termed 'mastering the basics'. Once these basics have been mastered, the remaining pieces can be slotted into place, and the information systems project optimized to provide the best possible chance of succeeding:

- Chapter 10 completes the failure model by introducing the foundations required for any successful project, including asking some fundamental questions about the project before it starts, and employing excellent project management.

- Chapter 11 updates the investment appraisal and benefits realization processes so that organizations are better placed to execute the right project, recognize and manage the risks, and take an active stance in the realization of the benefits.

- Chapter 12 takes a detailed look at how the culture gap between the business and IT can be resolved.

- Chapter 13 assesses the short- and medium-term solutions to information politics, including how, through the use of effective IT, problems associated with information sharing and availability can be significantly reduced.

- Chapter 14 identifies approaches that will allow an organization to recognize the warning signs of over-commitment and, more importantly, do something about it.

- Chapter 15 reviews the legal accountabilities for defective software, and introduces a process for assessing accountability for the failure of internal software projects.

- Chapter 16 highlights how organizations can avoid the silver bullet syndrome by taking more care when selecting new tools and techniques, and, more importantly, understanding what to expect.

CHAPTER TEN

Mastering the basics in four, not so easy, steps

To manage the complexity associated with the issues raised within Part I, one first has to manage, and manage very well, some basics. There are four cornerstones to delivering an information system effectively. Once in place, these can serve to generate the necessary sensitivity to deal with the issues raised within Part I. The four cornerstones are:

1. Understanding that the introduction, application or extension of information systems is not only about the upside. IT presents risks as well as benefits, and understanding this is a necessary step to ensure that the over-exuberance associated with technology is dampened and placed within a more realistic frame of reference. This is not to say that technology is bad, but to recognize that there is a downside as well as an upside. A balanced view is required.

2. In recognizing that technology can present significant risk, it is necessary to ask some basic and quite searching questions prior to embarking on the project itself. This should allow the organization to consider very carefully the investment on which it is about to embark. It also forces the business and IT professionals to consider both sides of the project equation, rather than in isolation, or not at all.

3. It is important to appoint the best project manager to run the project, and not fall into the common trap of appointing someone who is a great technician, but a lousy project manager. Techno-centric project managers are not necessarily the best people to run IT projects, for all the reasons discussed in Part I. Managing a major information systems project requires a focus on project management, not technology management. If the project is to succeed, these skills should be first class. Having first-class skills – which includes those covering the less tangible, political and behavioural aspects of the project – should mean that the project manager is equipped to recognize and manage some of the early warning signs of failure.

4. Having appointed the best project manager, it is crucial that excellent project management disciplines are applied throughout the project. It is obvious from the classic advice given when projects fail, that the core project management disciplines are often lacking. Despite this advice, project failure and overruns are more common than outright success.

I would strongly argue that without these four cornerstones, an information systems project is unlikely to fall within the 16 per cent of projects considered successful. Indeed, it is unfortunate that many of the inexperienced, incompetent and techno-centric project managers lack even these basic competencies. Having these cornerstones in place is, of course, only the beginning, because the inherent dangers associated with poor investment decisions, the culture gap, lack of accountability, the silver bullet syndrome, irrational behaviour, escalation and information politics still represent major obstacles to success. However, it does mean that the sensitivity required to deal with these problems is greatly enhanced, and the opportunity for success substantially increased. It is in everyone's interest to ensure that the foundations for success are laid so that they provide the necessary basis for managing the added complexities of an information systems project.

STEP 1: RECOGNIZE THE RISKS OF SOFTWARE DEPENDENCY

The early chapters of this book outlined some of the investment trends associated with IT, and highlighted the increase in IT dependency within many organizations. Because IT is able to speed up product life cycles and markets in general, it has created a business environment which itself is speeding up. Change comes more rapidly now than it did, say, fifty years ago, and with it, comes major implications for the working and economic environments. This increasing speed has been the result of advances in technology, and principally those associated with information and communication technologies. Rapid change in connectivity is a double-edged sword. For example, the connectivity of the global economic system allowed the late 1990s economic crisis in Asia to spread to the other weak economies across the globe, including Russia and South America, in a very short space of time. It was through the interconnected IT systems, which include media and data feeds provided by, amongst others, Reuters, that the markets were able to respond so rapidly to the local events in Asia. Equally, the response from the world's major economies, such as the United States, and the wider economic community including the International Monetary Fund, allowed the severity of the crisis to be alleviated and helped to prevent a world-wide recession and possible depression.

If the world's economy is not immune from the impacts of technology, neither are organizations. But because organizations tend to see their business survival through the application of IT, they fall into the trap of believing that every business problem can be solved by IT. As a result, they tend to see just the upside. But to apply IT more effectively, organizations must become more aware of the associated risks. They must be prepared to ask themselves some fundamental questions about the consequences of their IT investments on their organization. This is, of course, not to say that they should not be investing in IT, but time should be taken to consider the investment in a

wider context, including the risks. The statistics in Chapter 2 suggest that the degree to which this analysis has taken place has, to date, been limited. So what types of questions should organizations ask themselves when considering their next major investment in IT? Lauren Wiener in her book *Digital Woes* highlights 13 major risks that come with software dependency – the 13 tales of digital woe.[1] Combining these with some of the observations and concerns of Part I, I have come up with three questions which organizations should ask themselves before they embark on their next IT investment. Organizations should use these to develop a more realistic perspective on the consequences of their investment, and also adjust the business case to include some of these hidden extras so often omitted.

1. HOW DEPENDENT WILL YOU BE ON THE NEW SYSTEM, AND WHAT ARE THE IMPLICATIONS OF FAILURE?

On 22 July 1962, a program with a tiny omission in an equation cost US taxpayers $18.5 million when an Atlas-Agena rocket was destroyed in error.[2] In 1983, when the Aegis Navy battle management system underwent its first operational testing, it was only capable of shooting down six out of seventeen targets when presented three at a time. It was designed to shoot down twenty targets but failed because of a software error. This system was latterly linked to the shooting down of the Iranian Airbus 320 by the USS *Vincennes* in 1988; the software incorrectly identified the Airbus as an F-14 military jet.[3]

Tiny errors can have significant impacts, especially when the software controls an organizational or, as in the case of the USS *Vincennes*, military function. This is a particular problem with very complex software systems, and something that can seemingly never be resolved. Therefore, when considering the next investment in a major information systems project, organizations should ask themselves how dependent they will be on this new system. If its failure at a future date presents no significant operational problems, the level of business continuity planning around the new system can be minimal. However, where the system is critical to the operation of the business – because it might be safety-critical, provide enterprise-wide data, or be operationally vital – the level of business continuity planning must, as a consequence, be much higher.

It would make sense if such requirements were built into the business case and project plan, and not considered as an afterthought. Understanding the level of dependency also allows the organization to assess the likely risks associated with failure. The level of software dependency is not always obvious to organizations as it often creeps up on them through the general intensification of IT. Considering the implications of software dependency and the consequence of systems failure is a valuable thing. But failing to consider the implications can result in chaos when systems fail, as the following examples demonstrate:

- During the peak months for passport applications in the United Kingdom, the system controlling the applications and despatch failed to cope with demand. The ensuing chaos resulted in people camping outside passport offices in order to guarantee getting their passports before going on holiday. Because of the public outcry, the Deputy Prime Minister had to intervene to establish a solution that used the UK post office network.[4]
- Less than a week later, there were problems in the Department of Social Security's national insurance system (NIRS2) which resulted in benefit claimants not receiving the money they were entitled to.[5]
- In August 1999, hundreds of customers of the UK retailer, Tesco, were cut off from the supermarket's Internet shopping service for over a week when the software failed. People who had become dependent on the software found that it repeatedly failed after it had been upgraded.[6]

In each case, it seems that not enough consideration had been given to the impacts of system failure, either on the internal operational efficiencies of the respective departments, or of the external perception of the organization. These problems also highlight how time savings promised by new technology can sometimes be offset by the time wasted in problem solving, even when there is expert help available.

2. KNOWING THE ANSWER TO QUESTION 1, HOW MUCH TIME SHOULD BE GIVEN TO TESTING THE SOFTWARE?

Clearly, if an organization can assess how dependent it might be on a new system, it ought to be able to estimate the level of testing that should be undertaken to ensure the system is as reliable as it needs to be. This is perhaps an impossible question to answer for many reasons, and not least because of the invisible and complex nature of software. For example, the software which operates the US space shuttle runs to 25 600 000 lines, itself a testing nightmare. And, because of the nature of the shuttle, it is controlled by five separate systems, even though it only needs one to operate it. The four additional systems provide the necessary level of redundancy to ensure that if one system fails, another can take over – clearly a good example of tailoring business continuity planning to the level of software dependency.[7] It is, of course, well known that even the thorough testing of a relatively small system can take literally thousands of years if every possible path through the software is tested. As a result, organizations have adopted various approaches in order to test software as much as they can, whilst still delivering it within a reasonable time frame. For example, the use of redundancy which relies on the probability of two identical components failing being less than the probability of one component failing, can ensure systems are less likely to fail. Thus the space shuttle, which has four redundant systems, has a low probability of failure. Another technique, known as diversity, is particularly important for safety-critical systems. Here, the same system functionality is built using different hardware and software. Therefore if the primary system fails, it is unlikely that the secondary, back-up system would fail in the same way because it would not contain the same systematic faults.[8] Again, in order to safeguard the space shuttle and its crew, its controlling software includes this additional safety net. Care in testing is vital, and it is important to recognize that even small changes can have major consequences, as DSC Communications found in June and early July 1991, when the standard 14-week testing cycle was omitted after a software change. The resultant outages affected telephone users along the eastern seaboard of the United States.

3.   WHAT ARE THE EXTERNAL IMPLICATIONS OF SOFTWARE ERROR?

In an increasingly wired world, where business is conducted electronically, the implications of software failure, or the transfer of poor information can be significant. For example, on 20 November 1985, a bug cost the Bank of New York $5 million when the software tracking government securities transactions from the Federal Reserve suddenly began to write new information on to the old. When the software bug hit the system, it was impossible for the bank to identify who owed what, and at the close of business on 20 November, it was $32 billion overdrawn with the Federal Reserve. The software error was located and corrected in just two days, but at a cost of $5 million – to cover short-term interest on the $32 billion loan.[9] As well as the financial dimension to the failure, there was an associated loss of confidence in the bank, something that was difficult to recover from. Therefore, as organizations become increasingly dependent on software, considering the external risks of software failure should become second nature. Assessing the external risks of software failure before the project starts can be used to frame the criteria under which the information system will be accepted once completed.

Step 1 is therefore all about forcing the organization to consider the wider impacts of computerization on itself and its external relationships. In a business environment that is increasingly IT-dependent, this is vital, and it is always worth having the following in the back of your mind:

- every technology has side effects, and thus risks;
- technology acts as an organizing force around which are mobilized massive physical, human and fiscal resources. Participants tend to exploit technology to promote self-interest in terms of wealth or power because they recognize that whoever controls technology controls the future;
- all technological choices involve trade-offs – between benefits, risks and costs; between short and long run outcomes; and between different parties;
- before you leap, look ahead for harmful consequences so as to balance long- with short-range benefits and costs, and become aware of distinctions among impacted parties.[10]

STEP 2: CONSIDER IF THIS IS THE RIGHT PROJECT

Having recognized the risks that computerization can bring to the wider organization, and its external business environment, the next step is to focus on the project itself. With continuous advances in computer technology, it can be difficult for organizations to judge the validity and compatibility of the latest technology. Sometimes the allure of being first to market with a new technology, or using the latest technological advance in the belief that it will become a catch-all for organizational success, causes companies to cut corners, marginalize the business users, and make too many quality trade-offs. Technical optimism should mean, in practice, the ability to recognize bad surprises early enough to do something about them, and not techno-worship.

When the business case for the next information systems project is being developed, it is worth adding some additional entries, beyond the answers to the three questions of Step 1. Wiener in her book *Digital Woes*,[11] once again provides some additional food for thought in this respect, and highlights seven questions, of which three are particularly relevant to this second step. The value of adding the following three questions to any business case lies in their ability to force the IT and business communities to consider the merits of the project beyond the hard financial measures usually used to appraise a project. Moreover, they can be used to generate some early dialogue between those who will be ultimately using the information system, and those who will be developing it.

1. IS THE CHOSEN SYSTEM RIGHT STRATEGICALLY AND OPERATIONALLY?

It is always tempting to throw technology at a problem, but some problems cannot be solved that way, as we saw in the previous chapter when General Motors embarked on their automation programme. It is also tempting to follow the advice of the technology sales personnel who make IT seem so powerful and effective. Equally, the allure of following the competition and mirroring their IT investments can be compelling. But it is clear from the examples provided in Part I that this is not always the right strategy to adopt. Believing that technology is the only arbiter of success can be a mistake, as some systems don't achieve anything. Therefore, when considering the case for the latest information systems project, senior managers ought to request additional information about why the system is the right one for the business. Answers such as 'the competition have just implemented a similar system', 'the computer press are raving about it', or 'it will solve all our data problems once and for all' are insufficient, and arguably indefensible blanket statements with little substance. It is important to know what alternatives have been considered, and why they have been rejected. This should not take long if the appropriate level of rigour has been applied in creating the business case, and clearly adds value to the decision-making process. Very often, however, the primary area of concentration lies in the creation of financial data required to meet the organization's hurdle rate; this alone cannot provide any real indication that the system is right for the organization. If, for example, the system does not fit in with the organization's strategic direction, or does not provide a good operational fit (that is, the ability to add significant operational value), some questions should be raised about the system's viability. This presupposes, of course, that the organization has a strategic direction in the first place.

As a coarse measure of a system's fit, the

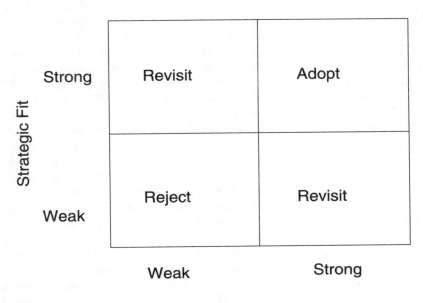

Figure 10.1
Investment fit

matrix in Figure 10.1 can be used to place any new IT investment in the context of strategic and operational fit, and hence act as a simple decision support tool to determine whether the investment is the correct one.

The two dimensions of operational and strategic fit are quite important, as they provide the balance between the here and now requirements of the organization, and the future direction of the business. Naturally, in cases where the intention is to change the working practices of the organization, the operational fit should be assessed against the new operating model, not the existing one. Where the coupling between these two dimensions is either strong or weak, the decision to adopt or reject the new investment should be quite straightforward. However, where they are not, this can be used to force the organization to question the value in more detail, and demand more in the way of justification. Hence, where the strategic and operational fit are out of alignment, it is not a case of rejection, but one of further investigation which should either lead to a project's rejection or adoption. The ultimate goal should be to establish a definite (that is, adopt or reject) outcome, as opposed to a 'let's suck it and see' approach to accepting the project.

2. WHAT ARE THE IMPLICATIONS ON THE EXISTING TECHNICAL AND ORGANIZATIONAL INFRASTRUCTURES?

IT systems are rarely isolated and, as a consequence, they are likely to impact more than just the business environment: the systems environment is increasingly an important factor to consider. When a new system is introduced, it is likely that it will alter the existing mode of operations – new relationships must be built, new interfaces created, new processes and information flows developed. It is necessary, therefore, to take an holistic approach to understanding the impact a new information system is likely to have on the business. This requires not only a deeper analysis of the role which the system is expected to play, but also an understanding of what other systems have to be altered, and what constraints these existing systems may impose on the new system as it is

being developed. All of this can add value, and hence provide balance to any business case because it reveals some of the additional project work, and associated costs. It will also provide a better indication of the investment required to achieve the anticipated returns.

3. HAVE THE HUMAN CONSEQUENCES OF THE SYSTEM BEEN FULLY CONSIDERED?

It seems trite to say, but people are an important part of any information system. The technical determinism of IT often seeks to minimize both their input during the project, and their involvement with the system once implemented. Any information system project should be about the optimization of technology and the human capital of the organization. Why? People have strengths and weaknesses, but their greatest asset is that they are motivated by outcomes, are especially good at recognizing patterns, and are able to take into account factors which are external to the system. Computers, on the other hand, are bad at these things, and dispassionate about outcomes. Although it is obvious to suggest that the relative strengths of the two should be optimized, for the last forty years, there has been limited success in this respect – technology has always won. Even within sophisticated computer systems, the most fault-tolerant and robust element is the operator. However, reducing their input to troubleshooting when systems malfunction is not a good use of the operator's skills, particularly when these systems are safety-critical. This can pose significant risks, especially when we consider how little people know about the inner workings of the system, or the business processes it supports. As more of an organization's business processes are subsumed within these black boxes, this lack of understanding will increase, and make it difficult for organizations to adjust and add to their systems without making them unstable. I have come across situations where business-critical systems have not been enhanced because people do not know how they work – indeed, there is a very real risk of system failure if they don't. One must always remember that information systems are designed by fallible human beings. Eliminating human contact within the key business processes of an organization can be highly dangerous, especially when the technology breaks down. It is not, therefore, unreasonable to consider the impacts on the staff at the time of the business case. Naturally, the introduction of a new information system may lead to a reduction in headcount, but for those who remain, it would be worth considering how their roles in the organization will be affected. This is, of course, not just about training, but job content and satisfaction. But, it must be said, this is rarely considered as organizations attempt to complete their information systems projects on time. Indeed, those who believe the computerization of the workplace is creating an electronic sweatshop are not far from the truth. For example, people who work in call centres, which currently employ approximately 350 000 people in the United Kingdom, endure conditions that can lead to musculoskeletal disorders, migraines and eye strain. In addition, they are monitored electronically and, in extreme cases, have to ask permission to go to the lavatory. It should come as no surprise that call centres suffer from high absenteeism and staff turnover.[12]

These three basic questions discussed above are worth asking, if only to provide a firmer and wider basis for the business case. Conversely, failing to consider these aspects at this stage of the project ensures they will remain hidden from view for the rest of the project. Unfortunately, it is rare to find a business case that considers these issues fully enough, if at all. But with the increasing dependency on interconnected information systems, the impact of ignoring these is going to be severe.

In order to bring into sharp relief the possibility and impacts of the project failing or running late, one further question is worth asking at this stage of the project.

4. CAN YOU AFFORD THE PROJECT TO BE LATE, OR FAIL, AND WHAT ARE THE IMPLICATIONS?

This is a question which is rarely asked, but I believe is very necessary. Asking this question before the project commences can be very enlightening. Clearly, if this project is strategically important, the organization would not wish it to fail, and may not tolerate it being late. For example, Enterprise Resource Planning systems (such as SAP, BAAN and PeopleSoft) are currently seen as being pivotal to running today's complex businesses. The projects which implement these systems are major undertakings and are often seen as being strategically important, and yet, according to new research, are usually late, over budget, fail to meet business expectations, and miss their return on investment targets.[13] Equally, the current gold rush into e-commerce is wholly dependent upon the success of the technology once implemented, and with the current trend towards integrating e-commerce with enterprise resource planning, the risk of real-time problems occurring in the future is very high.[14] When a project is running late, it is ultimately impacting its return on investment. If the project is significantly over budget and late, its viability must come into question, because cost and time overruns will dramatically reduce the ability to achieve the benefits. Therefore, as organizations develop their next business case, five scenarios should be added to force an assessment of the implications of the project running late, being over budget or failing:

1. The project runs to time and budget, and delivers all that is expected of it.
2. The project is late and/or over budget but delivers all of the expected functionality.
3. The project runs to time and budget, but is de-scoped to meet the time and cost constraints.
4. The project is late and/or over budget but delivers a reduced functionality.
5. The project fails, and is terminated before, or shortly after, implementation.

When assessing these, it is necessary to identify the financial, internal organizational and external business implications of each scenario. Once completed, they can provide immense benefit to the organization's decision makers as they weigh up their next IT investment. I will come back to this in the next chapter.

STEP 3: FIND A FIRST-CLASS PROJECT MANAGER

Having created a robust basis on which to decide to invest in the project, the next task is to appoint an excellent project manager. Pretty easy? Maybe not.

First-class project managers are hard to come by, and first-class IT project managers especially so. There are unfortunately, many projects being run today by what I call the 'Titanic project managers'. These are people who, at the first sign of trouble, will leave their post in order to tackle an interesting technical problem. As captain, their job is to steer the project through the usually turbulent waters, not to manage technical issues. As soon as they leave their post, there is a real danger that the project will run into difficulties because there is no one leading it. This is, of course, not the only reason why the project might fail, but given the complexities that must be managed on a typical project, this behaviour is particularly damaging because it detracts from the constant vigilance required to make it a success.

The first-class information systems project manager is one who recognizes that he can no longer rely just on his technical knowledge to deliver the project. With an increasing move to large, cross-functional projects, involving a mix of technical and non-technical activity, the IT aspects are fast becoming a small, but critical, component to the overall project's success. Therefore, relying solely on technological skills and know-how to deliver such projects is unlikely to be successful. But the problem is that there are too many Titanic project managers who are unwilling to let go of their technical comfort blanket. This unwillingness is not, of course, entirely their fault, as professional bodies and organizations fall into the same trap: they too believe that technology is of primary importance. For example, the British Computer Society does not usually recognize degrees that lack a strong technical component, even though they may cover the vitally important non-technical, organizational, business and behavioural issues. Such myopia serves to reinforce the technophile geeky image of IT,

which turns off potential candidates from joining the IT profession, and leads to the skills crises and shortages that affect organizations with ever increasing frequency.

It is also clear that organizations fall into this techno-centric trap. How many times do adverts in the IT and national press claim to want project managers, when what they appear to want are technical experts: 'Wanted: top flight project manager for major blue chip client. Must have in-depth knowledge of Java, C++, Oracle, workflow and ERP systems.' Obviously, they are looking for a programmer, or perhaps a technical analyst or consultant. What is clear from these advertisements is that they are not looking for a project manager.

Apart from the failure to position the role of the project manager correctly, other problems tend to persist, which are primarily associated with the way in which the projects are executed. For example, all too often, it is the failure of project managers to adhere to the basic principles such as project planning, estimation of costs and assessing/managing risks, that sets the project on the path to failure. Add to this the failure to choose and motivate the right staff, manage the associated organizational politics and consult with and build relationships with the stakeholders – it should come as no surprise that only 16 per cent of projects are successful. Project managers are also notorious for leaving problems too late, by which time it becomes impossible to take corrective action. For example, the criticality of the $175 million automated baggage system at Denver City Airport was not appreciated until it was too late because information was not reaching the key influencers at the right time.[15]

There is, therefore a much needed shift in thinking within project management (see Table 10.1), which includes the move toward more hybrid business, technical and project management skills. As projects grow in their complexity, and as IT becomes deeply embedded within business processes, there is less need for the technical project manager.

So how can you recognize the first-class information systems project manager? I believe possession of the following are good indicators:

Table 10.1 Project managers – new and old

Old-style Project Manager	New-style Project Manager
Technically focused	Organizationally focused
Hard quantitative skills	Strong qualitative skills
Automates existing processes	Changes business processes
Change insensitive	Change sensitive
Politically naïve	Politically adept
Frequently a technical expert	Frequently a business–technical hybrid

- first and foremost, a good grounding in project management, its associated skills and disciplines;
- a sensitivity for the organizational and behavioural elements of the project as opposed to just the technical elements;
- the ability to understand the business benefit of technology;
- the ability to motivate the team and wider stakeholder community through leadership, personal action, passion and enthusiasm;
- personal presence and the ability to command respect; and
- the skill to adapt their craft to the organizational circumstances, rather than having an obsession for a particular method or methodology.

There are naturally many more, but these should be sufficient to identify (and retain) the best the organization has to offer.

STEP 4: APPLY FIRST-CLASS PROJECT MANAGEMENT DISCIPLINES

Once found and appointed, the first-class project manager must apply their craft and deliver the project. As well as depending on the types of skills and behaviours identified above, there is the need to apply very well the basic project management disciplines. But what constitutes first-class project management skills? With so many books and journals dedicated to the subject, this should be obvious, and I will not belabour these too much.

However, there is one aspect that is rarely considered, and that is the organizational environment in which the project manager is able to perform. This too has to be first class. Unfortunately, many organizations do not provide an environment in which project management skills can be applied appropriately, either spending little or no time on training, or failing to accept the importance of the role. A recent survey by Asta Development Corporation confirms this and highlights an unacceptable scale of wasted resources, time and money through project management inefficiencies, and a lack of understanding of what project management is, and what it can offer.[16] The survey also highlighted a lack of training or investment in what many business leaders regard as an increasingly critical business tool. This lack of value leads organizations to throw people into project management roles without first providing them with some basic training – learning on the job is the order of the day. This leads to major inconsistencies in approach even within a single organization, and tends to result in an unacceptably high level of failure.

Some recent research conducted in the United States provides some further insight into this organizational dimension of project management. The research, which focused on best practices for controlling technology projects, identified 25 reasons why project management tools and techniques were underused or rejected.[17] Here are just a few:

- lack of understanding of how to use tools properly;

- general anxiety over methods and information use and misuse;
- use of tool requires too much work, is too time-consuming, and requires too much paperwork;
- tools reduce personal drive and willingness to fix *ad hoc* problems and contingencies;
- too busy to learn new tools or techniques;
- tools don't help control, but help to maintain status quo when project performance deteriorates;
- reduces face-to-face communications and complex decision making;
- tools isolate team members and their leaders; and
- tools weaken managerial power.

These problems are less about the tools and techniques of project management, and more to do with the lack of training, experience and acceptance of the need for professional project management by the organization. This clearly needs to be addressed before projects can become more successful.

So what constitutes first-class project management? I believe the following:

- A focus on planning – This means investing sufficient time in planning the project, and not leaping straight into the scheduling tool (such as Microsoft Project). Planning is more than just creating a Gantt chart, it involves determining what the project is to achieve, what it is going to produce, what techniques and tools it is to apply, and what resources it requires to achieve these. This is not an overnight process, nor is it something that the project manager should do in isolation. Engaging the project team and wider stakeholder community during the planning process can provide many benefits.

- A focus on monitoring, control, and visibility – Once started, the project must be monitored and controlled. Monitoring and controlling typically involve the management of the plan, the resources and the constraints under which the project is executed – usually time and money, and occasionally quality. Ensuring this is visible to the project stakeholders is very important. Visibility, however, is not about distributing the Gantt chart. In general, the Gantt is only designed to serve the project manager and their immediate team, as it allows the tasks and their duration to be tracked. Visibility is about ensuring that the mechanism, be it primarily graphical or data-based, allows the project's status and prognosis to be clearly understood by all project stakeholders.

- A focus on communication – Communication is the lifeblood of any project. It must be continuous and depends to a great extent on the project manager. Uncommunicative project managers, who are unwilling to talk to their team or their project stakeholders, are a significant danger to the project. Communication at team level should be daily, and the adoption of a 15-minute meeting at the start of each working day can be beneficial. The meeting is especially useful during times of intense activity, such as when the project nears completion. Equally, having one-to-one meetings with the principal stakeholders is a must, as these meetings can highlight potential areas of difficulty, especially associated with politics or power. It also allows some of the private views about the project to be fed back to the project manager.

- A focus on benefits – Benefits realization should be the only reason why projects are initiated. Too many projects fail to deliver any significant benefits, and even when they do these are usually way below those which were anticipated at the time of the business case. Being able to report on the status of the project from a benefits perspective is a valuable addition to project reporting, and demonstrates to senior management that the project manager is concerned about the outcomes of the project, and not just the project itself.

- A sensitivity for power and politics – Many

project managers shy away from power and politics because they believe they are difficult to manage, or feel that they are unimportant – as long as they deliver the project everything will be fine. There is plenty of evidence to suggest the opposite is true, as major projects involve a varying degree of power and politics. Being attuned to this, and managing it in a sensitive way, allows the project manager to steer the project through the often turbulent political waters.

These five elements of project management are vital to the successful delivery of any project, and, as we will see in the subsequent chapters, they constitute the bedrock for being able to manage the particular tensions associated with information systems projects.

The purpose of this chapter has been to develop the final piece of the information systems project jigsaw puzzle. An early organizational focus on the implications of the project is clearly worth having, if organizations are to bet on the right horse. Equally, recognizing and embracing professional project management disciplines is also fundamental to success. Without these, there may be little hope in improving the success rate of information systems projects. With these, however, comes the opportunity to tackle and minimize the effects of the issues identified in Part I. With this assumption in mind, we can now address these issues one by one.

CHAPTER ELEVEN

Guaranteeing returns from high-investment information systems projects

A recent *Financial Times* front-page article carried the headline 'Government to probe its IT failures'.[1] The article announced the launch of an inquiry by the United Kingdom's Cabinet Office into why so many of the government's information technology projects were going wrong and struggling to deliver value for money. As well as taking the unprecedented step of reviewing projects already underway, the inquiry will also be examining private sector IT projects. But one has to ask how much value they will get from this analysis, as the private sector finds it just as difficult to achieve value for money as the public sector.

This move is part of a general trend, as organizations begin to wake up to the need to achieve real investment returns from their IT projects. Indeed, as this realization has grown, there has been a corresponding increase in seminars, books and conferences dedicated to the subject of how to achieve investment return from IT. A common theme that is increasingly evident from all of this interest is the importance of managing the benefits realization process from the cradle to the grave. Without the active management of the benefits, it is very unlikely that the full value of an information system project will ever be realized. After all, in the absence of process and rigour, it is easy for the project manager, sponsor, senior manager and operational manager to delude themselves that they have done as much as they can. But, in adopting this attitude, they only deliver paltry returns on increasingly large investments. However, to kid oneself that the benefits will realize themselves is extremely difficult where there is due process and accountability. Executing a project that has no discernible benefit or one in which no one is expected to take accountability for the benefits realization process is missing the point of choosing to execute the project in the first place. However logical this might seem, many organizations do not really know how they can make this happen – there is little historical information available, and there is seemingly no one around to make it happen. So what can organizations do?

THREE STEPS TO HEAVEN

Realizing business benefits from information system projects should not be difficult, as long as some care and vigilance is applied. There are, as far as I can see, just three steps to achieving real investment return – and of course, all three must be applied if the benefits are to be realized:

1. The application of a rigorous and consistent project appraisal mechanism in which some of the basic questions mentioned in the last chapter are answered – These, of course, are in addition to the financial measures (which must themselves encapsulate some form of sensitivity analysis around the project itself).

2. The monitoring of benefits as part of the project management and control process – This includes an ongoing review of benefits to see if they are likely to materialize, and also the identification of additional benefits as the project progresses. This adds dynamism to the benefits realization process, and provides greater realism to the expected returns as the project nears completion.

3. The introduction of a consistent process plus associated accountability for realizing the business benefits, and hence their continued monitoring once the project has

completed – As well as being an important component to the process, it also allows additional opportunities to be spotted where further investment can provide more benefits.

In the majority of organizations, one, two, or all three of these crucial elements are missing, and hence the full benefits are never realized. What is also remarkable is that organizations are so willing to commit to projects which promise jam tomorrow (at significant cost) and yet are so unwilling to follow through in making sure the benefits are realized. This can and must change. The remainder of this chapter describes each of these critical steps in more detail.

STEP 1: APPRAISING PROJECTS – BACKING THE RIGHT HORSE

The previous chapter identified a number of questions an organization should ask itself before embarking on its next major information systems project. Such questions are designed to enhance the business case and, more importantly, generate information geared toward the outcomes of the project, rather than focusing purely on the inputs. Coupling the necessity for inputs with project outcomes – both positive and negative – should ensure that key decision makers have the necessary information on which to apply their judgement. As a result, they should be capable of selecting projects that are more likely to provide them with the benefits they, as leaders of their organizations, seek. It should also force them to consider the wider implications of their IT investments, and especially the internal and external impacts. Naturally, any business case is incomplete without the financial analysis, and it is to this I will now briefly turn. At the end of this section I will return to what constitutes a good justification process.

According to Henry Lucas, in his book *Information Technology and the Productivity Paradox*, the type of IT investment will vary considerably.[2] This concept is, of course, nothing new, as other researchers[3] and general observation have identified similar variations

(see Table 11.1). The benefit of such stratification lies in its ability to classify the types of IT investment and facilitate the decision-making process by comparing projects on an even footing.

It is necessary, however, to take this stratification one step further, and vary the investment appraisal approach to match the type of IT investment. This ensures that a more substantial and more accurate analysis and hence representation of the project and its benefits is achieved. With the well-known shortcomings of the standard investment appraisal techniques, such as Net Present Value and Return on Investment, some recent literature sheds light on the alternatives that can be used to appraise information systems projects. Furthermore, interest in the use of balanced scorecard techniques has allowed organizations to assess the value of their IT investments more widely by focusing on the non-financial benefits in a structured fashion.[4] It is therefore worth highlighting, albeit briefly, the types of approaches that can be applied to the different types of IT project. In their book *How to Assess your IT Investment*, Farbey, Land and Targett discuss in detail the importance of marrying the method used to evaluate a project to the type of IT investment.[5] They recommend the use of an approach which assesses the project from the dual perspectives of the role which IT is to adopt – which includes the types of benefit, the relationship of the project to the business and its certainty of impact, and the associated evaluation constraints – which include the timing of the evaluations, the nature of the decision-making process, the nature of the system, and the industry situation. The model allows the most appropriate appraisal method to be selected for a given type of information systems project, and from this provides the basis of a thorough appraisal. This helps to avoid the immediate rejection of projects which cannot be assessed on financial measures alone, or which have a combination of financial and non-financial benefits. The authors recommend that:

● Return on Investment should be applied in

Table 11.1 IT investment types

Project type	Characteristics
Mandatory	Typically externally driven, for example, through regulatory or political pressure/legislation. Decisions in such instances tend to be confined to choosing a design which meets these externally imposed requirements, whilst at the same time minimizing the costs to the organization.
Automation	Applications designed to replace existing methods and/or processes in order to reduce costs. They may provide little in the way of business innovation and may, apart from the reduction in headcount, have only a limited impact on the profitability of the business.
Direct value added	Applications which are designed to add direct value through a combination of cost reduction and leveraging value through innovation. Such projects are designed to make significant impacts on the organization's effectiveness and efficiency.
Management Information and decision support systems	Applications that provide information for planning, control and decision making. These are usually focused at senior and middle management, and are aimed at making general improvements in their efficiency.
Infrastructure	Applications that provide a general capability but may not be targeted at any specific functional area. This is one of the most difficult types of project to gain commitment and funding for, as it is hard to demonstrate a direct positive return on the investment. However, they do provide the foundation upon which further applications and investments can be made.
Inter-organizational systems	Systems which cross organizational boundaries and which are shared by more than one organization, chiefly trading partners. The value added may, however, be different for the cooperating parties. A good example would be the introduction of electronic data interchange between a supplier and their customers, and increasing e-commerce through business-to-business, and business-to-customer applications.
Strategic systems	Projects directed at achieving competitive advantage, improving organizational performance and productivity, enabling new organizational structures to be implemented or developing a new type of business. A good example of this would be the use of information and communication technologies to implement teleworking and hot-desking within the workplace. In general, the benefits can be quite difficult to assess and measure in this type of project.
Business transformation	Projects designed to enable change within an organization. These are specifically directed at transforming (and occasionally turning around) the organization and as such are expected to make significant impacts on profitability.

traditional cost-reduction projects, as the benefits are hard and very measurable. Because such projects typically involve the elimination of headcount and infrastructure they are simple to value, and hence easy to measure. Return on Investment is not, however, generally suited to projects which have high levels of uncertainty in either their cost or benefit projections.

- Cost–benefit analysis should be applied in well-defined circumstances. Unlike return on investment, it has the capability to deal with a wide range of benefits that are both tangible and intangible in nature – as long as there is consensus on how the intangibles are to be measured. The method typically fails where this consensus cannot be achieved, or where the realization of the intangible benefits seems unlikely.

- Multi-objective, multi-criteria methods should be used in more complex situations. These techniques recognize that there are other measures of value apart from money, that different stakeholders will have different views on the value of the proposed benefits, and that the majority of organizations find it easier to express their preferences in relative rather than absolute terms. As you would expect, such approaches require more effort to apply than the standard financial techniques, such as return on investment, but this effort is worth expending because they are designed to cope with large and complex projects that could have major organizational impacts. In order to achieve consensus and the required buy-in to the project, it is necessary to explore the concept of value as widely as possible, and in doing so, recognize that there are likely to be multiple objectives associated with the project, which themselves may require multiple criteria for their assessment. The application of Utility Theory can be helpful here, especially when it is difficult to gain agreement. Utility Theory is a model which specifies the ways in which people or organizations should act in order to attain their goals. It involves assigning arbitrary numbers to the desirability of different outcomes (their utilities) and prescribes how best to achieve one's goals to the maximum possible extent. Stuart Sutherland, in his book *Irrationality*,[6] provides a useful step-by-step guide to understanding Utility Theory which is repeated here with an additional stage (zero) added for completeness:

* Stage 0: Define a number of courses of action.
* Stage 1: List the possible outcomes of each course of action identified.
* Stage 2: Each person involved in the decision-making process assigns a number (utility) against each outcome.

This number may be positive indicating the outcome's desirability, negative indicating its undesirability, or zero if the answer is neutral.

* Stage 3: Because some outcomes are uncertain, the utility for each is multiplied by its probability of outcome, yielding the expected utility for that outcome.
* Stage 4: The expected utilities of each outcome are added together yielding a combined expected utility.
* Stage 5: The expected utilities of all options are then compared and the option with the largest combined expected utility is chosen.

The utilities assigned by the individual involves arbitrary numbers, but they must be consistent. For example, if outcome A was twice as desirable as outcome B, the decision maker can assign any number as long as A's is twice B's. According to Sutherland, Utility Theory has been shown to overcome irrationality because of its ability to force people to take account of evidence which is often counter to their own views. He goes on to cite an example from California associated with developing land by the sea in which the opposing camps of developers and environmentalists could not come to an amicable agreement. Because of this, decisions were often made using the wrong information or rushed through because of time constraints or when other key members of the committee were absent. The application of Utility Theory however allowed the two opposing camps to agree on development projects because it forced them to apply an objective framework that avoided the adoption of their usual stances. The use of Utility Theory had made each group pay attention to those factors which were contradictory to their own overall view, and which they usually ignored. Utility Theory has also been shown to minimize dispute and even shorten the time spent on committees.

- Where IT is to be applied in more radical

and leading-edge ways, many of the traditional approaches to its evaluation break down. Adopting a leap-of-faith approach is also insufficient to give the level of comfort with which to commit to the project. Evaluation methods in this case have to deal with systems which have a wide range of benefits and which themselves are probably large, have very significant organizational impacts, and involve significant sums of money – the London Stock Exchange's Taurus project would have fallen into this category. The use of Information Economics – which uses a combination of conventional return on investment techniques for those costs and benefits which are readily identified and measured, and a decision-making process based on a scoring technique for the more complex costs and benefits – is generally applicable here.[7]

Clearly, varying the appraisal technique as a means of assessing both financial and non-financial benefits can present problems to organizations, as each requires a deep understanding of how they should be best applied. Despite this obstacle, the opportunity to assess projects more comprehensively has distinct advantages, not least in the ability to compare projects on an even footing. If organizations are concerned about investing in the right project, they should really attempt to establish a balance in their approach. It would be practical to apply a hard, financially based, appraisal method, such as Net Present Value, or Return on Investment alongside an approach which focuses on, say, multi-objective, multi-criteria techniques. Through this, a dual approach to developing the investment appraisal could be established with which the organization could initially gain some invaluable experience, and more importantly, over time, ensure the right projects are accepted or rejected at the time of the business case.

Once the basic investment appraisal has been completed, another dimension worthy of inclusion within the business case is a sensitivity analysis. For example, it is useful to attach a probability to each appraisal that indicates the likelihood of the project delivering the benefits expected of it. It should be recognized that in many cases this might be below 100 per cent. This sensitivity analysis is particularly important because it asserts that the likelihood of a project achieving its investment returns is predicated, at least to some extent, on the type of project being undertaken and, more significantly, on the ability of the project team to deliver.

This is a useful addition to the business case because it suggests that the expectation of achieving 100 per cent investment return should not be assumed or even expected. Moreover, the return is likely to vary considerably, according to the type of system that is being developed. This is, of course, not to say that the investment will add no value at all to the organization, but expecting a return cannot, and should not, be guaranteed, especially when a minimum of effort is usually applied in achieving it. This type of sensitivity analysis fits well within Utility Theory where the probability of outcome is needed to derive the overall utility of an option.

I believe this sensitivity analysis should be taken one step further by incorporating the five scenarios of project outcome identified in the previous chapter and assessing the likely impacts of these on the project's costs and benefits (see Table 11.2). The advantage of including this is that it forces the business, IT and senior management to consider and question more carefully some of their underlying assumptions made when drawing together the cost and benefit data. More importantly, it forces them to think the unthinkable, and assess the consequences for the organization and, where applicable, its customers, of the late delivery or failure of their information systems project. In doing so, it brings into sharp relief the commitment required to make the project a success.

Bringing together the key points from this and the previous chapter allows a comprehensive business case to be developed that better serves the organization in its decision-making process. It should be stressed, however, that the responsibility for the development of the case should not reside

Table 11.2   Sensitivity analysis and project outcome

Project outcome	Impact on costs	Negative impact on benefits
The project runs to time and budget, and delivers all that is expected of it.	Nil.	Nil, assuming they are actually monitored and actively managed once the project has completed.
The project is late and/or over budget but delivers all of the expected functionality.	Moderate to significant depending on how late and over budget the project is.	Moderate to significant as delays would lead to a lag in the realization of the benefits. Furthermore, the increase in project costs will eat into the investment returns, and will serve to further reduce the benefits.
The project is on time and within budget, but is de-scoped to meet these constraints.	Nil.	Limited to significant, depending on the degree of de-scoping. Although the project will have completed on time and within budget, the impact of de-scoping will serve to limit the benefits achieved. Furthermore, some additional investment may be required to develop the full functionality, and hence meet the original benefit expectations.
The project is late and/or over budget and delivers a reduced functionality.	Moderate to significant depending on how late and over budget the project is.	Moderate to significant, as it is very likely that additional investment will be required to complete the remaining functionality. Hence there will be an immediate reduction in benefits because of the increase in costs, as well as a reduction in the longer term because of the reduced functionality. Interestingly, organizations usually tackle the problem of the additional investment under their IT maintenance budgets. This is, of course, misleading, and fails to provide a true representation of the total costs of developing the system.
The project fails, and is terminated before (or shortly after) implementation.	Moderate to very significant depending on where in the project life cycle the project is terminated. In general, there is a tendency toward the very significant end of the spectrum because of the impact of irrational behaviour and escalation.	Very significant, in that there will be no benefits.

purely with the IT department; it should be owned by the business and jointly developed with IT. Why? History has shown that delegating the production of the business case to IT can lead to an over-emphasis of the technological aspects of the project to the detriment of the organizational. Moreover, it allows the business to avoid taking any responsibility for project outcomes, which is itself an extremely common, albeit poor practice. Business accountability is essential, as it allows for a greater degree of buy-in to the project, as opposed to being on the periphery, and hence seeking out the natural scapegoat when projects fails – that is, IT. This of course achieves nothing apart from reinforcing the culture gap between business and IT.

Insisting that both IT and the business should be involved with the development of the business case recognizes that any information system is about the optimization of technology and the organization's human capital. At the time of completing the business case, a summary should be produced (see Figure 11.1, based on the CONFIRM project). The purpose of this summary is threefold. First, it provides the board with a summary of the salient points of the project, including the answers to the questions posed in the previous chapter. This can be used to gain an immediate insight into the project that they may be sponsoring. Second, it can act as an *aide-mémoire* for the principal stakeholders during the life of the project and allow them to keep all eyes on the return on investment prize. And, third, it can provide a vision for the project itself and be used as an effective and continuous motivator and reminder to the project team of what the project is all about, that is, creating business benefit, not just implementing some new technology.

Once the business case has been developed, it should be reviewed, along with all other information systems projects that require funding. In my mind, for this assessment to be successful, a simple two-step approach can be used, which would allow the organization to spend the right amount of time assessing each case in turn. This two-step approach would entail:

1. The establishment of an information systems project prioritization cell, comprising a mix of business and IT personnel at a sufficiently high level to ensure they are fully empowered to take executive decisions. The purpose of this cell is to review each business case in detail together with its summary and decide on those that are most valuable to the organization using the model of Figure 10.1 as the basis. Clearly, at this stage, there may be some merit in the IT and business sponsors meeting with the prioritization group to conduct a business case questions-and-answers session, the purpose of which would be to clarify ambiguities within the case and determine its full value to the organization. All projects that are accepted by the prioritization group would then progress to the next stage. In preparation for this, project summaries should be sent to the board or functional heads as appropriate.

2. All projects that require investment beyond a certain level, say £1 000 000 for large enterprises, and £100 000 (or lower) for smaller organizations, should make a formal presentation to the board (who would have seen the investment case summaries beforehand). This should put forward, among other details, what the project is going to achieve for the organization, the costs involved, and the risks associated with the investment. This is, in essence, a sales presentation and should be treated as such. It should not be delivered by IT, but by business and IT together. The sole purpose of the presentation is to ensure the board is fully aware of the organizational commitment that is required to make the project a success. In addition, it also provides an opportunity for the board to question their own commitment to a project which could complete over budget, late, deliver less than anticipated, and which might even fail. I believe the board must be the ultimate decision maker for all large projects, and should be fully accountable for their ultimate success. When I say board, I mean the entire board, not the chief information officer/IT director – it is not permissible to delegate such decisions to a technologist alone. For all projects below this threshold, a similar presentation should be made to functional heads. The objectives, of course, remain the same.

STEP 2: SAFEGUARDING THE BENEFITS – AN ADDITIONAL PROJECT MANAGEMENT ACTIVITY

Having taken the care to select an investment that is able to provide the organization with the business benefits it seeks, it is vital that the

Business Case Summary	
Project title: CONFIRM (Combined Travel Reservation System).	**Project description:** Development of a state-of-the-art combined travel reservation system capable of booking cars, hotels and lodgings on one system.
IT accountability: AMR Information Services (AMRIS).	**Business accountability:** Hilton National, Marriot, Budget Rent-A-Car (consortium)
Estimated investment required: $55.7 million	**Estimated benefits (financial):** Operating costs (cost per reservation) dropping from $1.05 per transaction to $0.40 in the fifth year of operation. With a reduction in operating costs, and an associated increase in transaction volumes, the operational profitability of the consortium members will be increased by 50%.
Pay-back period: Benefits achieved over a five-year period during which the operating costs will reduce significantly. Initial drop in transaction costs expected immediately.	**Other benefits (non-financial):** First to market, competitive advantage, increased market share. Opportunity to market the system world-wide. Opportunity to extend the system's capability and usage to include the wider leisure market.
Duration: 44 months (elapsed).	**Peak resourcing required:** 360 development and business staff.

Dependency implications (once implemented)	
Level of dependency: High. Once implemented the system will become the backbone of the consortium's operations.	**Implications of failure on the internal business:** Very significant. System failure and down-time could result in significant business disruption, which would include, amongst others, inactive staff, and possible paper-based backlogs.
External implications of software error: This would depend on how persistent the problem was. However, loss of confidence in the reservation system could result in a general loss of confidence in the consortium. A possible indirect consequence is a loss of custom, and if it is a persistent problem, of market share.	**Level of contingency planning required:** Must be high, given the expected level of dependency. Therefore, hot-standby and system mirroring may be required. A paper-based backup may not be viable given the anticipated level of daily transactions.

Project implications	
Is this the right system?: The current view from the industry is that there will be a significant increase in both business and leisure travel over the next 3–5 years. This will mean the ability to handle large volumes of reservations will be the key indicator of success. Probably the only way in which this can be achieved is through the introduction of a fast, reliable computer reservation system.	**What are the wider system implications?:** Significant effort is required to transfer existing client details (static data) into the new system. Changes to the network infrastructure are also required to increase the speed of communication between the travel agents and the data centre. In addition, changes to the existing accounting and general ledger applications will be necessary.
What will it require of the users?: Users will be expected to become travel advisers. Therefore, as well as operating the system, they will be expected to develop a wide understanding of the travel industry and the products and services of the three consortium members.	

Sensitivity Analysis	
Impact of late delivery: Reduction in benefits in the near term. In addition, there may be a short-term loss of confidence in the consortium's ability to operate their business effectively.	**Impact of failure:** Very significant. Investment wasted, damage to the consortium's reputation, and potential loss of market share. Cost of transactions remain high, and ability to handle increasing volumes of reservations will be difficult.
Impact of de-scoping: Depends on the degree of de-scoping, and whether there is an associated overrun in project costs and schedule. However, this is likely to affect both the timing and scale of the benefits, as well as the general system capabilities. For example, a reduction in the functionality may result in an inability to deliver all of the consortium's requirements simultaneously. If the system is de-scoped, further investment may be required to develop the remaining functionality, once implemented.	
Prioritization cell decision: Accept, pass to the board for final decision.	**Board decision:** Agreed. Costs must remain within target, and the risks must be managed.

Figure 11.1 A sample business case summary

project is executed by a competent project manager who is capable of protecting the investment, by delivering the project's benefits.

The purpose of project management is to ensure the completion of the project within the constraints set by the organization. Clearly, any project worth its salt is designed to deliver benefits to the organization, even where these may be considered less tangible in nature. However, it is often assumed, quite wrongly, that the benefits will be delivered automatically once the project has completed. Ensuring enduring value is achieved not only involves the active management of the benefits whilst the project is being executed, but also after it has completed. To achieve this means the development of a reception strategy – designed to prepare the organization for the change that will occur, but more importantly provide it with the tools with which to realise the benefits – early on within the project. As a result, the project manager's responsibility must encompass the protection of the business's investment and the active management of the benefits realization process early on within the project and well beyond its completion.

The starting point for this process is understanding how the project's deliverables link into the attainment of business benefit. Such benefit, as I have already stated, comes from the operational line, not the project – the

project is designed to provide the foundations for the benefits to be realized (see Figure 11.2a). The simple model shown in Figure 11.2a emphasizes the importance of having clear project objectives and benefit outcomes, as these help to frame the project plan, and ultimately its deliverables. The shaded section is where the effort of the project manager is usually focused and tends to concentrate on safeguarding the project's schedule, cost and deliverables. Historically, the monitoring and control activity of a project has been restricted to ensuring the project delivers to time and budget. As a result, the project manager has tended to focus on the capturing and reporting of costs and significant project achievements. Rarely, it seems, has the project manager monitored the benefits, and rarely has the project manager really engaged the organizational line in this process. The project boundary therefore acts as a brick wall to this involvement, and it is often exacerbated by the culture gap. As a result, the operational line only tends to get involved at the back-end of the project when there is some pre-implementation training or user acceptance testing to be undertaken. It should be stated that this does not always work very well, especially where the results are out of alignment with expectations.

Clearly, if the level of project success is to

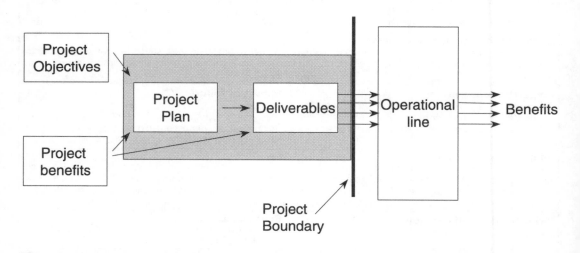

Figure 11.2a Protecting the investment – the classic view

increase, the project plan must also identify the benefits it is going to achieve and ensure there are tasks within the plan associated with their realization. With the majority of project benefits dependent on the operational line, the project manager must involve them early on within the process. Without this involvement, it is difficult to protect the organization's investment, and more importantly, generate the necessary commitment to manage and monitor the benefits once the project completes.

It should, of course, be recognized that realizing the benefits is not necessarily an easy task. For example, headcount reduction is one of the principal ways of justifying information systems projects, and yet it can be very difficult for the project manager to provide the basis for its reduction alone. Reductions in headcount can also seemingly allow any project pay-back within a year, and thus appear to be an obvious candidate for acceptance by the board (the Department of Social Security's Operational Strategy provides a good example of where this can go horribly wrong – see Chapter 4). Realizing the benefits from headcount reductions is more involved than project managers think, and typically involves managing the following:

- Union and employment law implications – These may lead to a protracted process of reduction, and to a potentially higher cost associated with paying staff as they leave.
- Trying to find displaced staff other internal work – Organizations typically try to find other jobs for those who want them prior to making them redundant. This can extend the period during which the headcount reductions are achieved, and also serves to reduce the potential benefits. Cost displacement as opposed to cost reduction is the result, with an associated reduction in the local budget, but no subsequent improvement in the organization's bottom line.
- Replacing lost skills – It is wrong to believe that an information system will be able to replace all of the employees' skills, given that they are often specialists in their field. Workloads may reduce as a result of the

newly implemented system, but the organization cannot always afford to lose their skills.
- Assessing the benefits of a reduction in workload – Replacing part of a person's role is unlikely to lead to a reduction in total headcount. Only where computerization is able to replace a whole person can the headcount argument be used.

This one illustration demonstrates just how difficult it can be to follow through from the business case, and ensure that the benefits claimed at the time of agreeing the investment are realized. Imagine how difficult this becomes with intangible benefits. Such difficulties put forward a very strong case for the monitoring of benefits during the life of a project. Moreover, the chief executive should be very concerned about how a major project will impact the business – not just at the end of the project, but for the duration of the project as well.

The model of Figure 11.2a thus requires updating to extend both the dialogue with the operational line during the project, and the monitoring of benefits as the project progresses. Unless a project is lengthy and is able to deliver benefit during its life, the benefits will only materialize once the project has completed. Despite this, the benefits can still be monitored in two ways: first, through assessing the impacts of a project's costs and timescales on the benefits. This can be done by mapping the project's deliverables (often termed 'products') to the benefits using a simple product-to-benefit modelling technique. This links each major project deliverable to the expected benefit, which can be described, and a monetary value attached to it. This can be used to track the impacts of increases in costs and timescales on the benefits and, where necessary, the impact of de-scoping the project. For example, it is well known that if the project is over budget, running late, or is de-scoped, it is highly likely that the benefits will be reduced, but without this simple technique, the full impacts would not be known.[8] The second approach involves assessing the operational line's attitude to the project as it progresses. This can be a valuable indicator of success. For example, if, over the life of the project, the attitude toward it changes for the worse, it is probable that the benefits will not be maximized and in extreme cases, the likelihood of rejection increased. There is a strong argument, therefore, to link the usual project stakeholder analysis and management to the benefits realization process in order to provide an additional sensitivity analysis.[9]

The project manager must not only involve those in the operational line who will be ultimately charged with the benefits realization process, but also constantly relate the project's progress and stakeholder attitude to the benefits. The project manager must also develop a shared understanding with the operational line of the project's benefits and help them to visualize and understand how they can be best achieved in the context of business as usual – which is the *raison d'être* of the operational line. To achieve this means changing the model of Figure 11.2a to that of 11.2b.

In this model, the natural project boundary has disappeared and the operational line has been included within the sphere of influence of the project. In addition, feedback loops have been included between the project deliverables, plan and benefits.

There are two components that underpin this enhanced model:

● Removing the project boundary eliminates the artificial barrier between the operational line's involvement in the benefits realization process. This is deliberate, in that it allows the perception of the project in the eyes of the project team and the operational line to change from one of pure delivery to one of benefit management. This recognizes that an early and continuous focus on the benefits can be valuable, and can be enhanced through the active involvement of the operational line. Such involvement cannot be merely rhetoric, but active and action oriented.

● Feedback from the operational line and from the general monitoring and controlling activities of the project should be reflected back on to the project's deliverables, plan and ultimately its benefits. If things around the project change, it may be necessary to change the plan or to reconsider the deliverables. As such, the benefits will change, and perhaps the project may no longer be viable. Such feedback should also extend to identifying other potential benefits as the operational line's understanding of the project increases.

The purpose of widening the project manager's monitoring and controlling role is to ensure focus remains on the benefits during the life of the project, and to make this a dynamic process. This, of course, is limited if the status of the benefits is not communicated to the senior management team. But monitoring the likelihood of achieving the benefits is of value because it provides another dimension of

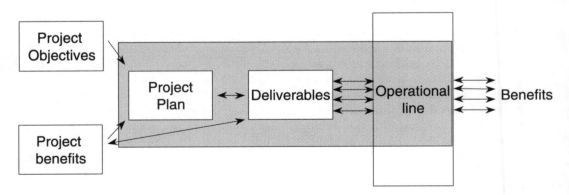

Figure 11.2b Protecting the investment – an updated approach

project activity that is usually invisible to the organization.

Assuming the project manager has delivered the project successfully, and co-developed the plan to realize the benefits, we can move to the final step of the benefits realization process.

STEP 3: FOLLOWING THROUGH – REALIZING THE BENEFITS ONCE THE PROJECT HAS FINISHED

The final element to the benefits realization process is to ensure there is sufficient accountability and responsibility for the ongoing, post-project, benefits capture. All too often this is only considered as an afterthought, or not considered at all. The problem with this is that if the persistence of monitoring and capturing is not established early on, it will fall away as other, more pressing, things come along. This limits the possible benefits that can be derived from the project because people lose interest, and robs the business of the much needed visibility of the benefits. An 'out of sight, out of mind' approach maintains the status quo of luck in benefits realization, rather than structure and rigour. It also hides the value which IT can bring to the organization, and hence reinforces the existing negative stereotypes.

The advantages of monitoring the benefits beyond the life of the project include:

- establishing a true perspective of the value the project has provided to the organization, and hence feedback into the selection of similar projects in the future, and into project metrics, if collected;
- gaining a better understanding of how benefits are realized within the operational line, and hence enhance the process for future projects;
- understanding how the changes within the organization caused by the project could be further exploited through additional project investment; and
- institutionalizing the focus on benefits as an ongoing organizational activity and demonstrating that it is serious about achieving real business value from IT.

The starting point for the ongoing monitoring of benefits rests with the project manager who must, in conjunction with the operational line, establish the plan and process for measuring them. Once the plan has been established, the responsibility and accountability for the post-project benefits realization process rests with the relevant senior manager(s) within the operational line. Given the importance of the benefits, these senior managers should have a direct reporting line into functional heads, or if the project is very significant, or business-critical, the board. The use of monthly or bi-monthly reporting showing how the benefits are performing against the plan and performance measures is a vital component to this. This establishes visibility on investment return and can be used to stimulate action where the benefits are either not being realized at the expected rate, or where they are not being realized at all. The use of a benefits realization risk register would be valuable in this respect as it would allow the high-risk areas to be managed proactively.

This process should continue until such time as the level of benefit delivery tails off, or where the original target has been met. In general, the former is the better option, as it allows the organization to establish a standard against which future projects can be measured, and assessed. For example, if the benefits from projects tail off well before the target value is met, it would suggest a general tendency to overstate the benefits when producing the business case. Equally, if more benefits are achieved, it might be possible to conclude that there is a tendency to understate the benefits. Whatever the outcome, this information can be fed back into the business case development process and allow a more realistic value to be attached to the benefits of future projects, hence providing more accurate information for the decision makers. Finally, to ensure the project manager and operational line are brought into the benefits realization process, a bonus pool should be established that is based on a percentage of total benefits realized. This can be used to generate greater commitment to achieving the benefits, and develop a greater sense of shared ownership.

High investment and high return – is it possible? Yes, I believe it is, as long as:

1. Organizations take care to appraise and hence select the right projects.
2. Project managers do more than just deliver the project to the usual time, cost and quality constraints. Projects must deliver business benefit, and the project manager is fundamental to achieving this.
3. The operational line take responsibility and accountability for actually delivering the benefits which the project has made possible.

Without these, IT projects will continue to deliver poor investment returns. With them, organizations will not only be able to spot their prize-winning projects, but also carry them through to the successful realization of the benefits. Fundamental to achieving this is the removal of the culture gap between the business and IT communities, which is the subject of the next chapter.

Eliminating the culture gap: business and IT working together

If you limit your view of a problem to choosing between two sides, you inevitably reject much that is true, and you narrow your field of vision to the limits of these two sides, making it unlikely you will pull back, widen your field of vision, and discover the paradigm shift that will permit truly new understanding.[1]

THE CONSEQUENCES OF THE CULTURE GAP

The creation of an information system involves significant human contact: if this contact is dysfunctional, the likelihood of achieving a satisfactory outcome for all stakeholders is unlikely. I believe that the culture gap can be considered to be a continuous dysfunctional influence on most information systems projects which, therefore, has a considerable impact on project outcome. Solving the problems that the culture gap presents must therefore be central to improving information systems project delivery. But key to its solution is recognizing that it is not a simple bipolar problem between two opposing camps, but a complex combination of internal and external factors. Because of this complexity, the culture gap cannot be resolved using a single approach – we have seen this fail with the introduction of the chief information officer/IT director, business analysts, the decentralization of the IT function, and even outsourcing. A richer approach which encapsulates these single-shot solutions is needed.

The approaches introduced within this chapter are directed at specific parts of the problem which itself must be viewed as a whole if the culture gap is to be reduced. Assuming any of these solutions is an isolated, one-off initiative is unlikely to be successful in reducing the effects of the culture gap. Bringing these together, however, will create an environment in which there is a positive working relationship between business and IT – the synergy that can result in world-beating information systems projects for world-beating organizations.

GRASPING THE CULTURE-GAP NETTLE

It seems that organizations and the wider IT profession are at last beginning to wake up to the need to address the issue of the culture gap. For example, the late 1990s skills crisis in the UK's IT community prompted the government to establish a working party to tackle the problem, and in particular to try and make the profession an exciting place to be for the country's brightest graduates. This action followed hot on the heels of a report which claimed that high-flying graduates were shunning the IT profession because they believed it offered limited career opportunities, and little in the way of interpersonal and management development, all of which are vital components of a stimulating and varied career.[2] The working party is, amongst other things, aiming to create a brand image for IT, and through this make it an exciting, non-geeky place to be. Creating a brand that is accepted within the wider market, like any others, requires the profession to consider the following:

- brand loyalty
- brand awareness
- brand associations
- its perceived quality.

Of these, it is the perceived quality that is of paramount importance in creating a consistent and acceptable brand image – brand value is created only if certain standards of performance are attained every time the buyer uses the services of an IT professional. The brand of the

IT profession will only have an enduring value if it has procedures to enforce quality standards.[3] Based upon the experience of the last forty years, however, I believe a lot needs to be done to create a brand for IT that people believe reflects the true professionalism expected of it.

Interestingly, in response to the announcement of the formation of the government working group, a leader in *Computer Weekly* suggested, that although branding was a necessary step, it was insufficient in itself to resolve the underlying problem of the skills shortage.[4] Much more is required than just rebranding the profession, because the problems with IT's image goes much deeper, and wider, than the government believes.

So what must the wider IT profession and organizations do to reduce, and ultimately rid themselves of, the culture gap? I believe the following:

1. Recognize and understand that the culture gap is not a straightforward 'us and them' problem, but one which touches on and involves the whole organization, the wider IT profession, and those that serve it including professional bodies, recruitment agencies and the education and training establishments. All play a part in the continuation of the culture gap, and all have a stake in its elimination. Therefore, identifying the extent of the culture gap is an important step to make in its elimination.

2. Create ways of breaking through the 'us and them' mindset which persists throughout organizations, in particular at the board and working levels. Although, as stated above, the culture gap extends far wider than these two principal groups, it is within the board, and at the working level, that it is most severe, and it is here where organizations need to concentrate their efforts.

3. Reframe the relationship between IT and the business into something that is energizing as opposed to debilitating, and through this achieve the prize of truly integrating IT into the business. To be successful, this process

must encapsulate the wider community identified under point 1, above.

4. Provide the IT community with fulfilling careers that are capable of meeting all of their expectations. This should include the classic technical career path, as well as a more business and generalist route. In the former, however, it must be recognized that technical experts can only be just that, technical experts. On no account should they end up on the board of directors, as it is unlikely they would have the requisite skills to be effective. This is not belittling the technical career route, but merely recognizing its limitations. One only needs to consider the problems experienced in trying to integrate the IT director/chief information officer into the board to realize that a purely technical expert is the last thing the board needs.[5]

5. Tackle the problem of the culture gap at its roots by enhancing the education system to encapsulate the wider issues associated with information systems. Doing this ought to provide the business and IT professionals of the future with the tools they need to ensure they maintain a healthy and productive working relationship. This is, of course, not an overnight issue, as it requires changes to university curricula which may themselves take a number of years to filter through to the student and working populations. That said, time is no excuse for inaction.

The remainder of the chapter looks at these five elements.

STEP 1: IDENTIFY THE EXTENT OF THE CULTURE GAP

The first step to eliminating the culture gap involves mapping the principal relationships and dependencies on which the wider acceptance and integration of IT depends (see Figure 12.1). As Figure 12.1 suggests, there is more to making the business–IT relationship work than just focusing on the board, the developers and business users of IT (the shaded

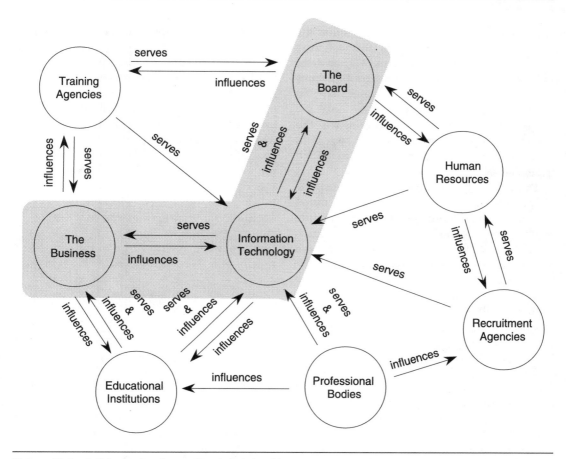

Figure 12.1 Building and understanding the relationships

portion of the model). The model also demonstrates that, in order to provide an environment in which business and IT can work well together, there needs to be a healthy two-way communication and flow of ideas across the stakeholder groups identified.

The model shows two basic relationships:

1. Serves – Here, one stakeholder group serves another by providing services or support. This includes the external, as well as internal providers, and embraces the usual IT products and services, together with training, education and other ancillary services such as recruitment and contracting.

2. Influences – Here, one stakeholder group influences another through thought leadership, specifying requirements or providing direction. Internally, this would

include the board of directors and the wider business community, whilst externally, this would include professional bodies and educational establishments.

In some cases there exists a more complex relationship in which one stakeholder group may both influence and serve another. For example, educational institutions, such as universities, serve the business and IT communities through the provision of entry-level and mid-career education, but also influence them through the research they conduct into IT and how it can be best utilized and effectively integrated within the organization.

Clearly, the model illustrated in Figure 12.1 goes much wider than a single organization might perceive its problems to be, but it is important for organizations to realize that the issue of the disconnect extends far beyond the narrow definition of business and IT. Naturally, any organization's web of relationships may vary from this model, and it is essential that these relationships are captured to make the model organizationally specific. Once the model has been tailored, the next step is to conduct a gap analysis across the identified relationships.

This gap analysis has two purposes. First, it is designed to establish the severity of the culture gap and understand its impacts on the organization. Second, it allows the organization to identify what actions are required to move from the existing situation to one in which the business and IT communities can work more productively together. This might, of course, include establishing new relationships which do not currently exist, and hence involve further updates to the relationship model in Figure 12.1.

The starting point for the gap analysis is to draw out the key issues and tensions that currently exist between each of the stakeholder groups, and also identify what the relationship ought to look like, assuming the culture gap no longer existed. This permits a series of outcomes to be established against which the redesign of the entire set of relationships can be based. The time taken to redesign the set of relationships will depend on the severity of the culture gap and the target relationships to which the organization aspires.

A word of caution is required here. It should be understood that the complete elimination of the culture gap may never be possible, because of the nature and impact of functional cultures. As discussed in Chapter 6, functional cultures will exist in all organizations, but it is how often they clash that will determine whether or not they are simple or difficult to resolve. The cultural differences associated with IT are a particular problem because IT touches every part of the organization. The purpose of the gap analysis is therefore to identify the best possible scenarios which could exist if the culture gap no longer existed – these are the possibilities.

Reaching these would be fantastic, but perhaps very difficult for some organizations and would fundamentally depend on how deep rooted was the cultural divide, or disconnect. However, reaching a point somewhere between the worst that the culture gap has to offer, and the nirvana of having no culture gap at all, will have an impact. Moreover, being able to articulate where an organization sits along this continuum should provide the opportunity for the establishment and communication of a vision, and an ability to measure progress towards achieving it. Therefore, if an organization is able to assess how severe its culture gap is now, and also set itself some targets of where it wants to be within a specified time period, it should be possible to set in train a series of positive actions designed to move it along the continuum. I will return to this aspect again under Step 3.

In order to illustrate the value such a gap analysis can provide, Tables 12.1 to 12.5 summarize some of the key tensions which currently persist within the lesser-known stakeholder groupings of Figure 12.1, plus the ideal relationship that ought to exist. This establishes the two ends of the culture gap continuum which can, for argument's sake, be considered isolated and integrated respectively.

The shaded portion of Figure 12.1 – that is, the business, information technology and the board – will be discussed in more detail under Step 2, below, for two reasons. First, this is where most of the problems associated with the culture gap tend to manifest, and second, because of the severity of the problem, each requires a more detailed review of how the tensions might be minimized.

HUMAN RESOURCES

See opposite page.

RECRUITMENT AGENCIES

See page 116.

PROFESSIONAL BODIES

See page 117.

Table 12.1   Relationships with Human Resources

Relationship with	Isolated	Integrated
The board	• little validation of business skills required to perform the IT director/chief information officer role. • typically emphasizes technical skills over business skills. • no predefined career route for IT specialists, particularly those with the desire to become an IT director.	• clear and unambiguous skills and experience match with potential board level candidates. • appropriate career structures and development frameworks in place that allow IT professionals to become effective directors (which includes experiences outside of IT).
Information Technology	• little effort to understand what skills are required beyond the technical. • limited verification of candidates entering the organization. They are often trusted to have the skills they say they have (which is not always true, especially if the skills they possess are very new, for example e-commerce). • no defined career route outside of the traditional technical path within IT.	• recognizes and balances the technical, business and soft skills. • thorough assessment, challenge and selection of candidates. • recognition that the world's best is usually unobtainable, and therefore sets realistic expectations of candidates. • multi-stream career routes which recognize the desire to retain technical skills as well as develop business, and hybrid, skills.
Recruitment agencies	• sets expectations too high, which tends to force candidates to over-embellish their skills. • uses agencies as body-shops, not strategically.	• sets realistic expectations and ensures there is a balance between the technical, business and softer skills. • strategic approach to resourcing, and use of agencies is subsequently value-adding.

EDUCATIONAL INSTITUTIONS

See page 118.

TRAINING AGENCIES

See page 119.

Having gained an understanding of the current state of the culture gap within the organization, it is useful to map its severity within a single model. The purpose of such a model is threefold:

1. It allows the full extent of the current culture gap to be modelled and visualized.
2. It allows the target relationships to be

established, and compared to those that currently exist.
3. It provides the mechanism through which progress toward the target model can be monitored.

The simple radar model in Figure 12.2 shows both the current and target models for the culture gap in a hypothetical organization. The radar is powerful because it provides a single view of the relative states of each of the stakeholder groups identified in Figure 12.1 and described in Tables 12.1 to 12.5. The way to interpret the model is to view the amount of grey as an indication of how connected each

Table 12.2   Relationships with recruitment agencies

Relationship with	Isolated	Integrated
Human Resources	• body-shopping, little effort is applied beyond a simplistic skills match. • no real consideration of business skills. • tendency to accept curriculum vitaes/resumes at face value with little or no validation or verification. • takes the lead from Human Resources, rather than adding value to the selection process.	• strategic positioning of staff based on an appropriate balance of business and technology skills. • application of value-based placements rather than body-shopping. • provides value to Human Resources by improving their understanding of the IT marketplace and the likely capabilities of candidates. • greater challenge and verification of curriculum vitaes/resumes.
Information Technology	• reactive and body-shopping approach to selection of candidates. • no challenge or value-adding in the relationship. • selection of candidates based on the latest technical buzzwords.	• prepared to challenge IT's requirements and expectations and move away from body-shopping. • adding value by maintaining a continuous view of technology within the marketplace and feeding opinion and viewpoints into IT. • selection based on an appropriate combination of generic and technical skills tailored to an organization's specific requirement, which itself is a mix of business and IT expertise.

stakeholder group is and therefore the amount of white indicates how much of a problem the culture gap is to the organization.

Naturally, as part of any programme to integrate the business and IT, it is important to establish a simple measurement system on which the extent of the disconnect can be assessed and measured on an ongoing basis. This does not have to be scientific, but it should be able to capture the broad status of the stakeholder group in relation to the culture gap. For example, the use of key performance indicators, balanced scorecards and questionnaires can be valuable tools. In particular, the balanced scorecard can be used to derive measures across each of its four quadrants (financial, customer, business

excellence, and innovation and learning) which can be monitored on an ongoing basis.

STEP 2: BREAKING THROUGH THE BOARD- AND WORKING-LEVEL CULTURE GAPS

There has been plenty of advice over the last ten years or so about how the culture gap can be eliminated, but it still seems to be as persistent as ever. Some believe, quite wrongly, that it will eventually solve itself as the level of computer literacy within the general population increases, and as the first, and subsequent, generations of computer literate directors reach the board. However, there is danger in assuming that the culture gap is merely a generation thing. There

Table 12.3 Relationships with professional bodies

Relationship with	Isolated	Integrated
Recruitment agencies	• limited, if any, influence exerted over the recruitment profession.	• provides advice and direction as to how best to manage the recruitment of technical staff, setting the standards and codes of conduct through influencing the recruitment profession.
Information Technology	• provides the basis of some professional development (such as the British Computer Society in the United Kingdom, and the Association of Computer Machinery in the United States). • offers special interest groups, which usually focus on the technical elements of the profession. • offers little incentive for joining; as there is no discernible benefit to the potential candidate. • still generally considered to be a second tier profession (when compared to the more established professions such as engineering, surveying, law and architecture).	• act as thought leaders to the profession through direction setting derived from a thorough analysis of IT's direction and impacts, lobbying and other associated activity. • extended career advice for the IT professional. • position IT as a tier one profession. • significant professional incentives for joining a body that is recognized by organizations as underwriting the professional standards of the IT profession.
Educational institutions	• limited influence, tends to be on a piecemeal basis rather than working strategically with, and across, the education system. • accreditation of degree courses focused on those which are strongly technical.	• provision of advice and direction on the types of course required to establish a full and productive career for IT professionals. • accreditation of courses which offer a much wider base to the student and which furnish them with a better basis with which to start their career.

will be benefit from a general rise in computer literacy, but the dangers of assuming that computer literacy equates to making the right investment decisions around IT, or being able to fully understand and question its value, is misguided. Increased computer literacy will not, in my opinion, mean that IT will be fully integrated into the business. Computer literacy essentially means that more people will accept IT, and these people will be more comfortable with its position in the workplace. It could also mean that in being more accepting, there may be a greater tendency to accept it at face value,

something that the current board of directors is guilty of, and something that has to change. We have also seen how strong the IT culture can be, and how, once working within the technical domain, business professionals can soon change their attitudes and assume the mantle of the techie (see Chapter 5). Being insensitive to the underlying complexities of information systems will also fail to create the much needed change in attitudes toward technology. Relying on future generations to solve the problem of the culture gap will not, in my opinion, work. True integration actually requires action and

Table 12.4   Relationships with educational institutions

Relationship with	Isolated	Integrated
The business	• MBAs provide some level of IT awareness from a strategic and managerial perspective. However, this tends to be restricted, as at least half do not provide compulsory IT courses. It is therefore possible to graduate with an MBA and have little or no understanding of how to manage IT.[6] • thought leadership through empirical research, covering both technical and business perspectives of IT; usually academic in nature.	• the implications and management of information technology (including failure) are taught as standard as a means of providing a balanced understanding of IT. • implications of thought leadership translated from the academic to the business environment.
Information Technology	• entry-level qualifications in computer science focus on the technicalities of applying information technology. • a limited number of courses (typically Masters level) exist which advance the knowledge of IT to include the managerial and organizational issues.	• much wider integration of IT with advanced level courses. • increased breadth of entry-level courses to cover the consequences of IT, including the principal issues associated with its development, management and failure.

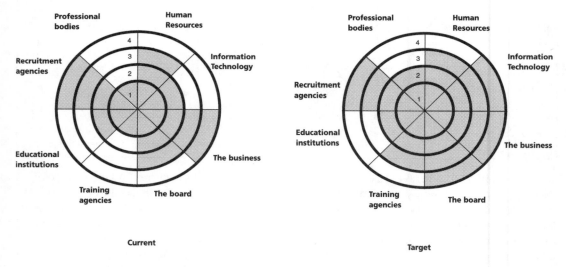

Figure 12.2   How connected are you?

effort from the organization – sitting back and waiting for it to sort itself out will only lead to disappointment. The shaded portion of Figure 12.1 is where the concentrated effort needs to be applied, and it is here where some efforts are already bearing fruit.

Table 12.5 Relationships with training agencies

Relationship with	Isolated	Integrated
The board	• in no position to help deliver the required skills. • not highly valued, low profit.	• an ongoing service to the board of directors designed to maintain their currency and understanding of technology from a business perspective.
Information Technology	• commoditized training, short-term and product focused.	• strategic training, and move away from product based training; a healthy mix is available. • dialogue with Human Resources to ensure courses are tailored to be organizationally specific.
The business	• typically limited to project management, and technical training (for example use of specific products).	• widen the umbrella to cover benefits, investment appraisals, challenging the IT investment case, impacts of IT (such as dependence) and managing IT.

TACKLING THE BOARD OF DIRECTORS

With the explosion of information technology, networking and communication technologies, senior executives, especially board members, have had to become more IT literate. IT used to be undervalued and misunderstood at board level; now its importance is appreciated, but it is still misunderstood. And, according to the chief executive of ICI, those who fail to develop an understanding of technology will lose their jobs.[7] However, such understanding seems to be rare, as two recent surveys seem to suggest. The first, by Cisco and Oracle in the United Kingdom, found that 50 per cent of directors fundamentally misunderstand technology, and believe conducting business on the Internet is someone else's responsibility. It also found that 50 per cent had never had a technology briefing, and 48 per cent never intend to have one.[8] The second, by Deloitte Consulting, found that only 13 per cent of company directors it surveyed had an IT-literate person on the board, and only 20 per cent believed the board had enough knowledge to make IT decisions.[9] How can the board lose their technophobia, and be more willing to challenge IT's hegemony over the business?

In some respects, the advent of the year 2000 has provided a much needed impetus to manage the relationship with IT more effectively: confidence in IT may be low, but the board has recognized it has a role in rejuvenating the mutual trust between business and IT. The year 2000 issue is probably one of the only IT programmes that has been able to unify the board, and although resolving this issue has been primarily geared toward business survival, it has brought into sharp relief the issue of benefits from IT especially considering the fallout – businesses world-wide believe that the $400 billion spent on avoiding the Millennium Bug has been totally wasted, particularly when there appeared to be little or no reported problems from those countries such as Russia, China and Italy, who had done very little or nothing to prepare for it.[10] If this new awareness is coupled with the general increase in the use of technology within businesses, the board has realized that IT can no longer be ignored.

To begin to tackle the culture gap, the board of directors must:

1. develop and maintain an understanding of the latest technologies which are being applied within theirs, and other, organizations;
2. be more ready to challenge IT from a 'value for money' perspective;

3. recognize that information systems cannot be built overnight, and information systems projects are increasingly highly complex undertakings. They must start to demand realistic project time scales, and set reasonable expectations of their project and programme managers;

4. take full accountability, along with the IT director/chief information officer, for the success of IT within their organization;

5. be willing to admit that they do not know everything about IT, and start to trust IT to add value to the organization without blaming IT for everything that goes wrong with technology. The current 'feeding frenzy' on the IT department prevents individuals from having a positive influence on organizational results – those who are unwilling to take risks do not contribute to progressing the organization. Therefore, the board should see how it could help in the delivery of information systems, not the other way around;[11]

6. be willing to learn from failure, and become more sensitive to it, rather than falling into the escalation trap; and

7. fully integrate the IT director/chief information officer into the board, and only appoint those who have the requisite business knowledge – never appoint the IT director/chief information officer on their technical skills alone.

THE EXECUTIVE STUDIO – INTEGRATING THE BOARD WITH IT

The West London Centre in the United Kingdom has developed an innovative approach to tackling the board-level culture gap.[12] The Executive Studio is laid out as a futuristic boardroom, with IT forming the hub. The Studio is specifically geared toward the non-IT director, including human resources, finance and marketing. Its purpose is threefold:

1. Through the innovative use of IT, the Executive Studio allows the IT-illiterate or semi-literate board member to gain some basic computer literacy, and through this allows them to become more comfortable with IT in general. This also starts to remove the air of mystery around IT, and hence allow board members to become more willing to tackle IT issues head on.

2. In bringing together board members from different companies, the Executive Studio provides an environment in which open and frank discussion about IT's value can take place. It therefore allows individual directors to raise their specific concerns with IT, and generate the much-needed cross-organizational information exchange of how best to apply it. This type of interorganizational learning is essential to make IT more effective, and also has the added benefit of generating increased confidence within the board community to challenge IT on issues such as value for money and appropriateness of investment.

3. Through the use of outside speakers, who are usually experts in their field, the Executive Studio provides an ongoing technology update in which board members can be brought up to speed with the latest innovations and, more importantly, understand how these can be of value to their organization. This, it must be said, is not a classic sales pitch, in which the silver-tongued salesman sells an inappropriate investment to the board, but rather a warts-and-all review of the technology which adds balance, and allows informed judgements to be developed. This therefore addresses one of the most common complaints directed at the board of directors, that is, their lack of currency and knowledge about IT.

In addition to the group facilities, individual computer literacy coaching is available, where directors can gain further insights into some of the basic and more sophisticated technologies. Indeed, there is an increasing trend toward personal coaching, as many directors do not want to make it obvious to their colleagues that they do not know enough about IT. Perhaps if they went public, the board as a whole would recognize their IT illiteracy as a common problem, and tackle it collectively. According to

Garrett,[13] boards which work well together are willing to learn from each other. It would make sense, therefore, if the IT-illiterate board members could learn from their experiences and as a result reduce the level of techno-illiteracy that currently exists across the entire board.

I believe that initiatives such as the Executive Studio are providing a very important and key service to the board of directors who not only feel uncomfortable with IT, but also feel unable to challenge it with any degree of confidence or certainty. This is reflected in its success. If the culture gap at board level is to be eliminated, similar initiatives are required, as there are many boards of directors who are crying out for such help. It is also important that these and other similar initiatives are not perceived to be just one-off events, but rather an ongoing service to the board of directors designed to maintain their currency in IT.

INTEGRATING THE IT DIRECTOR/CHIEF INFORMATION OFFICER INTO THE BOARD

Clearly, in order to rebuild the relationship at board level, the role of the IT director/chief information officer also must be revisited. And, just as the other directors must embrace technology, the IT director/chief information officer has to embrace the business – they can no longer rest on their technological laurels. Some research by Salford University in the United Kingdom is highly constructive in this respect, as it provides some direction to the budding IT director/chief information officer.[14] They conducted a series of surveys with the Institute of Directors in the late 1980s and early 1990s in which the role of the IT director/chief information officer was investigated. These surveys built on previous work that demonstrated a growing communication gap between the IT director/chief information officer and the rest of the board. The research concluded that IT directors/chief information officers must develop the capabilities required to function effectively at board level, something which a traditional career within IT failed to

prepare them for.

According to the UK's Institute of Directors, the ten most important qualities required at board level are: strategic awareness, objectivity, communication skills, individual responsibility, customer focus, self-discipline, teamwork, creativity, perspective and breadth.[15] With this set of attributes in mind, it is clear that any prospective IT director/chief information officer must overcome the external image their technical background has created. Indeed, most chief executives perceive their IT board member to be more technical and introverted than their colleagues, and lacking the softer skills so important for senior management positions. Therefore, prospective IT directors should take note and use these ten attributes as the basis for their career planning. Further, the board of directors, working with Human Resources, should use these same ten skills as the basis for developing their IT experts into rounded business professionals, and more importantly, use them as the basis for selecting the most appropriate candidates to the board.

Also, given the importance of strategic awareness to the role of any director, Wang has some sound advice for the chief executive officer that should ensure they use the IT director's/chief information officer's full capabilities within the strategic planning process. He recommends the following:

● Someone in the organization must link the technological capabilities of the organization to its strategic direction, and this someone must be able to represent information technology.
● The chief information officer must address the organization's information and technology needs strategically, and not as a set of individual, disconnected requirements.
● The chief information officer must have a cross-functional impact, just like the other board members.[16]

IT directors/chief information officers must grasp the nettle and take control over their careers in order to gain the necessary broad cross-functional experience required of any board member. In demonstrating this, they are more likely to be accepted into the board and be trusted to bring their technical and business judgement to bear on the job of directing the organization from a technical perspective.

The bottom line is that IT managers must act like business managers, lose their technical image and involve themselves in corporate affairs, which also includes the politics. This, along with initiatives directed toward the non-IT directors, will go a long way to bridging the gap at board level.

AT THE COAL FACE – IMPROVING THE RELATIONSHIP BETWEEN DEVELOPERS AND USERS

Solving the problems of the culture gap at the working level also requires an approach that brings IT and the business together into a closer and more productive working relationship. Because of the service-based relationship that exists between business and IT, the majority of the effort must come from the technologists. However, there are actions that the business community must undertake to make themselves more sensitive to the dynamics of information systems projects. As with the board-level culture gap, effort needs to be applied to ensure each party is sensitive to the other's language and tensions.

First to the technologists: a lot has been written and said about the need to develop the business–IT hybrid, but as yet they have not really materialized in sufficient numbers to make an impact. So, despite the strong cries that this is an important step towards making IT more business-focused and responsive, it appears that little or no effort has been directed at making this a reality. Equally, the received wisdom, that a resolution of the culture gap requires increased levels of communication between the business and IT camps, is also failing to eliminate the problem, as more communication is not the answer to poor communication.[17] Is this resolution therefore an impossible dream, or symptomatic of a profession that does not wish to concern itself with business issues?

David Jacobs, managing director of *profit for information*,[18] believes that it is possible to create a business–information hybrid. Recognizing that the tensions at this level are extreme, Jacobs believes it is important for the IT professional to adopt an attitude that is focused on getting the best for the business. This hybrid business–information professional, as he terms it, must provide first-class guidance at the interface between the business and IT. Although this may sound very similar to the role of business analyst, it in fact goes much wider. Whereas the typical business analyst concentrates on the translation of business requirements into technical specifications, the business information specialist has a much wider contribution to make to the overall management and organization of the project, including:

- ensuring that business and IT understand each other;
- helping to measure the current business value derived from IT and enhancing it;
- ensuring IT gives the business and its users maximum benefit;
- helping the business to develop its IT requirements whilst at the same time articulating their implications and feasibility;
- ensuring IT receives an accurate picture of the requirements and ensuring an effective response to the users is maintained throughout the project;
- advising on the respective responsibilities throughout the development of the information system;
- informing the business of the risks, uses and abuses of software production of which they are often unaware, and explaining the importance of placing IT into the correct context; and
- dovetailing the available business and IT skills to form an effective team for the duration of the project.

Jacobs believes that in having this business–information hybrid, organizations will be able to start to bridge their communication gap, and believes the benefits are compelling: shorter development times, early warnings of problems, higher likelihood of success, less maintenance and better morale.

So what else can the IT professional do to minimize the culture gap from the technician's perspective? First, the IT professional must understand the real importance of what they do and where this fits within the overall business strategy – which ought to come from the IT director/chief information officer. Second, they must learn to be more sympathetic to the user's requirements and help them, rather than out-tech or out-smart them. Third, IT should come clean about the risks and realities of software development – many systems are technically too ambitious and expectations unrealistically set. For example, the £2 billion project to equip the UK Army with new radios has been dogged by, amongst others, the rapid advance of technology, and as a result is now over six years behind schedule.[19] Where technology is risky, it is not technical skills that will have the most effect in minimizing the risk, but sensible business, objective-driven management. And, fourth, they must develop skills and knowledge beyond the technical domain, as recommended by one author: 'Many technical professionals don't have a real understanding of the marketplace, the competitive situation, and the economic climate. They will perform better with this knowledge – and have a fuller understanding of the value of their contributions.'[20]

The hybrid approach can be an effective mechanism to underwrite the overall quality of the information system being developed, and ensuring the correct level of communication is maintained as the project progresses.[21] But more than just hybrids are required, especially as they seem to be so small in number. For example, some researchers believe an approach which focuses on having the right blend of skills across the whole team would be preferable to employing individuals with such skills. Furthermore, multi-disciplined teams can have a direct impact on those whom, although not working on the project, can see the value it brings.

One area where the business–information professional can make significant impact is within the benefits realization process. Working closely with the project manager, the business–information hybrid can help to create clear and unambiguous benefits statements, together with the process through which they can be achieved and tracked. They should also liaise and work with the user/business communities to help them articulate how the benefits will be achieved from the new information system, and then work with them once the project has completed to realize the benefits. Hybrids can also provide a valuable role in tracking and reporting progress towards achieving the full benefits from the project, and help to spot potential areas for further development, and hence future benefits. In summary, the hybrid should be used to provide a continuous link between the business and IT communities (see Figure 12.3).

But what of the users? As part of the two-way relationship with the IT community, they must take time to understand the pressures which IT has to work under, as well as recognize that information systems projects are complex undertakings. The business must also begin to take more responsibility for the outcome of projects, rather than abdicating both their involvement in, and responsibility for, their success. Again, this is where the business–information specialist can help. Any project worth its salt requires persistence, perseverance and cooperation in order to succeed, and the business community is a vital component to this. Instead of abdication, the business must help to drive the project forward, and take an active part in setting its direction and making it a success. This means providing the resources necessary to achieve the project's objectives, and working with IT to develop an appropriate solution. It also means taking into account the limitations of the technology being used, and not over-engineering the end result by asking for functionality that is unnecessary and unsuitable. And, just as the non-IT director must gain a basic understanding of the various technologies open to the business, so must the business user. This is where the training agencies could help by providing courses which can add to the understanding of the non-IT expert.

Integrating business and IT can start at the project level, but with project outcome so

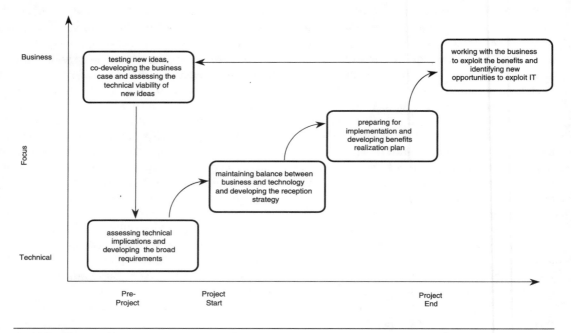

Figure 12.3   Using the hybrid business–information professional

dependent upon the general competencies of the project team, something more is needed. In essence, what is called for is an approach that is capable of integrating IT into the wider business environment.

STEP 3: REFRAMING THE RELATIONSHIP BETWEEN BUSINESS AND IT

There have been very few attempts at integrating technical functions into the business line, but there is one that has provided a useful insight into the steps through which this can be achieved. Adler believes there are three characteristics which indicate sustained technical accomplishment and business success.[22] These have been summarized from an IT perspective below:

1. The IT function's overall posture and direction are clearly stated in successively more detailed versions – mission, objective, strategic plans – and they are broadly accepted within the function and throughout the business.

2. The IT function manages itself as a business with due attention to its key processes, resources and internal and external linkages. Clearly articulated policies guide day-to-day decision making – policies that are comprehensive, compatible with strategic direction, compatible with each other, and useful as decision guides, not just bureaucratic hurdles.

3. The IT function can adapt as managers assess the strength and weaknesses of their function's capabilities against the opportunities and threats presented by the evolving market.

Adler has identified four stages toward full integration which allow an organization to assess where they sit along the continuum of an isolated IT function, to a fully integrated one:

● Isolated – The IT function has few links to the rest of the business and makes a minimal contribution. This reinforces the ivory tower image of IT, and the associated introverted boffin image that goes with it. It also perpetuates the myth that the issues involved in systems development are too technical for users to understand. Such stereotypes are kept alive through stories, jokes and slogans.[23]

- Reactive – The classic fire-fighting IT function responds to problems encountered by the rest of the business, but never identifies its own long-term strategy.
- Proactive – The IT function generates lots of new ideas and has a long-term strategy, but is not well tuned to the other functions' needs and expectations.
- Integrated – The IT function's activities both support the current business priorities and create new opportunities.

Many organizations lie somewhere between the isolated and reactive states, a few probably can be considered proactive, and fewer still are integrated. Adler identifies a number of attributes against which any technical function can measure its position along the isolated–integrated continuum, and more importantly, use them to establish the route map through which it can move toward becoming more integrated:

- identifying posture and setting direction, which includes the articulation of the mission, identifying the function's objectives and developing its strategic plan;
- processes, which embrace personnel recruitment, development and rewards, project selection, termination and project management, and quality assurance;
- resources, which includes dealing with intellectual property rights, departmental funding, facilities and equipment; and
- linkages, which covers the remaining components of functional structure, interfunctional linkages, external linkages and regulatory compliance.

The approach suggested by Adler can be used to establish a series of characteristics that describe the IT department and how it relates to the organization (see Figure 12.4). Combining this with the results of the culture gap analysis allows a comprehensive framework to be established which describes IT's relationship with the business. This can be used to help define the

target model of where the organization wishes to be, and hence can feed into a programme of work that will bring this about. Because of the importance of IT to the business, the work must be sponsored by the chief executive officer and have representation from the stakeholder groups identified in Figure 12.1.

The model in Figure 12.4 can be linked directly into the culture gap radar diagrams of Figure 12.2, with Level 4 mapping to the integrated state, Level 3 mapping to the proactive state, Level 2 to the reactive state and Level 1 to the isolated state. When brought together, these two models, along with Tables 12.1 to 12.5, can provide a powerful basis for understanding where along the isolated–integrated continuum an organization lies, and where it wants to be. The key point to making IT work effectively with the business is changing its culture from being perceived as isolated to being viewed as integrated. Because we are dealing with culture change, it is necessary to consider how we can measure this change as it occurs. The following activities are relevant to this process:

- development of a cultural map of the organization – Figure 12.1 should provide the starting point for this, and focus on the business–IT culture gap;
- assessment of the current culture against the organization's strategic objective, that is, the target culture to determine what needs to be changed and how feasible, and hence risky, this change is likely to be;
- establishment of a network of change agents across the organization – in this case the business information hybrids recommended by Jacobs; and
- creation of a blueprint of the organization to encapsulate the necessary structural, process and policy changes.[24]

STEP 4: PROVIDE IT PROFESSIONALS WITH ALTERNATIVE CAREER PATHS

It is insufficient to eliminate the culture gap without giving some attention to the career of the IT professional. Changing the way IT is perceived within the organization must also

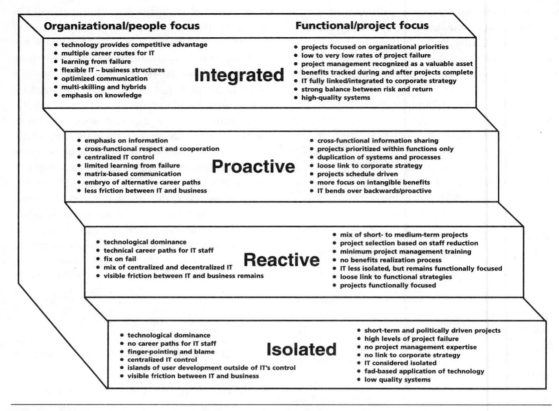

Figure 12.4 From isolated to integrated: characteristics of IT and its relationships with the business

include a reassessment and realignment of IT careers. If the organization wants IT to change, they must provide the opportunity for them to change. This means ensuring IT professionals are able to transition to higher-order roles outside of IT. Equally, the IT professional must recognize that his traditional career path is being eroded through competition from, amongst others, the Indian sub-continent, competent end users and the general increase in the number of packaged and desktop solutions.[25] Alternative career routes must be created, and Human Resources, together with the education and training establishments and professional bodies can help.

Naturally, when considering career paths, IT professionals should still have the opportunity to retain the traditional career ladder starting in a typically junior role and moving up the technical value chain. But if they want to progress outside of this technical domain, it is

necessary to recognize that the organizational competencies required to succeed – emotional intelligence, organizational understanding and interpersonal skills – will have to change, as the following illustrates:

> Two computer programmers are explaining how they go about doing their job, designing programs to fill the pressing business needs of their clients. Recounts one: 'I heard him say he needed all the data in a simple format that could fit on one page.' So the programmer followed through to deliver just that ... The second, however, seems to have trouble getting to the point. Unlike the first programmer, he doesn't mention the needs of his clients. Instead he launches into a litany of technical talk: 'The HP3000/30's BASIC computer

was too slow, so I went directly to a machine-language routine.' In other words, he focuses on machines not people.[26]

Therefore, if IT professionals wish to remain firmly rooted within the technical domain they should be allowed to do so. But, if they aspire to the higher-order roles, a transitional process is required (see Figure 12.5). This transition must ensure the technical expert develops other skills and understanding required to perform at these levels. As a result, he should be exposed to general operational management, gain experience of a number of other business functions and ensure that a wider understanding of the organization is achieved, and broader interpersonal skills developed. This may, in addition, be augmented by training in some of the basic business functions, such as finance and marketing.

Organizations must move away from the mindset that allows the Peter Principle to persist, in which a person rises to their level of incompetence – usually based on their technical, not business, capabilities. Instead, a developmental period is required in which the IT expert is able to augment his skills and become a rounded business professional. For example, David Jacobs of *profit for information* believes that someone with a good aptitude could be turned into an effective basic hybrid (business analyst) quite quickly, say, within twelve months. To be advanced, however, requires more mature experiences that would entail an increased understanding of business and information strategy and general business knowledge.

In providing alternative career paths to IT, organizations can demonstrate their commitment to the professional development of their IT staff, and help them to become integrated with the rest of the organization.

STEP 5: ELIMINATING THE CULTURE GAP AT SOURCE – THE ROLE OF EDUCATION

Educating the next generation of business and IT professionals is a task that should not be taken lightly. Ensuring education courses provide a healthy mix of technical, business and

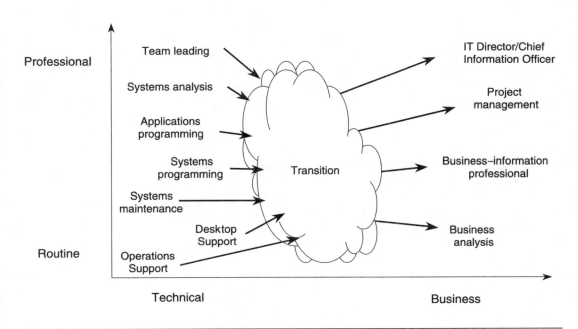

Figure 12.5 Career paths for IT experts

organizational understanding is essential in creating the rounded professionals required for the complex business environment we now work within. Both IT and business studies degrees need to be upgraded to ensure that a sufficient level of understanding about IT and business is embedded within their students. This means there ought to be a compulsory managing IT course within business studies degrees, and an introduction to business disciplines within technology degrees.

Current IT degrees are very good at preparing the would-be technologist for a technical career. In focusing on solving computational problems, such courses cover the usual technologies and associated processes. They also major on the underlying technological concepts, including databases, application and system programming, and some of the recent developments in IT, such as enterprise resource planning and e-commerce. But one has to ask whether these degrees provide the education necessary to solve organizational problems and develop information systems that are truly fit for purpose. Various commentators believe not, and I would tend to agree, as these courses do not cover the breadth of knowledge required to develop the much needed hybrid professionals or indeed the capability to develop effective systems. IT degree courses do not usually cover organizational development, or how organizations invest and make use of information systems. And, as we are all well aware, the impacts of poor systems can be very significant on an organization's productivity, effectiveness and, in some cases, viability: Kling points out that technical excellence alas does not guarantee that an information system will be effective in the organizational environment.[27]

Although computer science degrees offer subsidiary courses, these also tend to focus on technical, rather than business, subjects. So even if a student is particularly interested in the human and organizational aspects of IT, it is unlikely that he will be exposed to these very important topics. Moreover, discussing the principles of software engineers, although an essential component of any computer science degree, will fail to address the general success rate of information systems projects. Students must, in my opinion, be exposed to the implications of IT and IT dependence. Without this, the unhealthy, invincible perception of IT and its capabilities is likely to persist into the next generation of business leaders. This is why the generation argument to the elimination of the culture gap is unlikely to work. Unfortunately, most graduates leave university with the bias toward the right solution or the right technology which clouds their sensitivity to accept viewpoints from those who will ultimately manage or use the systems they develop. I read with interest one recommendation concerning computing curricula from the United States Association of Computer Machinery and the Institute of Electronic and Electrical Engineers: of the total contact time of 238 hours, only 11 were associated with the organizational or human elements of IT.[28] With it taking years, not months or weeks, to adjust existing IT courses, such recommendations are clearly worrying.

I believe technology degrees must begin to address some of the wider issues associated with computerization. Without this, graduates entering the employment market will retain the same techno-centric views that are already damaging corporations and turning bright students away from the IT profession. The culture gap is caused, at least in part, by the dominance of technology over all else, and therefore if it is to change, the entry-level professional must be better equipped. Enhancing technology degrees to include some of the elements below could go a long way to improving the profession's image discussed at the start of this chapter, and move beyond the superficial rebranding of a profession perceived to be techno-centric and nerdish:

● organizational analysis and development
● an introduction to the basic functions of a business
● the impacts of software dependency – both organizationally and socially
● the implications of software usage within organizations
● an exploration of organizational politics and its impacts on information systems projects

- managing the complexities of IT
- achieving benefits from information systems and IT in general
- exploring the dynamics of software development and information systems projects
- understanding why information systems projects fail.

It would, of course, be ridiculous to suggest that technology courses lose their technical core, as this would be missing the point. Instead, they should be augmented by topics that cover the wider issues associated with the application of IT within the modern enterprise which itself is more complex, subject to greater internal and external pressures, and is increasingly dependent on IT for its success. Without IT, an organization is liable to fail, and without an understanding of organizations, IT is liable to fail the organization.

As well as technology courses, there is a need for the general business course, and particularly MBAs, to have a greater component of IT within them. Such additions should be compulsory, as without them, students will be unable to manage the implications that IT dependency brings. Such changes would recognize the importance of IT within the modern corporation, and also prepare the business people of the future for a corporate life that is increasingly technically focused. Looking down the list of subjects which I have recommended for inclusion within technology degrees, it would make sense to have the same subjects in the MBA and undergraduate business studies degree. This would provide some common understanding between technology and business graduates which would filter into the working population. The only other addition I would make to business degrees and MBAs would be the inclusion of a course on working on information systems projects and with IT professionals. Developing an understanding and sensitivity for these would be invaluable in managing the tensions which currently exist between business and IT and, more importantly, ensure that the worst of the culture gap is bred out of both business and IT professionals.

SOLVING THE CULTURE GAP: A CONCERTED EFFORT IS REQUIRED

Returning to the model in Figure 12.1, and considering the types of activity which are both underway and needed, it can be seen that resolving the culture gap requires action from all of the identified stakeholders. Whilst there will be actions targeted at the wider profession, many will be directed at individual organizations, and key to solving the culture gap is to recognize that tackling the issue in an isolated fashion will not result in long-lasting success. Organizations should therefore consider bringing together recruitment agencies, training agencies, educational establishments and internal representatives to derive an approach which best serves them. I believe the education establishments and professional bodies have a major part to play in this process.

The culture gap is, in my opinion, soluble as long as action is taken in the widest possible sense, and the basis for short-, medium- and long-term improvements to the relationships between the business and IT communities established.

But before we leave the culture gap, and move on to the important topic of information politics, it is worth recalling the experience of a Japanese company that was bidding against American, British and German consortiums for the design and build of a chemical plant in Germany.

Although the Japanese bid was not the cheapest, or the most technically superior, they won the contract, to the surprise of the remaining bidders, who at this time were the Americans and the British; the Germans had failed at the first hurdle. Both the Americans and the British appealed against the decision, and unusually, the client invited them to discuss why they had lost the bid. Although both bids were of the highest quality, considered technically superior, and presented extremely professionally, they failed for one reason, and one reason only – client focus. The Japanese had taken the trouble to conduct all their dealings with the client in German, including the final presentation. This meant that, as well as producing the bid, the Japanese consortium had taken the trouble to learn German and ensure they fully understood the cultural aspects of their client. As a result, they were able to satisfy the technical aspects of the bid, but more importantly were able to demonstrate empathy and understanding of the client, their business issues and culture – a winning combination. This example demonstrates that technology is not the only indicator of success, and that it is the human and organizational aspects that can hold sway over success or failure.[29]

CHAPTER THIRTEEN

Short- and medium-term solutions to information politics

We are not in the Information Age, but in an age of information.[1]

Information is the life-blood of the modern corporation; in 1990 the typical Fortune 500 company stored 33 billion characters of electronic data, and in 2010 this is expected to be 400 trillion.[2] To achieve such a significant increase in data over such a comparatively short space of time, it is assumed that it increases by a compound rate of 60 per cent per annum. When viewed graphically, as in Figure 13.1, it can be seen just how rapidly data can increase. Also, according to the US analyst, the Meta Group, the volume of corporate information is doubling every twelve months, and is accelerating.[3] If this is true, then the graph in Figure 13.1 can be considered to be somewhat conservative. Whether these projections are accurate is, of course, questionable, as many similar projections within the technology arena have proved to be wide of the mark. However, the message that such projections portray is significant: as organizations produce more and more data, it can very rapidly spiral out of control, especially when there is no one to keep it in check, to ensure it is the right data, that it is current, accurate and adding value to the organization. Furthermore, as the lines of communication within organizations have become more sophisticated, the amount of information to process has increased and, more importantly, so has the time required to make decisions.

What is in no doubt, however, is that the amount of information in the modern corporation is growing, and growing fast. Organizations have an insatiable appetite for information as they drive to seek customer satisfaction, increase market share and improve operational efficiencies. If being in business is all about gaining and retaining customers and providing them with the products and services they need, then information, and lots of it, is what organizations need. But organizations should take great care. Although lots of information can add value, if it is the wrong information, or it is managed incompetently, then their investment in this information and its associated IT infrastructure may be wasted. An organization must therefore be competent in its information management, especially if it is to survive in a business environment where information can yield significant competitive advantage. If an organization is to be competent at managing its information, it must also be prepared to manage the associated politics.

As we have seen from Chapter 6, the reasons why managing the politics of information is so important has a lot to do with the prevalence of the old culture of personal ownership. But, until such time as information sharing is embedded within organizations, and the old cultures dispelled, managing the politics of information and knowledge will be an important skill for any information systems project manager. Furthermore, to be able to succeed in realizing the benefits from information systems, business users, IT professionals and senior managers alike must be sensitive to the politics of information. Such sensitivity will ensure that both business and IT professionals are working towards a common aim, which must be the effective exploitation of information to service both external customers and internal operational needs.

Research has highlighted that organizations typically focus over 80 per cent of their investment in information on information technology. But, according to this same research, technology only determines 10 per cent of an organization's information

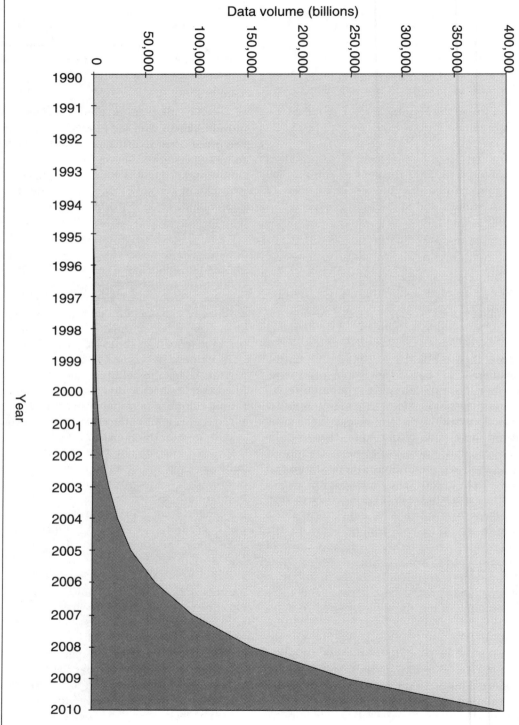

Data volume (billions)

Year

Figure 13.1 The exponential growth of data

competency. This suggests that technology is only a small component in achieving information mastery, as people, process, organizational structure, culture and leadership all have their part to play.[4] Concentrating on the technological aspects alone will never allow organizations to achieve the excellence they seek, be it in customer management, supplier service or operational efficiency. Furthermore, focusing on technology at the expense of these other aspects allows the political behaviours identified in Chapter 6 to go unchecked. As a result, information will be captured, created, hoarded and protected without creating any intrinsic value to the organization. The politics of information is here to stay, at least for the short term, and organizations must learn to manage it until such time they can address these non-technical elements in concert.

Recognizing that eliminating the politics around information is not an overnight process, organizations must approach the effective management of information from two distinct directions:

1. In the short term, they must embrace the concept of information politics, manage the tensions around it, and work within this new political environment. This means accepting that information politics exists within the modern corporation and developing an appropriate response to minimize its worst excesses. This will allow information systems to be developed that are able to meet the organization's information needs as opposed to an individual function's pet requirements. It should also serve to limit the unnecessary duplication of data, itself often the result of political desires rather than genuine organizational need.

2. In the medium term, organizations must start to work on minimizing the consequences of information politics through the creation of a federal approach to its management, that is, an approach in which the core belief within the organization is one of information sharing, not hoarding. To achieve this requires changes in the underlying IT–business relationships,

discussed in the previous chapter, as well as re-engineering the underlying IT infrastructure to support and facilitate the effective management and exploitation of the organization's information. It also requires an attitudinal shift in the way information is viewed within the organization, particularly by those who create and consume it.

The remainder of this chapter reviews these activities.

SHORT-TERM STRATEGIES FOR DEALING WITH INFORMATION POLITICS

As there is unlikely to be any overnight change in the way information and knowledge are used for political advantage, it is necessary to develop a sensitivity for, and an ability to manage, the politics of information. This will establish a stronger basis for creating IT solutions that are better able to exploit the information that is genuinely needed by the organization as a whole. It will also allow the destructive behaviours associated with information politics to be more readily identified and tackled earlier within the project life cycle. It is obvious that avoiding political behaviour must start with the requirements-definition phase of the project, because this is where it starts to manifest. In extreme cases, this can delay projects for months, as conflicting requirements are discussed and debated at length; we have seen this within the London Stock Exchange's Taurus project, where the Siscot Committee had little choice but to make significant compromises that ultimately alienated a number of key stakeholders. Furthermore, if such political issues cannot be tackled early on within the project, this can result in further delays downstream as functions deliberately delay and snipe at the project. I have known some projects where the requirements specification is only signed off at implementation; not exactly a healthy way to conduct a project.

If organizations wish to manage the politics around information more effectively, where do they begin? In my mind, the starting point must be the identification of the principal types of information that are used by the organization. This will highlight where the tensions, and hence the political hot spots are likely to be and, to aid this analysis, it should also include who, from a functional perspective, produces, consumes and changes information (see Figure 13.2).

It should be apparent from this simple summary that political behaviour around the ownership of information is a natural response to the difficulties experienced in trying to share common information between functions. When different functions consume similar, but often different, variants of the same information, there is plenty of opportunity for conflict. In many cases, functions hold on to the core information and update it locally, and often inconsistently with the rest of the organization. This leads to data drift and a reduction in quality. This degradation in quality has implications, because data can soon lose its currency and value and, in extreme circumstances, this can lead to major issues within the organization, as no one knows which data to use. For example, customers may be contacted by various functions at similar times, using slightly different information about them. Having witnessed first hand the problems that such islands of information cause, and how much effort is needed to recentralize such data, I can testify to just how frustrated and annoyed customers can get. Very often, this situation is compounded by the general inadequacies of the IT systems on which the functions depend to supply them with the information they need. These IT systems are often overly complex, unresponsive and do not always meet their exact information requirements. Therefore, to meet their specific needs, functions collect their own data and store and manipulate it locally. This also explains why IT projects are so often hijacked by powerful functions who bully their way into getting their requirements and information needs satisfied above anyone else's. This behaviour results in an information system that is only capable of satisfying one interest group, leading the others to seek alternative ways to get the information they require. This usually means developing systems outside the control of IT to meet their own islands of

Information Type	Created, consumed and updated by
Business relationships	Sales, Marketing
Personnel	Human Resources, IT (if centralized). This may also vary if the organization is heavily decentralized
Skills and competencies	Human Resources, IT Sales, Marketing, Production, Operations, Procurement
Customer	Sales, Marketing, Operations
Sales	Sales, Marketing
Marketing	Sales, Marketing
Financial	Finance, Marketing Sales, IT, Production
Logistics	Operations, Logistics, IT, Production
Supplier	Operations, Logistics, IT, Sales, Human Resources, Procurement
Competitor	Operations, Logistics, IT, Production, Marketing, Sales
Operational (internal business management)	Operations, Logistics, IT, Sales, Human Resources, Procurement
Strategic	Senior management, planning cells if they exist (usually focused within each function)
Process	Operations, Logistics, IT, Sales, Human Resources, Procurement

Figure 13.2   Information types

information, or having special, stand-alone systems developed to support their information requirements.

It should come as no surprise that functions will apply different political strategies in order to get and retain the information that they need to perform their duties. This is, of course, also designed to retain their power base within the organization, especially within those functions that are information intensive. As suggested earlier, in the short term, information politics can only be responded to in a tactical manner by sensitizing the project manager to the common political behaviours so that they can attempt to reduce them during the project's life. To some extent, the corporate-level issue with dysfunctional information behaviours is outside of the project manager's control. But those at functional level are not. Adjusting corporate-level behaviours must be the focus of the board.

TACKLING INFORMATION POLITICS AT THE CORPORATE LEVEL

There are a number of reasons why addressing the problems of information politics must start with the senior management of the organization:

● Behaviours associated with information at the highest levels in an organization tend to filter down through the organization. If the senior managers display dysfunctional attitudes toward information, these same behaviours will usually be reflected in the attitudes and behaviours of their subordinates. Thus, if middle management see senior management adopting dysfunctional behaviours they will emulate these, as they assume that these are acceptable and will allow them to progress within the organization.

● Any manager in fear of losing their job will hold on to anything they can to justify their existence. This includes information. The greater this fear, the greater the desire to hoard and not share information.

● The structure of the organization, its use of

technology and the way in which strategies are formulated will impact the degree to which dysfunctional behaviours exist. Strongly functional organizations are more likely to exhibit the whole raft of political behaviours around information than those which are flatter – if nothing else, it is possible to act in isolation from other functions and focus on information that provides them with a source of power.

The improvement of the organization's information culture lies in educating senior and middle management, and then helping them to adapt their information behaviour to the prevailing business environment. Being able to respond to the external signals is increasingly important within a world that is constantly shifting. The consequences of not having a sensitivity toward information can be dramatic, as we have seen in recently in the United Kingdom. Over the last year, we have witnessed the fall from grace of a number of household names in the retail sector, including Marks and Spencer, and the food retailer, Sainsbury. These companies were considered the bastion of the retail market, but have suffered because they took their eye off the customer and competitor balls. This has resulted in them losing market share, and exposing them to takeover. Indeed, in response to the continued decline in its fortunes, Marks and Spencer has split itself into seven business units to improve focus on its customers.[5] As boards of directors are the leadership engine of the organization, they must keep their eyes on the external environment and use this to determine the information they need to remain competitive. Knowing that, they can then direct the organization so that it can respond appropriately to the challenges they face.

Educating senior management is a two-stage process: awareness, followed by ownership. Making senior managers aware should be a simple exercise, as the evidence is probably all around them, and in some cases overwhelming. Engaging them to create a sense of ownership to act and adjust their behaviour is a little harder. However, there are some short-term actions they can take to ensure the organization's information culture is at least partially aligned to the business environment. According to Marchland, this alignment is key, as without it the intensity of information politics will increase. Marchland believes such alignment can be achieved by considering the degree of uncertainty and complexity within an organization's operations, and recommends:

● Where the market is stable and uncertainty is low, it is best to adopt a controlling behaviour as a means of ensuring the right information exists and is used correctly.
● Where uncertainty is low, and complexity high, it is necessary to adopt a sharing culture.
● Where uncertainty is high and complexity low, an inquiring culture is necessary. This means keeping an eye on the changing information needs of the organization and responding appropriately.
● Where both complexity and uncertainty are high, organizations need to adapt quickly to the changing business environment.[6]

Flexing the approach to information based upon the external business environment is a useful stance to adopt, but it may be difficult to instil, particularly when the functional information behaviours come into the equation. Furthermore, it would be very difficult to achieve a rapid response to the information needs if the IT infrastructure was not equally as responsive. Creating a responsive IT infrastructure is part of the medium-term solution.

TACKLING INFORMATION POLITICS AT THE FUNCTIONAL LEVEL

As already suggested, an organization's top-level information culture is likely to have some influence on functional information behaviour. It is this that will have the greatest impact on the execution of an information systems project, because it is within the function that the information system, and hence information, will be used.

With this in mind, it is worth exploring how each of the four functional information behaviours identified in Chapter 6 (monarchy, feudalism, anarchy and utopianism) manifest themselves within each of the four organizational information cultures (reactive, fixation, paralysis and reactive). This exploration draws out some of the subtleties of each functional culture and provides the basis for a tactical response to minimize their negative effects. In general, the reinforcing effect of the perceived information need and level of control will result in one functional culture dominating in each of the organizational cultures: the shaded boxes of Figure 13.3. Because of this, the dominant culture may be the hardest to deal with from a tactical perspective. However, in some cases, one of the non-dominant functional cultures may help to limit the worst excesses of both the corporate-level information culture and that of the dominant function. In this case, the tactical response would be to promote the alternate culture and use it to develop balance.

Each of these corporate-level information behaviours will influence the development of the underlying functional cultures. And because of the potential variety of political behaviours, the information systems project manager and the chief information officer/IT director should become familiar with them. The tactical responses identified can be used until such time that a full and thorough solution to the problem is available.

REACTIVE CULTURES

Recalling from Chapter 6 that the reactive culture is one in which there is usually little or no control over what information is collected and consumed by the organization, it should be expected that each of the four functional cultures will exhibit subtle differences in how this lack of control is manifested. Within this state, it is the utopian culture that tends to dominate through the reinforcement of the reactive culture itself. Figure 13.4 summarizes the particular functional environments that exist within the reactive state, together with the tactical responses that could be used to limit their impacts and avoid potential disasters within information systems projects.

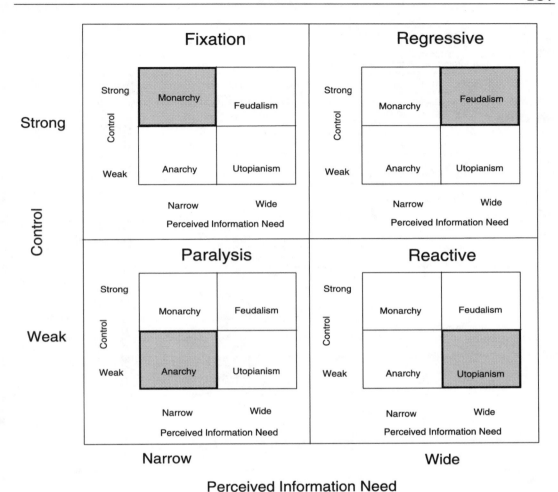

Figure 13.3 Dominant functional information cultures

REGRESSIVE CULTURES

In the case of the regressive culture, the focus is on maintaining large volumes of information and, unlike the reactive culture, maintaining excessive control over it. Paralysis by analysis tends to predominate as individuals are expected to use as much information as possible to assess a problem prior to making any decision. The dominant functional culture in the regressive state is feudalism, as the function hides behind its functional walls, and is unwilling to share information with anyone outside. The resultant functional behaviours, together with the tactical approach to managing them, are detailed in Figure 13.5.

PARALYSED CULTURES

In the case of the paralysed culture, anarchy rules. As a result, no new information is accepted, and so the organization is unwilling to improve the currency of its information – at least not collectively. In some functions, there tends to be an over-emphasis on traditions and outdated views of information which is usually coupled with an unwillingness to embrace the information age. This view tends to be self-fulfilling as the technical infrastructure is usually in no position to support the wider use of information across the firm. However, with a weak control over its information, pockets of resistance are likely to develop, especially where the functional culture is utopian.

	Narrow	Wide
Strong	**Monarchy** Situation: Although in a culture that has little control over information, in the monarchy it is generally held by only a few functional members. Most others within the function are excluded from this group and are starved of information. Information is usually hoarded and only shared if it provides those sharing it with greater organizational power. Response: 1. Develop systems that are capable of breaking the personal stranglehold on information. 2. Empower the function's staff to seek out other information and use it. 3. Incentivize the sharing of information. 4. Attempt to re-educate the information power brokers, and if this fails, attempt to have them removed from their posts.	**Feudalism** Situation: The function sucks in large amounts of information, but little is shared outside of the business area. Information is generally fiercely protected, and information systems projects are swamped with requests which have no value to the organization but a perceived need for the function. Response: 1. Force the function to focus on cross-functional information requirements. 2. Create systems that are able to communicate with sources of data and information outside of the function. 3. Closely link requirements to benefits in order to eliminate unnecessary information.
Weak	**Anarchy** Situation: Without any effective control over information, anything goes. Islands of information aimed at satisfying personal needs predominate. Information is shared only if it provides some reciprocal benefit. Information systems are fragmented and projects lack any coherent strategy. Response: 1. Concentrate on developing a functional data repository, with a technological infrastructure to support it. 2. Focus on the value of information and retire that which is out of date and irrelevant. 3. Place information systems projects into the wider organizational context.	**Utopianism** Situation: Obsessive application of technology irrespective of its ability to add value. Significant duplication of effort and systems. Information is considered to be of secondary importance to technology. Prevalence of project failure due to the leading-edge nature of the technology. Response: 1. Focus on information not technology need. 2. Focus on the value that technology is bringing to the management of information. 3. Assess and reuse existing technology where appropriate. 4. Attempt to centralize some of the locally held information and build the technology around this to avoid duplication of effort.

(Vertical axis label: **Control**)

Narrow　　　　　　　　　　　　　　**Wide**

Perceived Information Need

Figure 13.4　Tactical solutions within reactive information cultures

However, the dominant culture is anarchy, as without any real control, anything goes. Figure 13.6 summarizes the typical functional behaviours that manifest themselves within such a culture.

FIXATION CULTURES

Organizations which display the fixation information culture can be considered an extreme version of the paralysed culture. Unlike the paralysed culture, however, this one exhibits a strong control over the information it believes it needs. As a result, it not only refuses to embrace the Information Age, but also fails to accept any information that is capable of providing additional value. The dominant culture in this case is the monarchy, and it is the true embodiment of the old, 'information is

power' culture. Like most monarchies, the function is unwilling to move with the times, and can soon become out of touch, ineffective and unprofitable. Figure 13.7 highlights the typical functional environments.

THE SOLUTION TO INFORMATION POLITICS: A FEDERAL APPROACH TO INFORMATION

Although it is important for organizations to become sensitive to the subtleties of information politics, it is also important to tackle the underlying causes of this political behaviour at source. It should be made clear at this point that information politics within organizations will persist because of its ability to provide an

Monarchy	Feudalism
Situation: Monarchies can thrive in the regressive environment, but with such high levels of information, the 'information is power' culture tends to be diluted. The focus is on satisfying narrow information needs at the expense of the wider needs that might benefit the function. Valuable information can be lost, as control is achieved by narrowing in on information that only benefits the few. **Response:** 1. Widen the narrow focus on information by assessing its value. Cut out all that is non-value adding, and retain/expand the rest. 2. Dilute the 'information is power' culture further by developing systems which facilitate access, such as corporate and functional intranets.	**Situation:** Empires are built on large volumes of information and data, but in this case the control of this is very strict because of the dominance of the organizational culture. Information is only shared within the function, and its volume slows down the decision-making processes. As a result, the function becomes inefficient and ineffective. Information systems projects tend to stall at the requirements-gathering stage. **Response:** 1. Free up the decision-making process through the introduction of decision support systems and, where possible, data warehouses. 2. Adopt a rapid prototyping, or evolutionary approach, to information systems development to speed up the requirements-gathering process.
Anarchy	Utopianism
Situation: Under conditions of strict control, anarchy in this sense involves undermining control through hijacking information systems projects, failing to collect and maintain information, or avoiding controlling the proliferation of information and projects. **Response:** 1. Introduce a functional IT and information architecture. 2. Establish firmer controls on how technology is used and what information is consumed by the function. 3. Replace local management with business–technology hybrids to establish control and stability.	**Situation:** Application of technology dominates, but is restricted through a tough stance on the use of IT. An IT strategy might exist, but the function tries to circumvent the standard controls and develops information systems away from centralized control. Projects tend to be funded from within the function and information is collected without reference to the centre. **Response:** 1. Provide a link back to the corporate IT strategy, and ensure all major systems are either developed by, or have input from, the centralized IT department. 2. Make the spend on IT and associated information transparent as a means of minimizing unnecessary spend and duplication.

Left axis: **Strong** / **Control** / **Weak**

Bottom axis: **Narrow** — **Wide**

Perceived Information Need

Figure 13.5 Tactical solutions within regressive information cultures

alternative route to positional and status power for those that seek it. But, in general, it ought to be possible to create a culture that facilitates the sharing of information across the organization. Instilling such a culture would mean re-engineering the underlying IT infrastructure, as this is a necessary component towards the elimination of islands of information, duplication of data and the protection of information for political means. Until such time IT is able to respond to the local information needs, individuals will continue to adopt a stance that best serves themselves. Local spreadsheets and databases will continue to proliferate and create problems for all concerned and, it must be said, increasingly from a data-integrity perspective. Restructuring the IT

infrastructure, if managed appropriately, would also reinforce the value that IT can bring, and aid in the elimination of the culture gap.

Davenport believes that a federal approach to the management of information is most appropriate for the modern enterprise, because without it, the culture of sharing information would be unattainable.[7] Key factors within this federal approach include:

- the use of negotiation to bring potentially competing and non-cooperating parties together;
- recognition of the importance of politics and embracing it accordingly; and
- the application of strong leadership and culture that encourages cooperation and learning.

	Narrow — Monarchy	Wide — Feudalism
Strong	**Monarchy** **Situation:** Information held by the few is generally out of date and hence decisions based on this information are generally unsound. In addition, the general level of data integrity is poor, and customers are poorly managed. Very little information of real value exists, and that which does is retained by those in power **Response:** 1. Undertake a complete information audit as a means of driving out old and potentially worthless information, and identifying that which will benefit the function. 2. Educate the holders of information in the importance of information currency, accuracy and integrity. 3. Develop centralized databases and establish processes for maintaining data currency.	**Feudalism** **Situation:** In an organizational environment that has a narrow focus on information and a weak level of control, the feudal function is able to source and retain information that best serves itself. Although information is retained and rarely shared, the wider focus can be of value. **Response:** 1. Consider extending the wider information perspective across the rest of the organization (recognizing that this will also help to limit the unwillingness of the feudal culture to share its information).
Weak	**Anarchy** **Situation:** Without any effective control over information, anything goes. Because the information need is perceived to be narrow, the function grinds to a halt because no one is taking care of what information is needed by whom. The function appears chaotic to the outsider. Without any coherent information strategy, the underlying IT infrastructure consists of incompatible systems that are unable to support current business activity. **Response:** 1. Undertake an information audit in which the true needs of the function are established – try to widen their perception of information. 2. Start to unify the systems through the creation of an IT backbone, and develop systems capable of meeting the wider information needs.	**Utopianism** **Situation:** With a weak span of control over how information is controlled, the utopian function is able to develop its own technical infrastructure unseen from the rest of the business. This function typically outperforms the others because it has more information to hand. Although the utopian culture is typically techno-centric, with a generally low level of technical expertise within the organization as a whole, it remains in check. **Response:** 1. Attempt to apply technologies and infrastructure beyond this one function.

(Vertical axis label: **Control** — with **Strong** and **Weak**)

Narrow   **Wide**

Perceived Information Need

Figure 13.6   Tactical solutions within paralysis information cultures

According to McKean, a shift to the federal model can only occur if each of the following dimensions are tackled: people, process, organization, culture, leadership, information and technology.[8] I have added an eighth, information politics, as any change must also consider how political behaviours around information can be eliminated through the establishment of an appropriate technical, process and organizational environment. Figure 13.8 identifies these eight elements.

Each of the model's component parts are described in more detail in the following sections.

INFORMATION

Taking into account the rapid rise of data and information within corporations, information should be treated like any other organizational asset. This means assessing its benefits as well as its cost of maintenance. Because information politics inhibits the effective management of information, it is essential that it is de-politicized. This can be achieved through the adoption and institutionalizing of an information life cycle[9] – designed to harness information that is of benefit to the organization and retire that which is too costly to maintain, or adds no intrinsic value to the execution of its business. The beauty of such a life cycle is that it allows an objective assessment of information's value, rather than the typical political bias that tends to persist within organizations (see Figure 13.9).

Monarchy	Feudalism
Situation: This is the classic monarchy. The strong control coupled with the weak perceived information need in an organization that has the same attributes means that the monarch can thrive without challenge. Almost total information power resides with the people at the top of the function and, in this case, the organization. Little or no effort is made to keep in touch either with the external or internal environments, and as a result the monarchy soon becomes out of touch.	**Situation:** The feudal function is able to survive without challenge within the fixation culture as long as it can focus on the core information considered important by the organization. Hidden from view, it tends to collect information that best serves itself. As a result, it is generally more effective than the monarchy culture, because of its wider use of information. However, as with the monarchy, it controls the information very tightly, ensuring very little of outside benefit is shared.
Response: 1. Use shock tactics to wake up the function (and organization) to the needs of the modern business. 2. Educate the function in the types of information it needs to survive within the changing business environment.	**Response:** 1. Assess the additional information collected by the function and share where possible. 2. Develop information systems that are able to meet other functions' needs, whilst still retaining the necessary level of control.
Anarchy	Utopianism
Situation: The anarchic function within the fixation culture is one in which the strong control over the information resource is ignored (user-declared independence). Alternative information requirements develop, although these are equally limited, and a local IT infrastructure is created to support these needs (usually outside of the centralized control of IT). However, the function suffers from an inconsistent use of IT.	**Situation:** In an environment which considers its information needs to be limited, and that also exerts a strong control, the utopian culture can offer a valuable antidote. With a wider focus on information coupled with its freer movement, the utopian culture is more able to respond to the internal and external information needs. The greater focus on technology tends to support rather than hinder the use of information.
Response: 1. Assess whether the information collected and exploited within the function is of use to the wider community. 2. Assess value of the local IT solutions and rationalize.	**Response:** 1. Attempt to widen the utopian culture by demonstrating the benefits of information sharing, and the appropriate use of technology.

Rows labelled on the left: **Strong** / **Weak** under **Control**; columns labelled **Narrow** / **Wide** under **Perceived Information Need**.

Figure 13.7 Tactical solutions within fixation information cultures

The adoption of an information life cycle can be a very useful tool in reducing the problems of information overload, which, according to two recent articles in the *Financial Times*, is likely to get worse before it gets better. According to the first, information overload is fuelled by organizations that constantly update their Internet gateways to accept more and more data. In addition, as electronic mail flies around the organization in ever increasing volumes, the amount of information that people have to contend with is increasing sharply.[10] The article suggests that it is the increasing bandwidth of networks that is tempting users to gather far more information than they actually need. The second article highlighted the results of a survey by the UK Institute of Management that

suggested that 54 per cent of managers suffer from information overload.[11] Recognizing that the sign of a good decision maker is their ability to apply judgement, and that the majority do not need enormous amounts of information to make good decisions, one of the advantages of the federal model is its ability to maintain the reliability of information and limit the degree of information overload through the information life cycle. Accepting the axiom of 'less is more', and only focusing on information that adds value, will speed up the decision-making process for the simple reason of having reliable, accurate and valuable information to hand.

Therefore, in providing the basis for assessing information from a business-benefit perspective, the information life cycle should

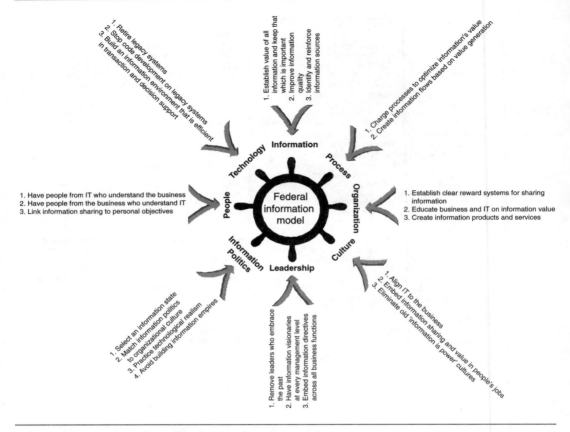

Figure 13.8   Key components of the federal information model

ensure that organizations retain information which is useful and valuable to them, and retire that which is no longer worth retaining. This simple act should limit the severity of information overload.

With an increasing volume of information, there is an increased risk of poor data integrity affecting the smooth operation of the business. Without any clear information policy, the risk of a severe data degradation is very real. Putting this into the context of Figure 13.1 should send alarm bells ringing in all major corporations: if organizations depend on having accurate, timely and relevant information in order to deliver business and operational excellence, they must have high levels of data quality. The adoption of an active information life cycle is a positive step to make, as it will begin to address some of these issues. Couple this with the adoption of an underlying technical architecture

that exploits core data, whilst at the same time offering ease and speed of access, and the issue of data integrity will begin to disappear as islands of information are eliminated and functions use data from a verified single source.

TECHNOLOGY

It is within the technological domain where some of the recent advances within technology can help to promote the federal model of information management. To do so, however, requires the technology to be placed within the context of the information life cycle illustrated in Figure 13.9, so that it facilitates the identification of information that can be exploited and retired. Figure 13.10 highlights one such configuration. The principal components of this are discussed in the following paragraphs.

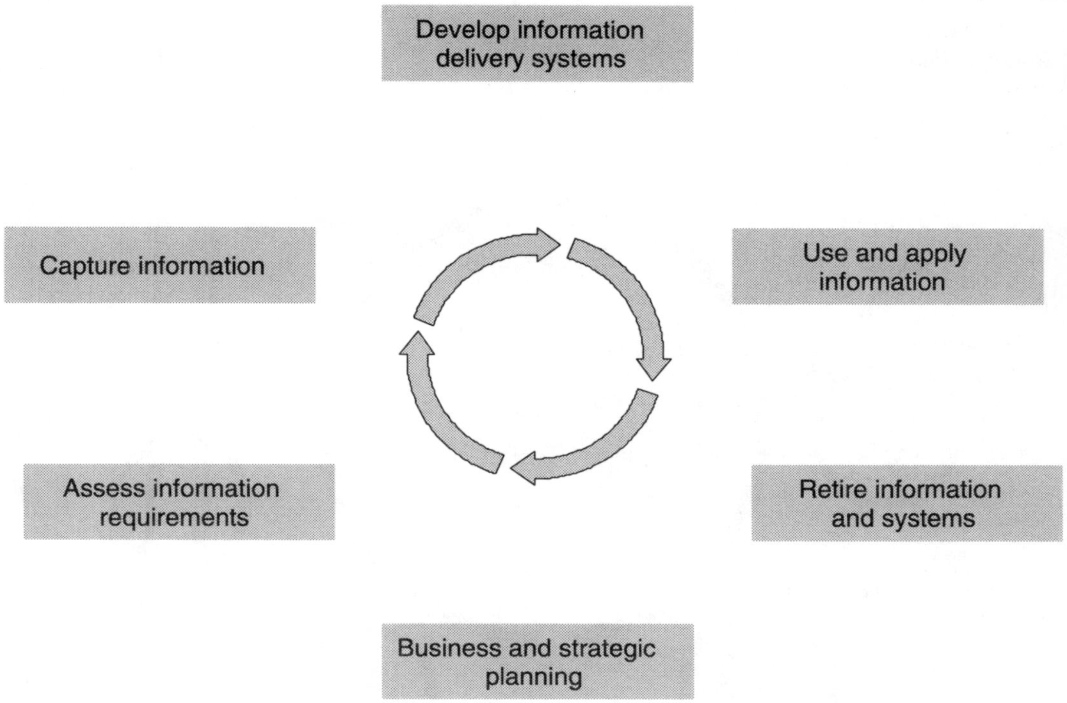

Figure 13.9 The information life cycle

- The core data repository – This is where the primary information of the organization is stored. As an important corporate asset, it is maintained in terms of its currency, accuracy and quality by a dedicated team of information experts. The size of the team will be dependent upon the volume of information the organization must manage. For example, a three- to five-person team for an organization of 1 000 plus employees would feel about right. The purpose of the core data repository is to ensure that information which is of general use to the business is stored once and used many times, and is readily available in its raw form. In that way, each function can take the core data it needs and add to it as required.

- The intelligent information hub and local information hub – This is the network or delivery mechanism to the business. It can be imagined to be a constant flow of data and information across the organization,

always available to be drawn off for local needs. As the information is generic, and single-sourced, it should present no accessibility problems. Also, with the increasing levels of data flowing around the organization, this intelligent information hub should be of the highest bandwidth possible. The intelligent information hub is designed to reduce the increasing amount of traffic that clogs up the organization's networks, most of which, it must be said, goes unused. This is achieved by monitoring the core data centrally using the information value cell. I believe that in freeing up bandwidth by limiting the amount of unnecessary network traffic, some of the productivity problems that have dogged IT and organizations over the last three decades should start to reduce as information becomes more readily available, and at high speed. The intelligence comes from the use of intelligent agents that filter out information

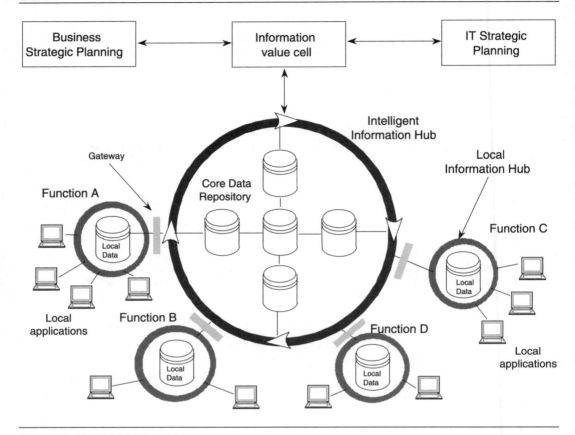

Figure 13.10　Sharing information

needed by the functions. Gateways link the local and corporate environments, and act as the interface between the main and local hubs supplying information. The local information hub operates on similar principles as the intelligent information hub, but is focused on the local, and typically functional, needs.

- Local data – Recognizing that each function will require variants of the basic organizational data, local repositories are available to provide access to data that is consumed locally. With the availability of new forms of software that are able to carry out the extraction, organization and selection of data for the needs of individual users, it should be possible for it to be automatically piped from the main information hub into the local information hub and finally into the local data

repository. The relationship between the local and core data should be considered a two-way street: local information that is considered to be of value to other areas of the business should become globally available by adding it to the core data repository.

- Information value cell – The information value cell fulfils an important function by integrating the information life cycle of Figure 14.9 into the technology infrastructure. Its purpose is to ensure the organization retains and maintains core information that is considered vital to the smooth operation of its business. It must also ensure that all core data and information is accurate, up to date, and still providing value to the organization. Where information is no longer required, it will be tagged for retirement, along with any information systems that support it. To work effectively, the information value cell links directly into the business and IT strategic planning processes. It is here where the cell can add significant value by providing an in-depth understanding of the information needs of the business and linking these into the business operations and IT. This not only ensures that the organization maintains a focus on the value its information provides, but also develops the responsive information behaviours discussed earlier. The creation of the cell is also designed to keep in check the proliferation of information systems servicing local information needs and identify where these can be serviced by other systems elsewhere within the organization. The information value cell uses the same intelligent agents and filters as the functions to maintain a regular check on the information held within the core data repository.

The adoption of a technical infrastructure that supports the effective and efficient sharing and management of information has many advantages, including:

- a reduction in the duplication of data and information;
- a reduction in the costs of maintaining data and information, not only in terms of information systems themselves, but also in terms of the people required to update them;
- a reduction in information overload through the effective supply of information;
- an increase in the level of data integrity, which includes consistency, accuracy and relevance;
- the creation of a flexible mix of centralized and decentralized information systems and information supply mechanisms allowing control to be balanced with flexibility; and
- an ability to focus on information and data that is of value to the organization, and hence focus the organization's IT investment more appropriately.

Clearly, in changing the underlying technological and information infrastructures, there will be an implied change in culture. But focusing on the technological aspects alone will not allow such a change to take place – we need to address the 90 per cent of mastering information that is not related to technology. It is therefore necessary to consider the remaining elements of the federal model carefully.

PROCESS

If we accept that the fundamental tenets of business process re-engineering involve focusing organizations on streamlining their business processes and systems, then we can see there is a link with the federal model of information management. In this case, it means organizations moving away from a functionally driven view of information towards one in which it is viewed organizationally. As with business process re-engineering, it means looking beyond the functional walls to assess information needs. It also means using process to drive out their information needs, since in general, people are more able to identify with the processes they use than the information they consume. Hence, there is value in adopting some of the basic principles of business process re-engineering. By identifying important processes and breaking these down into their constituent information components, organizations will to be able to capture their most important information. If this process is linked to the concept of the information value cell and the assessment of information in terms of business value, processes that are non-value adding can be eliminated along with the information they consume. A similar approach can be used within each of the functions to clear out information that has no value to it. Having completed this task, functions and the organization as a whole will be in a much better position to assess their current portfolio of information systems, and begin to determine which systems facilitate the effective use of information, which do not, and where new ones are required. This will allow the scarce IT resources to be applied more effectively, and directed at those areas where they can add the most value. During the rationalization process, some information systems will be retired, and others will be consolidated, but the net effect will be a streamlined and value-adding IT infrastructure.

A word of caution is needed here. Experience from the business re-engineering initiatives of the 1990s suggests the achievement of a federal model can be difficult. As Hammer points out, despite the significant successes of the pioneering companies who re-engineered their business in the early 1990s, the aftermath for these and the many organizations that followed in their wake was less positive. Many found that they were no longer able to understand how to manage their businesses. This was because re-engineering had turned their organizations ninety degrees on their sides, resulting in the traditional management processes being no longer applicable.[12]

In summary, the process component of the federal model must instil the necessary process excellence around the sharing, maintaining and retiring of information. Without these, the value provided by the adoption of the federal model can soon be lost.

ORGANIZATION

Because the move to information sharing will result in a new organizational dynamic, it is essential to focus the organization on viewing information as an asset. To achieve this involves the creation of a reward system that promotes information sharing and switches the 'information is power' culture to one of 'information sharing is power'. As well as changing the culture, it is also necessary to educate employees in the implications of the Information Age. This education must focus on the importance of information to an organization's success, how it can be exploited, what it means to the way the organization works, how the functions should cooperate, and what the implications are for the staff. In tandem with the education process, staff should have personal objectives tied to the sharing and exploitation of information. This should include the identification of information that can add value to the organization, as well as highlighting information that should be retired.

CULTURE

The underlying culture change required to support the federal model is not necessarily going to be an easy transition to make for some organizations. The importance of instilling a culture that promotes the sharing and exploitation of information is a common theme in both the academic community and popular press. For example, according to one research report, the successful exploitation of intranets depends on an underlying business culture that is positive toward information sharing.[13] This, as we have seen, is an important component of the federal model. The culture change requires that the organization embraces teamwork, information sharing and a focus on leveraging the value from its information. The Information Age dictates that these must be in place for success. But for true culture change, these behaviours have to be embedded within the day-to-day operation of the business, and one of the best ways to achieve this is to link them into hard-edged performance measures and the reward system.[14]

Creating an information-rich organization is fundamentally about changing the business culture to one that values learning and sharing. For example, Davenport believes those organizations which are able to make the necessary cultural shifts that underpin the federal model are those that have already implemented total quality programmes, or those which are attuned to customer satisfaction. Establishing the right culture also means that organizations have to make some hard decisions. If the old culture of 'information is power' is no longer valid, then those who still hold on to it and refuse to make the required change in behaviour must be re-educated, and if this fails, removed from the firm. Although this might appear harsh, organizations have little option but to take these types of action, as the old cultures will inhibit their success in the new information economy.

LEADERSHIP

Leadership is vital to establishing the federal model for a number of reasons. First, strong leadership is necessary to manage the resistance from those functions that wish to hold onto the old 'information is power' culture. Second, leadership will be necessary to tackle the change in status of IT, who will lose their dominant role in the organization as information becomes the critical element. Third, in recognizing that senior managers significantly influence the behaviour of their subordinates, it is essential they demonstrate the behaviours they expect of their subordinates themselves. As with any form of organizational change, if the senior management team maintains their old behaviours, whilst expecting their staff to make the change in behaviour, the process will fail. As a result, the change will fall into the fake change outcome described by Clarkson – the belief that the change is fundamental, when it is cosmetic, and old behaviours usually reappear at the first crisis.[15]

If senior managers are serious about being able to exploit information for competitive advantage, they must embrace the philosophy behind the federal model. A remuneration system that rewards the sharing of information, and the achievement of information-based objectives should be established, and start at the top. I believe that such a link should remain as a continuous reminder and incentive to maintain the disciplines and attitudes of information sharing. Associating incentives with change is a useful approach to take, as people rarely want to move outside of their comfort zone. Appealing to the latent greed of individuals is one way to bring them into this new territory and once there it can be difficult for them to return. Equally, it may be necessary for the leadership to impose sanctions on those who are unwilling to commit to this new regime. Tough leadership and example setting is required.

As it is necessary to re-educate business and IT in how information is valued by the organization, it would be a good idea for the leadership to set some guiding rules to establish the basis for successfully transforming the organization, for example:

- Only use information that can add value to the business processes you operate.
- Do not create islands of information.

- Apply IT appropriately, and only allow it to be information-, not technology-led.
- Information sharing is power.
- Highlight information that is valuable, and also that which is no longer needed.

INFORMATION POLITICS

The key thing to mention under this component of the federal model is to understand that the politics of information will never fully disappear. Some of the tactical responses introduced in this chapter will still have to be applied, but to a lesser extent than they do now. Davenport provides some useful advice in this respect:

> Unless the politics of information are identified and managed, companies will not move into the Information Age. Information will not be shared freely nor used effectively by decision makers. No amount of data modelling, no number of relational databases, and no invocation of 'the information-based organization' will bring about a new political order of information. Rather it will take what politics always take: negotiation, influence-exercising, back room deals, coalition-building and occasionally war. If information is truly to become the most valued commodity in the business of the future, we cannot expect to acquire it without the occasional struggle.[16]

FROM OUR WAR CORRESPONDENT

It is possible to achieve wonders in the management of information, and an illustration of what can be achieved is provided by the 1990 Gulf War. Although the circumstances were clearly war related, which itself allowed equipment, resources and money to be thrown at the problem, the ability to achieve so much in such a short space of time is compelling. The following extract from James Adams' book, *The Next World War*, summarizes the achievement:

> Thus began one of the most innovative, seat-of-the-pants operations ever

undertaken. As more and more units were deployed in theater, the scientist, computer nerds and whiz kids had to patch together a voice and data network using whatever came to hand, while in the United States their support services scrambled to pull together and ship out the hardware they needed. In the end, over 200 sorties by C-141 Starfighter transport aircraft were required to carry the equipment to the Gulf, in the process virtually draining the USAF of tactical and strategic communications equipment. In the end, the communications effort involved 2,300 personnel, 12 combat communications squadrons, 7,000 radio frequencies, 1,000 miles of land links, 59 communications centers, over 29 million calls, all in support of the 350,000 air operations in Desert Shield and the 225,000 in Desert Storm. It is testament to the skill and imagination of the technicians involved that the system worked, because nothing on that size or scale had ever been envisioned, let alone created.[17]

What can this tell us? First, it is possible to focus on information that is valuable to an enterprise, and marshal the right resources to source and exploit it. All other information, although important, is either discarded or ignored. Second, it is possible to use technology appropriately, in a focused way to achieve stunning results. Third, it is possible for those who hold the information to share it for the common good of the enterprise. And, finally, it is possible for the technologists and the business to work together in harmony and develop something which is of immense value to the organization.

In summary, for organizations and their managers to succeed in managing both the short-term politics associated with information and the medium-term goal of introducing a federal approach to the management and sharing of information, they must unlearn the following:

- that cooperation is less desirable than competition
- that information is power and can be shared only to one's detriment
- that trusting others makes one vulnerable.

As a final point, Pfeffer and Sutton in their book, *The Knowing–Doing Gap*,[18] summarize ways of overcoming destructive internal competition within organizations. A number of the points they make are particularly applicable in the resolution of information politics, namely:

- Punish those that only act in their own self-interest. This includes demotion, firing and any other sanction considered appropriate by the organization.
- Focus energy on defeating the competition, not fighting internal turf wars.
- Establish measures that are able to assess internal cooperation and use these to identify problem areas.
- Model and actively promote the behaviours of those leaders who act collaboratively, share information and help others.
- Use a combination of power and authority to get people and business units to share information, learn from each other and work collaboratively to enhance the organization's overall performance.

Stopping the escalator: ensuring your information systems projects are successful

When competent, sensible people do something stupid, the smartest move is to try to figure out, first, what kept them from seeing it coming and, second, how to prevent the problem from happening again.[1]

Software problems and some kinds of medical problems are similar in three basic respects:

1. *Prevention is more effective than curative treatment.*
2. *Early discovery of the problem leads to a higher recovery rate.*
3. *If left untreated, the problem will seldom go away.*[2]

The three most significant dangers within any large undertaking are:

- the inability to see when it is going wrong
- not being willing to pull out once it becomes clear that things are going wrong
- the unwillingness to learn from the resulting failure.

The power of irrationality and over-commitment within large-scale information systems projects is a major problem. The finger-pointing that takes place when projects fail is a powerful motivator to hide, cover up and generally ignore problems when they arise, and not learn from failures when they occur. Unfortunately, focusing on blame distracts organizations from exploring why the project went wrong and how the information systems delivery processes and general attitudes towards information systems projects can be improved. Organizations must break through this mindset if they are to achieve consistency in project outcome – in this case, project success after project success.

It is important to remember here that success might also mean the early termination of a project that is failing. Widening the perception of success to include the termination of a project can only be a good thing, as it stimulates learning and feedback, and drives home the fact that IT is not as infallible as most organizations would like to believe. The need to terminate a project also recognizes that recovery may not always be possible, especially if the problems are too severe or have surfaced too late to do anything about them. The alternative of maintaining commitment to a failing project can only lead to cover-ups, escalation, blame and finger-pointing. This is not to say that accountability does not matter, because clearly it does, and the IT profession has a significant accountability deficit to address – the topic of accountability will be dealt with in the next chapter, since accountability within law, and from an organizational perspective, is a necessary component to unravelling any IT project disaster. What accountability does mean however, is that when a project fails, resources are directed to understanding why. And, where this analysis yields something that is of wider benefit, it is fed back into future projects. In this way the same mistakes should be avoided.

Stopping the escalator means:

1. being sensitive to the irrational and escalatory behaviours that go hand-in-hand with a failing project;
2. having an objective measurement system that is able to demonstrate that a project is failing – important because those within the project may be unable to see why the project is failing, or believe the evidence when confronted by it; and
3. eliminating the negative and confrontational

blaming and finger-pointing associated with troubled projects.

The remainder of this chapter examines these three areas in more detail.

GENERAL INDICATORS OF ESCALATION

Many of the major information systems project disasters discussed in this book have common attributes that suggest certain projects are more likely to suffer from escalation than others. This is useful, as it can provide those organizations who are willing to learn from others' past mistakes and errors of judgement, a sensitivity they would otherwise lack. These attributes are:

- the imposition of tight and unrealistic timescales – This includes those imposed by the organization on their internal IT department or external vendor, those that are self-imposed by a third-party IT supplier in order to win the contract, or those that are the result of external market pressure – such as a sudden change in the economic climate, or the need to address regulatory requirements.
- the need for significant capital and non-capital investment;
- the expectation of significant returns on investment – This might be imposed by the organization through investment appraisal hurdle rates, expected because of one or two high-profile and well-publicized successes, or stated as achievable by a third-party supplier wanting to win the business.
- the use of leading-edge technologies (or technologies that are at the boundary of an organization's capability), to break into new markets, or to introduce major organizational change;
- where the future of the business depends on the successful outcome of the project, or the project is considered business-critical – Such projects typically must succeed, no matter what the cost.
- where the careers of senior managers depend on the successful outcome of the project; and

- where the project has been publicly announced, either within the organization, to the wider business population or, in the case of government projects, to the general population.

For completeness, I have brought together a number of well-known failures and assessed these against the predictors of escalation (see Table 14.1).

Table 14.1 demonstrates that many of these failures exhibited some, if not all, of the factors that are likely to escalate a project to the point of failure. Many previous analyses into why major information systems projects failed have tended to concentrate on what I consider to be some of the fundamentals of project success (the classic advice, outlined in Chapter 2). These factors include ambiguous user requirements, the general lack of senior management involvement, poor planning and so on. But, in my mind, these are technical reasons why the project may not have delivered, and indicate a general lack of project management competence, or poor information systems development processes. They do not, in any significant way, provide a valid reason as to why the commitment to the project was sustained over what was usually a lengthy period of time, and often despite mounting evidence pointing to a disaster in the making. Organizations would be wise to recognize these factors the next time they commit to a major IT investment.

Taking Table 14.1 and converting these seven factors into questions (Figure 14.1) can be used to augment the business case assessment process discussed in Chapter 11. The questions can be used as a simple check-list at the start of a project to raise the level of awareness about the potential risk of escalating commitment.

It is rare to find a project suffering from escalation from just one of the factors identified in Figure 14.1. For example, if the project had been publicly announced, but had been set realistic expectations in terms of costs, benefits and timescales, and had a competent project manager at its head, it would be very unlikely to escalate out of control. As a simple rule of thumb, if the response to 50 per cent or more of

Table 14.1 Predictors of project escalation

Project	Tight, or unrealistic, timescales	Significant capital and non-capital costs	Significant return on investment expectations	Application of leading edge technological solutions	Seen as business-critical	Career dependent	Public decisions
London Ambulance Automated despatch system	✓			✓	✓	✓	✓
Westpac CS90		✓	✓	✓	✓		✓
CONFIRM travel reservation system	✓	✓	✓	✓	✓	✓	✓
Bank of America Trust accounts system	✓	✓	✓	✓	✓	✓	✓
Department of Motor Vehicles Vehicle licensing system	✓	✓	✓				✓
Performing rights society PROMS project	✓	✓	✓	✓	✓		
DSS Operational Strategy		✓	✓	✓	✓		✓
London Stock Exchange Taurus project		✓	✓	✓	✓		✓
State of Florida benefits system		✓	✓	✓	✓		
Wessex Health Authority RISP project	✓	✓	✓			✓	✓

these questions is yes, then the project may be susceptible to escalation. Organizations would therefore be wise to develop a sensitivity to the factors of Table 14.1 and use the questions of Figure 14.1 to assess the risk of escalating their commitment to a project, both at the beginning, and during its execution, not at its end when it is too late.

ARE YOU ON THE ESCALATOR?

The starting point for any organization concerned about the possibility of over-committing to an information systems project has to be its past experience of projects and, in particular, project failure. If, for example, the organization has a poor track record in information systems project delivery, and hence a high prevalence of failure, it is more likely to fail in future projects. Understanding why this is the case is an important step to take, as it ought to be possible to build in a level of awareness into its project and senior management staff to prevent it from happening again. Some of the

Question	Response	
1. Are the project timescales tight, and possibly unrealistic?	Yes	No
2. Are significant capital and non-capital costs involved?	Yes	No
3. Are there significant benefit expectations?	Yes	No
4. Does the project involve the application of leading-edge technologies, or technologies that are at the boundary of the organization's capability to either break into new markets or introduce major organizational change?	Yes	No
5. Is the project seen as business-critical?	Yes	No
6. Are people's careers (especially senior managers) dependent on the successful completion of the project?	Yes	No
7. Are there likely to be any significant public decisions made on the project?	Yes	No

Figure 14.1 Is the project likely to escalate?

reasons why information system projects have failed will clearly fall into the realms of the classic advice outlined in Chapter 2, and others will be due to the issues alluded to within Part I of this book. Therefore, if we add to this a sensitivity of escalation using the seven questions in Figure 14.1, then the overall sensitivity to failure should increase.

But this is not enough on its own, as organizations must be able to assess whether they are over-committing to a project once it has commenced. Understanding these dynamics in large-scale information system projects is particularly important, as this is where over-commitment can be especially damaging. The path of over-commitment and failure is fairly consistent (see Figure 14.2).

Usually, at the start of a project, the project team and sponsor will do their utmost to generate the necessary commitment to ensure that the project gains momentum and acceptance within the wider organization. This is vital if the project is to get off the ground. The level of commitment reaches its optimum when the project enters the crucial stage between the middle of development and the end of implementation. Naturally, it is necessary to maintain a high level of commitment during this period to ensure that the effort required to complete the project is sustained. Equally, it should be expected that the level of commitment will vary during this

phase, as problems are encountered and resolved.

If the project team are trusted, and commitment is maintained – both within the team and the wider stakeholder community – the project has a good chance of succeeding (the dotted line in Figure 14.2). However, where severe problems are encountered and the project team, together with the wider stakeholder community, are unwilling to recognize the warning signs, then escalation can lead to commitment increasing beyond that which is considered healthy. Usually associated with a lengthening in project timescales, and problems in developing or delivering functionality, focus is typically placed on both the costs (having already spent a vast amount, why pull the plug now?), and benefits (the expectation of significant benefits is still strong – a case of jam tomorrow, although in this case tomorrow will never come). Escalation continues, and results in the project team and wider stakeholder community believing that they can still deliver the project. However, there comes a moment of truth, when reality dawns on the project team and the organization that the project will not deliver. When this happens, the project is terminated, the recriminations start, and the hunt for scapegoats begins. This, as we have seen in some of the examples within previous chapters, can be a very messy affair.

As well as the common route to escalation,

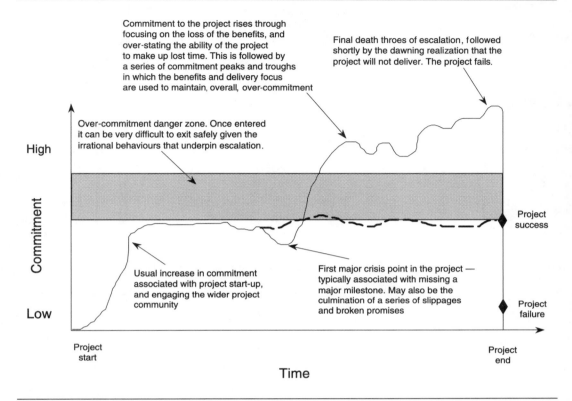

Figure 14.2   The pattern of over-commitment

there is another simple measure that can be used to indicate problems with commitment and over-commitment to a project. Observation suggests that a simple relationship ought to exist between commitment and project performance (see Figure 14.3). Projects that are healthy are likely to maintain a healthy level of commitment, that is, both performance and commitment will move together. Equally, one ought to expect that when a project's performance wanes, so should the commitment to it. This is also healthy, as it ensures that organizations terminate projects that are failing to deliver.

However, where a project's performance deteriorates, the level of commitment may increase significantly as more time is spent promising jam tomorrow and convincing the stakeholder community that the project is still viable, rather than tackling the problems. This is especially true of large information systems projects, and was a common theme in the

London Ambulance failure, the London Stock Exchange Taurus project, CONFIRM and Westpac CS90. This situation is unhealthy, as it means the organization is failing to see how the project is likely to end; in this case, failure. Equally unhealthy is the instance where the commitment to a high-performing project is reducing. Although this is usually the result of poor stakeholder and expectation management by the project manager, it can also be due to other factors, such as an inability of the organization to terminate projects it considers no longer relevant. Instead of stopping them, they ignore them, hoping the project team will get the message and give up. Surprisingly, this happens quite often. Letting a perfectly healthy project peter out is just as much of a waste as failing to terminate unhealthy ones.

Knowing that over-commitment follows a fairly standard pattern and that commitment and project performance go hand-in-hand, it would be extremely useful for organizations to

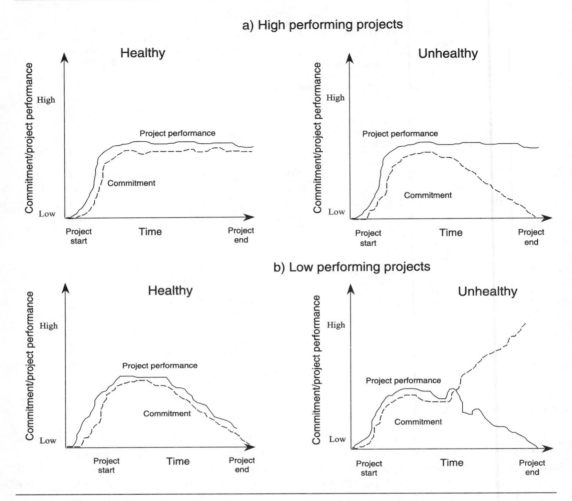

Figure 14.3   The relationship between commitment and project performance

be able to assess whether they were over-committing to a project that was clearly failing. Such information can then be used to determine if intervention is required to bring the project back on track, or whether termination would be the better option.

WHEN TO INTERVENE?

Knowing when to intervene in a project that is believed to be under-performing can be difficult because of the need to maintain the balance between trust and concern. But before moving on to an intervention approach, it is necessary to cover briefly the topic of project health checks. Many organizations use these to assess

the general effectiveness of their project management processes, and the health of individual projects.[3] Although health checks are supposed to form the basis of an intervention within a troubled project, they very often fail, for a number of reasons:

● They fail to uncover major project problems; instead the result is a superficial check-list and a tick-box approach to assessing a project's ongoing performance and viability. The majority involve determining, amongst others, whether the project has a plan and risk register, and if it is doing the standard sort of procedures you would expect of any information systems project. All clearly important elements to any project, but what about the underlying factors that might cause the project to fail? Checking for the presence of certain elements and procedures is therefore not enough, and ultimately fails the organization because failing projects are allowed to continue.

- They are usually performed by some kind of quality assurance function, often staffed by people who have a limited experience of projects, and who are generally unable to challenge the project manager – even an average manager is able to run rings around them.

- They tend to have overly complex scoring methods, thereby making the whole process a pseudo-science, rather than an effective tool. Such complex scoring methods can often hide the true problems, because effort is spent discussing individual scores rather than the issues; thereby allowing the project to continue.

- When issues are found, they tend to be superficial, ignored, or explained away by the project team.

- They fail to address the factors associated with irrational behaviour and escalating commitment.

For health checks to be as effective as their designers would like, they should be performed by experienced project managers, who are not only able to apply their professional judgement, but are also sensitive to the tell-tale signs of escalatory behaviour.

As stated previously, the first step in the intervention process is to determine when to intervene, and at which level (project manager, project team, sponsor, senior management, wider stakeholder community and so on). Figures 14.4a and 14.4b provide two simple questionnaires that combine the good components of project health checks, plus the added element of escalation. These questionnaires are designed to assess first whether a project is under-performing, and second, for those projects that are considered to

be out of control, assess the degree of over-commitment. Rather than make it overly complex with scoring mechanisms, the questions are of the yes/no variety, thereby making them binary and avoiding any debate about the value assigned to a specific variable. This also forces the assessor to apply their judgement.

The process of assessment should involve a combination of project analysis and interviews, using the questions listed in Figures 14.4a and 14.4b. Within the interviews, it should be possible to make judgements about the confidence of the interviewee by observing their body language, and assessing whether it is congruent with what they are saying. The project manager, the team and the immediate sponsor should be interviewed at this stage. Hard data is also required to support the assessment and would include an analysis of the plan, progress to date, and a projection of the current rate of progress to assess likely completion date. Such analysis would also include an assessment of costs and likelihood of meeting the benefits.

With the application of project management judgement, and an understanding of irrational and escalatory behaviour, it should be possible to make an assessment of a medium to large project within one to two weeks with a team of three to four people. The assessment will provide an indication of the general state of the project (healthy, unhealthy or terminal), together with an assessment of the degree to which commitment is congruent with performance (aligned or misaligned).

Although the questions are designed to make an independent assessment of the project, there is good reason for the project manager to use these to take the occasional step back and make an honest assessment of his progress. It can be hard for project managers to do this, because it requires them to be brutally honest about how well their project is progressing.

ASSESSING PROJECT PERFORMANCE

The purpose of this first set of questions is to assess the project's health. To make a reasonable assessment, it is necessary to understand the

Questions to assess the general health of the project	Response	
1. Does the project have a robust and believable project plan?	Yes	No
2. Based on the plan, does the project have sufficient resources under its direct control to deliver the project (IT and business)?	Yes	No
3. Are project team members expected to work more than 8–10 hours per day to complete the project?	Yes	No
4. Is the project under any significant time constraints?	Yes	No
5. Is the project under any significant budget constraints?	Yes	No
6. Based on questions 1–5 above, does the progress to date (meeting milestones, quality of deliverables and so on) suggest the project is on track for completing on time and within budget?	Yes	No
7. Is the project using skills or technology that are at the edge of the project team's comprehension or ability?	Yes	No
8. Are there visibility mechanisms in place that ensure progress is highly visible, and simple to assess by the project team, wider stakeholder community and sponsor?	Yes	No
9. Are the project manager, and project team open and honest about the project's true status?	Yes	No
10. Is the project sponsor, and wider stakeholder community, aware of the project's true status?	Yes	No
11. Has the project experienced any significant problems to date?	Yes	No
If yes,		
11a. Have these been dealt with appropriately?	Yes	No
11b. Have the impacts of these been reflected in the project plan?	Yes	No
11c. Have any changes to the plan been fully communicated?	Yes	No
11d. Have any changes to the delivery time frame been accepted by senior management?	Yes	No
12. Are there any signs of friction between the IT and non-IT staff working on the project?	Yes	No
13. Are there any signs of political manoeuvring, particularly around information?	Yes	No
14. Are there third parties involved with the project?	Yes	No
If, yes,		
14a. Are they fully aware of their commitment?	Yes	No
14b. Is this commitment reflected in their work?	Yes	No
14c. Can the work be delivered in the time they say it can?	Yes	No
14d. Is the third-party plan available for inspection?	Yes	No
14e. Is third-party progress visible?	Yes	No
14f. Does the project manager have access to third-party deliverables?	Yes	No
14g. Is progress to date in alignment with expectations?	Yes	No
14h. If there have been any problems with the supplier, have they been managed appropriately (see question 11)?	Yes	No
15. Are project deliverables available for inspection?	Yes	No
16. Can the project team (including the project manager) articulate when the project is expected to finish?	Yes	No

Figure 14.4a   Project performance questions

Questions relating to poor performing projects (designed to assess the degree of escalation)	Response	
1. Do the project manager, project team, sponsors and key stakeholders believe the project is achievable and are fully committed to making it successful?	Yes	No
2. Have public statements about the need to complete this project been made by senior management?	Yes	No
3. Is there a belief that lost time can be made up by the project team?	Yes	No
4. When questioned on the slippage, does the project manager (or external supplier) focus on the benefits, and emphasize these above all else?	Yes	No
5. Has there been a reduction in the level of project visibility over the course of the project?	Yes	No
6. Is success considered to be the only outcome by the project team, sponsor and wider organization?	Yes	No
7. Despite the project missing major milestones, is anyone prepared to challenge its viability and recommend termination?	Yes	No
8. Has the true status of the project been suppressed?	Yes	No
9. Is there a belief that people who highlight poor project performance will be removed from the project?	Yes	No
10. Are management unwilling to hear that the project is in trouble?	Yes	No
11. If the project is experiencing continued problems, is the organization still committed to it?	Yes	No
If yes, why?		
11a. Too much money has been spent already, and they are unwilling to consider termination.	Yes	No
11b. The desire to attain the expected benefits is too strong.	Yes	No
11c. The belief that the project will still deliver remains strong.	Yes	No
11d. The outcome of the project is business-critical, and failure is not an option.	Yes	No

Figure 14.4b   Commitment questions

viability of some of the general mechanisms of the project, such as planning, the attitudes of the stakeholder community towards the project, and the constraints under which it is operating. Although these questions are not exhaustive, I believe they are sufficient to assess the health of a project to a degree that will allow conclusions to be drawn. In answering these questions, it would be necessary to interview the project team, assess project data to acquire hard evidence of status, and determine the likely prognosis of the project.

When assessing the answers to these questions, if the majority – greater than 70 per cent – are yes, then the project is possibly terminal in nature. Between 20 and 50 per cent, and the performance can be considered unhealthy. Anything below 20 per cent can be viewed as healthy, although there is no room for complacency. This is a simple rule of thumb, and judgement needs to be applied when taking account of individual project circumstances.

ASSESSING COMMITMENT

The purpose of this second set of questions is to assess the degree to which the organization is over-committed to an unhealthy or terminal project. Unlike the first set of questions, which can be supported by hard project data, this set can be considered to be more qualitative and judgemental in nature. In reality, over-commitment has less to do with actual project performance and more to do with how people feel towards it, and the implications it may have on their careers and the organization as a whole. This is very important, because in the end it is people's perception towards the project that will sustain its life, even when failing. The first question is particularly key, as it will indicate how severe the over-commitment is, or is likely to be.

These questions are specifically directed at those projects that are either unhealthy or terminal, and are designed to assess whether the commitment to the project is either aligned or misaligned. With respect to the problems associated with escalation, it is where commitment is misaligned with an unhealthy or terminal project that is the focus of our concern. Therefore, if a project is unhealthy or terminal, and the majority of questions in Figure 14.4b are responded to with a 'yes', there would be every reason to believe that the level of commitment is misaligned with the project's performance.

Having completed the assessment, it is important to draw conclusions as to the likely prognosis of the project, and make these as clear-cut as possible. Figure 14.5 provides the basis for this summary, although additional information would be required to support the conclusions.

WHAT SHOULD YOU DO WHEN YOU INTERVENE?

Having made the assessment and drawn the conclusions, it is necessary to follow this up with actions. For all but the healthy, aligned project, some action is required. In the case of the unhealthy and terminal misaligned project, this is likely to be significant because it requires action to tackle both poor project performance and misaligned commitment. Before discussing the actions required to address these, I will first turn to those required when commitment is in alignment.

ADDRESSING THE UNHEALTHY PROJECT WITH ALIGNED COMMITMENT

Where the performance of a project is under par, but the organization still believes it is worth completing, the actions highlighted below should be undertaken to bring the project back on track.[4] Because commitment is in alignment, the focus of this activity should be around the project itself, since once it is performing at a higher level, commitment to it should start to increase.

There are usually good reasons why a project

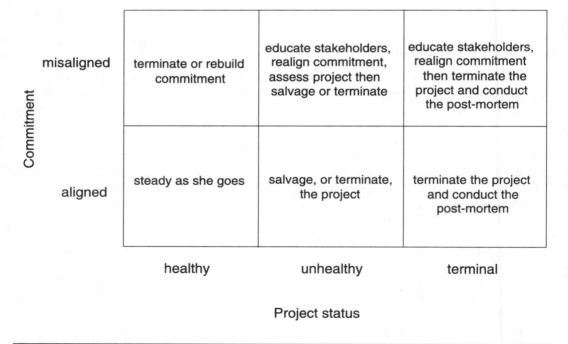

Figure 14.5 Project performance versus alignment of commitment

is performing poorly, and these are normally associated with a general loss of control, and the inappropriate application of project management, or software development practices. The key actions in this instance are:

- Fix the parts of the development process that are not working. This includes the standard project management and software development activities such as risk and issue management, configuration management, planning, reporting and testing.

- Create detailed milestones for the remainder of the project. Focusing the project on short, sharp deliverables is vital, so that control can be re-established. A new schedule linking these milestones together should also be created, as it will provide an indication of how long the activities will take to complete, and highlight the dependencies between them.

- Make these milestones visible, and ensure that they are reported against at least every week, and where required, more frequently. As well as detailing achievements, the report should also include reasons why milestones have been missed. This will establish trends. For example, if the milestones are consistently missed by individual team members, it would suggest that the original productivity assumptions on which the effort required to complete the work were incorrect. In revising these assumptions, there will be a subsequent impact on the schedule, as additional time will be required to complete the remaining work.

- Stabilize and freeze the requirements, especially if these have been changing frequently during the project.

- Consider reducing the functionality. If this is necessary, it is best to link the functionality to the benefits. Cutting functionality where there is little or no benefit is a good starting point. However, care should be taken where functionality associated with major benefit streams is to be cut, as this could lead to the project becoming no longer viable from a cost–benefit perspective.

- Remove any functionality that is of poor quality.

- Monitor and control the number of defects by tracking and tackling them through stringent code reviews.

- Maintain regular communication with the project's stakeholder community, and ensure they are fully aware of progress and issues as they arise.

- Try not to add more staff to the project, as this will lead to a lengthening of project schedule – one of the classic Brooks' laws.[5] Care should also be taken where staff are to be removed from the team because of poor performance. Before doing so, it is recommended that the impact on the remainder of the team be gauged, as such an action may have significant, and negative, repercussions on morale and productivity.

- Once the project has completed, conduct a post-mortem to assess why its performance wavered. This should be used to draw out any changes that need to be made to the project management and software development processes, and fed into future projects.

ADDRESSING THE TERMINAL PROJECT WITH ALIGNED COMMITMENT

When the project is considered terminal, it is essential that it is closed down as quickly as possible using the following actions as the basis:

- All project activity ceases as soon as possible, and the project is brought to a tidy conclusion. This includes bringing all of the project documentation together in preparation for its analysis, moving the project team back into the organizational line, terminating any third-party supplier contracts, and so on. This must be carried out carefully and sensitively, especially where third parties are involved.

- Conduct an analysis of the project, in terms

of its performance, key events, and how problems were addressed. At this stage, it may be necessary to interview members of the project team, stakeholders and the sponsor, together with any third-party suppliers, in order to understand some of the dynamics of the project which are not obvious from the raw project data.

- Assess the principal causes of the failure, and from this, establish where accountability may lie. If the failure involved a third party, legal advice may be required (see Chapter 16). The purpose of assessing accountability is to ensure that, if there is a genuine case of negligence, this is dealt with appropriately.

- Assess the contribution of other factors to the failure and update processes, procedures and the skills of project personnel accordingly, including business people as well as IT.

- Ensure that any lessons that can be learnt from the failure are fed back into the wider project community to prevent the same mistakes being made in the future.

- Avoid the temptation to seek out scapegoats. This is unnecessary, and a waste of time and energy. Moreover, it tends to lead to cover-ups and the widening of the recrimination process. Managing the process calmly, carefully and sensitively is essential. This sends out an important message to the wider project community that failure is not dealt with in a knee-jerk, reactionary fashion, and is therefore more likely to lead to the earlier identification of problems.

WHAT TO DO IN CASES OF MISALIGNED COMMITMENT

The real concern for organizations is where commitment to a project is misaligned, especially when associated with unhealthy or terminal projects. When this misalignment is linked to a healthy project, the focus of the assessment is to understand why and, depending on the outcome,

the action is to either terminate the project, or re-establish an appropriate level of commitment to it. The former can be achieved by following the advice outlined in the previous paragraph, whilst the latter can be achieved through a series of interviews with the wider stakeholder community. These should seek to understand why support for the project waned, and ascertain if the project is no longer important to the organization. If this is the case, termination is the best answer. If the project is still considered important, however, effort should be directed at improving the project's visibility, including communicating its objectives and successes. This should allow the commitment to the project to be realigned.

In my mind, it is where the level of commitment is too high for an unhealthy or terminal project that needs the most attention. Before some of the actions related to project turnaround or termination described above can be undertaken, it is necessary to realign commitment. To achieve this requires a combination of hard evidence, and persuasion, to bring about the necessary realization that the project is unlikely to complete successfully. This will typically mean addressing each of the principal stakeholder groups separately and working with them to reflect on the current status and likely prognosis of the project. It will also mean that each group is forced to confront the degree to which they are behaving irrationally. It can, however, be difficult to achieve a consistent consensus if the process is handled haphazardly. For example, even though the chief executive of the London Stock Exchange could see that the Taurus project was failing, he could do very little about it, because the wider project community either failed to see it, or were unwilling to acknowledge it.

When addressing the stakeholder groups it is best to start with the project manager and work outwards (see Figure 14.6).

Following a defined order is a useful strategy for two reasons. First, it starts the process at the source of the problem – usually the project itself – and second, it creates a growing body of people who believe the project will not succeed, and which therefore allows commitment to be realigned. Speed is of the essence, as the

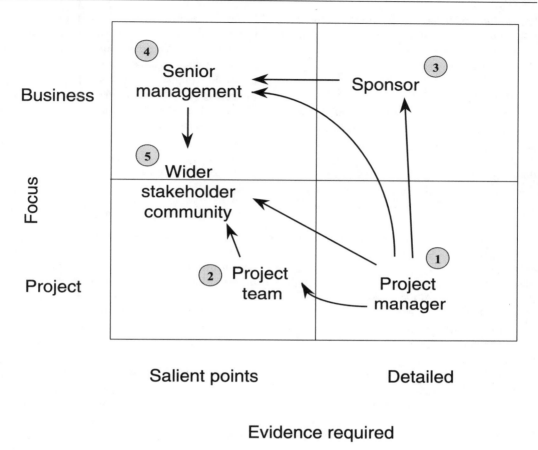

Figure 14.6 Addressing over-commitment

opportunity for rumours to spread about a failing project is usually high. The following paragraphs describe in more detail the actions required at each of the individuals/groups outlined in Figure 14.6.

1. TACKLING THE PROJECT MANAGER

Where the project is unhealthy or terminal, the project manager is likely to be suffering from over-commitment. Being so close to the project, it is possible he will either fail to recognize the warning signs, or believe, quite wrongly, that he can still deliver the project within is original constraints. The use of an independent review by an experienced project manager, coupled with a hard look at the evidence, should be sufficient to make the project manager realize the project is unlikely to succeed.

Where the outcome of the project is linked to the project manager's career, the opportunity for distortion and not wishing to speak up and admit defeat should not be under-estimated. Therefore, to succeed in making the project manager recognize the problems, the evidence must be sufficiently detailed so that it becomes indisputable. If it is not detailed enough, project managers will typically ignore it, distort it, or explain it away. For example, projecting current productivity, cost and achievement data forward using earned value can provide an unequivocal insight into the final costs and completion date of the project. This can be very difficult to ignore, even when the project manager believes the project team can still claw back lost time. Breaking the irrational belief that the project can still complete on time is a major step forward to being able to limit the irrational behaviours identified in Chapter 8, but in particular conformity error, misplaced consistency, ignoring and distorting the evidence.

2. TACKLING THE PROJECT TEAM

Depending on the morale and general cohesiveness of the team, and their relationship with the project manager, they will be relatively easy to convince. Although close to the project, they are often able to see that it is failing. Where the team is strong, and group behaviour dominant – itself the result of a dominant project manager – it can be more difficult for the team to open up and acknowledge the problems with the project. Unlike the project manager, however, the key hurdle to overcome with the project team is group think. Groups, especially if they are cohesive, do not wish to speak out, particularly if they believe they will be subject to sanctions if they do – loss of job, negative impacts on careers and so on (see the CONFIRM project description in Chapter 8 for a good example of this). Whistle-blowers are not generally well thought of. Groups also tend to suppress bad news as this is often seen as a way of coping with the issue – in a similar manner as the example of Italian Jews cited in Chapter 8. Finally, within strong groups, there is also a tendency for project heroics, in which the team believes it can retrieve the project and work inhuman hours and weekends to do so. This only leads to more errors and greater fatigue, as the team collectively becomes unproductive and more error-prone.

When addressing the team, it is best that the reality check comes from the project manager. This assumes the project manager has the respect of the team, and if this is not the case, it might be advisable if the news came from the independent assessor, with the project manager present. Once the realization has dawned within the team, it is worth spending time exploring the options available to the project, particularly if salvage remains a possibility. Such information will be required by the project manager when meeting with the sponsor and, latterly, when the project's problems are discussed with the senior executives of the organization.

The principal purpose of addressing the project's performance with the whole team is to allow them to recognize that they can think and say what they believe to be unthinkable and unsayable: that the project is failing. Being able to express this without recrimination is essential as it not only allows them to express their true fears about the project, but also provides them with the opportunity to assess the various options open to them. This in itself may lead to an improved performance should the project continue.

3. TACKLING THE SPONSOR

In general terms, the sponsor, by virtue of their positional power within the project and organization, is unlikely to be told the truth. In many instances they are told what they want to hear, rather than what they ought to hear. This can be compounded if the project manager has a fear of failure. Because of the sponsor's relationship with the project, and the possible issues that failure may present to them personally, they are often similarly disposed as the project manager. Not wishing to fail in senior management's eyes, they will endorse project heroics, and believe the project is recoverable.

To break the irrational behaviours of distorting and ignoring the evidence, it is essential to have the project manager present the news to the sponsor. Although using an independent assessor to analyse the status and prognosis of the project is always the right approach to adopt when making the original assessment, they should not be used to deliver the results and consequences to senior managers and sponsors. In many cases, these independent analyses are either suppressed or rejected – such as within the London Ambulance and Westpac CS90 projects. Ensuring the project manager takes ownership of assessment's outcome is vital, as this gives more credibility to the delivery of its results to the sponsor. Again, this does depend on how well respected they are.

As with the project manager, it is necessary to focus on some of the details that support the conclusion. In this case, however, the focus must be more business-based – cost, benefit and business impact and so on. At this stage, it is worth the project manager and sponsor spending time developing the strategy for breaking the news to the senior executives, and in particular, determining what the key messages will be. This is especially important where the project may be recoverable, as a sceptical management will require a lot of convincing if they are expected to endorse additional spending. If termination is to be recommended, it will be necessary to emphasize the importance of understanding why and how this learning will be used to prevent future disasters. Again, sceptical senior managers, who are unlikely to be pleased that the project has failed, may be unwilling to invest in the time and effort to do this properly. Emphasizing the value that such learning can bring is the key to gaining their commitment. There will, of course, be instances where senior management will not want to terminate the project, and will be unwilling to face up to the reality of failure. In this case, the evidence must be conclusive, and will typically be a more detailed mix of project and business data.

4.   TACKLING THE SENIOR EXECUTIVES

The senior executives will typically encapsulate the board of directors, particularly if the project is business-critical. Their major concern will focus on the impact the failing project will have on the business, and what actions are required to minimize it. They will, in general, be less concerned with the mechanics of what went wrong, unless there is a legal impact. Thus presenting cost, benefit and business-impact information will be necessary, and this will be typically at a high level. They will, as with the other groups involved with the project, be unwilling to hear the messages, and if they are over-committed, may well pressurize the sponsor and project manager to continue with the project. As a result, it may be necessary to drill down into detailed project data to support the case. We all know from history that such persistence is foolhardy. Therefore, to ensure the board realizes this, the evidence must be conclusive. Drawing on other major failures can be of use here to demonstrate that continuing

with a failing project is an unwise thing to do. In addition, if the measures outlined in Chapter 11 have been adopted, a degree of sensitivity to failure may have already been established, and the board may be more willing to terminate the project for the right reasons. As with the sponsor, it is vital that the next actions are outlined, and where a project is recoverable, it will be necessary to convince them that the same mistakes will not be repeated in the future.

5.   TACKLING THE WIDER STAKEHOLDER COMMUNITY

With potentially many different functions involved, each with different agendas, the perception of the project and its failure will vary quite widely. In this instance, it is best to use all available resources to cover the entire community as quickly as possible. Engaging the project manager, sponsor, senior executives and project team in this task provides the commonality of message necessary to prevent rumours from starting and spreading.

THE IMPORTANCE OF VALUING LEARNING AND FEEDBACK

There is no doubt that organizations must be more willing to accept the value that failure can bring. No matter how painful, it is better to learn from mistakes than pretend that they never happened and then repeat them at a later stage. Equally, indiscriminately sacking members of the project team serves no purpose other than to stifle innovation. A healthy attitude toward failure is required as it allows organizations to become more innovative, take calculated risks, and learn when things do not go as well as planned. To be successful at this requires a number of shifts in the way organizations act when project failure occurs. These include:

- committing to the termination of projects for the right reasons;
- committing to learning from failures, as a means of improving future projects;
- committing to the appropriate management of project personnel once a project has failed, rather than indiscriminately sacking people;

- committing to the sharing of knowledge of failure across the organization as a means of increasing the sensitivity of staff towards it; and
- recognizing that failure will always be a potential outcome of any project and as a result maintain the vigilance required to prevent it from happening.

As Abdel-Hamid and Madnick suggest, every failure has a silver lining, because through experience and costly errors, managers develop the effective intuitive judgement needed to prevent further failures.[6] Organizations would do well to embrace this, but also to go one step further and institutionalize the practice of learning from failure. Intuitive judgement, often gained through experience, is normally a personal thing. Making this intuition widely available in the organization is one of the keys to preventing over-commitment and failure within information systems projects.

CHAPTER FIFTEEN

Rehabilitating accountability

We have a legal system based on physical possession of property. Yet we are in a virtual world with virtual property.[1]

In their professional practice, engineers universally recognize the need to update technical methods because of advances in scientific knowledge. Today, however, there is a compelling obligation to consider also a new environment for practice – the social, economic, legal, political and ecological ramifications that impose design constraints. Such demands arise because technology exercises such a potent influence on modern human affairs, because every technology generates side effects and imposes risks and because the public expects higher levels of risk management, accountability and legal liability.[2]

The legal and professional frameworks have found it difficult to keep up with the implications of a computerized world. The sheer pace of technological change and, in particular, the implications of electronic commerce and the Internet have meant that both have constantly had to play catch-up. From a professional standpoint, there seems little to demonstrate that the IT industry has developed a positive attitude toward the formal recognition of the risks that software poses to the typical organization – the many project failures and software problems discussed in Part I point to a continuing problem of managing the risks associated with software projects. Unfortunately, this impacts the way the IT profession is perceived by the business community: a recent survey by Kennedy Information Research placed IT consultants last amongst all clients in terms of client satisfaction.[3]

In addition, the legal system has found it difficult to maintain the currency of its framework. Although significant headway has been made, it seems that, just as the legal system

has caught up with one aspect of computer technology, a new one opens up. This also means it is often difficult to mete out justice when software causes harm. The key reason for this is the change from a physical to a virtual world that has come about with the emergence of information and communication technologies. Without the familiarity of physical intuition, it can be very difficult to apply legal judgement to a product that does not fit comfortably within the physical world.

Establishing accountability for defective software and poorly implemented systems is an important component in improving the outcome of software projects, especially given the increasing dependence on IT. Establishing accountability, however, does not just rest with the legal system; organizations and the wider IT profession also have their part to play. In any case, it is wrong to rely on the legal system to resolve issues created by the lack of accountability. Accountability brings professional pride and sensitivity toward the outcomes of the software development process. Embracing accountability not only improves the practices of the IT professional, but also improves the general image of the profession as a whole. It also underwrites its importance to organizations and society, and makes it generally more attractive to prospective candidates. In essence, it improves the trust between those that develop software and those that use it – something that is sorely in need of being rebuilt. Acting with integrity is one of the cornerstones of trust, and I believe it is essential that the IT professional starts to act with some – this means taking responsibility for his work, and being held accountable for errors and failures that may result.

To achieve the level of accountability required to improve both the degree of trust between business and IT professionals, and the success rates of information systems projects, the following is needed:

- an objective framework in which accountability for project failure and defective software can be established;
- a sensitivity for the legalities associated with the delivery of third-party systems;
- the introduction of accountability within organizations to facilitate the objective assessment of failed information systems projects; and
- the creation of a robust professional environment in which the practices of the IT practitioner can be controlled, and the perception of the profession improved.

WHY HAVE ACCOUNTABILITY AND HOW TO MEASURE IT?

Accountability means that a public or private agency entering into a contractual agreement to perform a service will be held answerable for performing to agreed upon terms, within an established time period, and with a stipulated use of resources and performance standards.[4]

In general terms, there are three areas for which institutions, organizations and individuals should be held accountable,[5] and these are especially applicable to software projects:

- Management practices – Organizations need to show that they are doing what their mission or objectives suggest they should be doing.
- Efficiency and productivity – Organizations should be as productive as possible, by maximizing output and minimizing input.
- Acting with honesty and integrity in their dealings with their stakeholders – This behaviour generates trust, and trust is the cornerstone of healthy business relationships, particularly within professional services.

In order to assess accountability in an objective fashion, it is essential to develop an assessment mechanism through which the accountability for a failed project or defective software can be determined. This can be achieved by:

- identifying the important components of

the project that is to be evaluated (the indicators);
- gathering information about the project that has failed (the evidence);
- assessing this information against some standard (the criteria); and
- making decisions based on each of the components above (the judgement).[6]

I will come back to this framework later, as it can be used to assess accountability for the failure of internally managed software projects. First, it is necessary to highlight the legal framework in which the delivery of third-party software products systems is judged. This knowledge is important because it is in the interests of everyone who employs third parties to develop and implement information systems, to familiarize themselves with the protection provided by law.

ACCOUNTABILITY IN LAW

Although the legal implications of a software-dominated world are extensive, the principal focus when it comes to externally delivered information systems projects is associated with the failure to deliver a software project adequately, or where the software developed turns out to be defective.

Although there is no room here to cover this complex topic as thoroughly as I would like, there are a number of books dedicated to the subject of computer law, and I would point anyone who wishes to explore this area in more detail to these publications.[7] Even at summary level, it is still worth outlining the principal components of the legal framework because it provides a level of general awareness that will allow organizations to avoid some of the more obvious pitfalls. The following paragraphs summarize the key aspects surrounding the legal accountabilities for defective software in the United States and Canada, and the United Kingdom. In addition, I have included a short summary of a landmark case in the United Kingdom involving the supply of defective software by International Computers Limited (ICL).

THE UNITED STATES AND CANADA

In the United States and Canada, computer programs are treated as literary works and, according to John Ramsey,[8] liability for defective software could arise from the following scenarios:

- The software is not performing at all.
- The software is not performing as well as any other comparable package on the market.
- The software is not performing to customer expectations.
- The software contains errors in its processes.
- A third party claims the software infringes its intellectual property rights.

Ramsey states that, should any of these defects appear within a licensed copy of a software product, the creators may be held liable when there has been:

- A breach of express contractual warranty – Express contractual warranties are those that promise a certain level of performance, and may be written or oral. They often include disclaimers stating what is not warranted. A breach of express warranty therefore entails the software performing to a lower level than stated.
- A breach of a warranty implied by law – This covers the implied breach of warranty that arises from the interpretation of statutes that have been passed, and case law that has been established – often around the expected quality of a product or service.
- A fundamental breach of contract – This is where the software fails to function at all, or is so defective that it is, for all intents and purposes, useless. Software suppliers often attempt to limit this liability though restriction clauses within their contract. This was, for example, an important element to the St Albans City and District Council versus ICL judgement, discussed later.
- Negligence – This applies where the software supplier has failed to exercise reasonable care to prevent damage or injury arising from the use of the product.

- Infringement of intellectual property rights – This usually occurs when the software infringes the patent or copyright rights of someone else, or uses information that was received in confidence.

THE UNITED KINGDOM

In the United Kingdom, the legal implications of defective software, or the failure to deliver effective software systems as part of a contract, are open to similar interpretations as in the United States and Canada. But unlike the United States and Canada, the software product is treated differently, depending on whether it is classed as a product, or a service. According to Bainbridge,[9] where loss or damage is associated with defective software, the following areas of the legal system may apply:

- The law of contract – A third-party supplier can be held liable under the law of contract if there is a breach of condition or warranty. A breach of a condition allows the recipient of the service to terminate the contract and claim damages. This includes the costs of implementing the system that was never delivered by the current supplier, with another, and lost revenue arising from the failure to deliver the system within the time specified in the contract. A breach of warranty is usually less serious because it rarely involves a catastrophic event, and as a result compensation is limited to damages only. And, unlike a breach of condition, the contract remains in force and must still be completed by both parties.

- The law of negligence – This is associated with a loss that has arisen from a breach of a duty of care. In the case of software, this may arise where a software system or product has malfunctioned and resulted in loss or harm. If this malfunction was due to its negligent manufacture, then there may be a case to hear.

- Where there has been negligent mis-statements – This is similar to the breach of express contractual warranty in the United States, in which the statements made about the software product turn out to be untrue.

- Product liability – The producer of a defective product is liable for damage resulting from a defect contained within it.

Because of the limited amount of case law to support legal cases associated with software failure, legal actions tend to be long and complex affairs, and it can be difficult to resolve a dispute without incurring significant financial and reputational costs. For example, a complex High Court hearing can cost in the region of £500 000.[10] And, if the case is sufficiently large to attract public attention, the reputational risks can be significant. Organizations are therefore unwilling to take the matter to court unless there are significant sums involved, or they are confident of winning. Even when they do, there is a tendency to settle before a final judgement is made, to ensure the full extent of the case is never made public.

Depending on individual circumstances, the legal implications of defective software will vary. The key distinction under English law is whether the software was delivered as a service, or as a product, because different laws apply when buying goods and services. For example, an artist who paints your portrait is classed as supplying a service because it is based on his expertise and skill. Buying a suit from a tailor, however, is classed as supplying goods because the customer is paying for the suit, and not the tailor's expertise.[11] This type of interpretation can become problematic when applied to software, because of the way in which hardware and software are classified under law: the delivery of hardware is typically classed as a product, whilst software is classed as a service.

Under English law, the failure to deliver software systems (including hardware) via a contract are principally dealt with by the following Acts:[12]

- The Unfair Contract Terms Act 1977 – This provides protection against unfair contractual conditions and exclusions. Therefore, if a contract is signed which contains such conditions, and later turns out to be unreasonable, the third party will still retain liability.

- The Sales of Goods Act 1979 – This protects the consumer against clauses that exempt the supplier from liability from faulty or defective goods. There are three tests that can be applied under the Act. First, are the goods fit for purpose? Second, are the goods of poor quality? And finally, are the goods as described? The third party is also bound by the Misrepresentation Act 1967, which is designed to enforce the accurate description of goods.

- The Supply of Goods and Services Act 1982 – As with the Sale of Goods Act, there are a number of tests that apply. The first is whether the work had been carried out to a proper standard. A person who follows a trade or profession must exercise the skill of a reasonably competent member of that trade or profession (although it can be very difficult to define exactly what constitutes a reasonable standard of workmanship). Second, have suitable materials been used in the provision of the service? Third, have goods, whilst in the care of the third party, been lost, stolen or damaged? And, finally, despite the work being delivered satisfactorily was it what was asked for or specified at the time of the contract?

Before leaving the subject of accountability in law, it is necessary to outline the particular dangers associated with exclusion and limitation clauses. These serve to limit or restrict liability when there is a breach of contract. Under contract law, there is an important distinction made between exclusion clauses in which total exemption from a breach of contract is provided, and limitation clauses that limit the liability to a specified amount. The former is typical of software licences, where as soon as the seal is broken on the packet containing the diskettes, liability for any loss incurred through the software's malfunction rests with the user, not the creator, of the software. Within contracts, exclusion clauses are usually associated with *force majeure* and other events that are outside the direct control of the service provider, such as industrial action. It is usual to find limitation clauses within software contracts which cap the amount payable at a much lower level than the likely losses. But where the variance between the cap and the actual losses is significant, the contract can be considered unreasonable by a court of law. Exclusion and limited liability clauses can be considered to be one-sided contracts in which the supplier of the service has the upper hand. However, there have been one or two notable cases that have turned this one-sided arrangement into something a bit more balanced, as the following example demonstrates.

In 1988, ICL signed a contract with St Albans City & District Council to develop and deliver a community charge payment recording system. This system was intended to maintain records of all community charge payers that fell under the council's responsibility, and raise the necessary bills. The software was delivered in 1989, and only after the number of community charge payers had been calculated, and the corresponding local tax been set, was an error found in the calculations. On investigation, it was found that the error was the result of a software bug, and it was this that led to the number of community charge payers being over-estimated by 2966. This meant that the council's tax receipts would be £484 000 less than anticipated, and the payments to its county council (in this case, Hertfordshire) almost £1.8 million higher. The actual loss to the council once other factors had been considered was a little over £1.3 million. The original contract signed by the council contained a limit on the liability that ICL would pay should the software prove to be defective. This set the maximum payable at £100 000 – significantly less than the £1.3 million loss faced by the Council. During the ensuing court case, it was judged that ICL were in breach of contract because the software had failed to provide correct figures relating to population numbers. The judge found in favour of the council and awarded damages against ICL amounting to the full loss, plus costs. ICL appealed, and the subsequent Appeal Court decision upheld the original judgement, although the damages were reduced by £600 000, as it was ruled that the council's losses had been overstated.[13]

Despite the reduction in damages, the case sent an important message to both the business and IT communities: the former could no longer be held to unreasonable contracts, and the latter could no longer follow anything less than best practice, including making detailed, specific and unambiguous requirements, and instituting effective change management processes.

Organizations would be wise to familiarize themselves with the protection afforded to them under law. They would also be advised to consider very carefully the legal framework when entering into any agreement with a third-party supplier to develop and deliver a software system. Because of the difficulties associated with assessing the software product when a project fails, organizations must be smarter at the way they administer their contracts, and recognize the value the legal system can provide when encountering problems with software suppliers.

ESTABLISHING ACCOUNTABILITY WITHIN ORGANIZATIONS

The accountability for poorly developed information systems within organizations usually lies outside of the legal framework, and as such must be addressed within the boundaries of the organization. Unfortunately, organizations rarely assess accountability carefully enough when their internal information systems projects fail, usually resorting to blaming those involved with the project, forgetting the failure ever happened, or sanitizing the results of post-mortems. Learning would be a much better option. But how can organizations introduce a level of accountability that is suitably objective to avoid the temptation of blaming those associated with the project, sanitizing and down-playing the results, and forgetting it ever happened?

I believe that by adopting and tailoring the framework introduced at the start of this chapter, accountability can be rapidly established, and if used correctly, can limit the typical responses to failure; that is, blame, sanitize and forget. In addition, having such an objective framework will allow organizations to learn from their mistakes in an environment that is not focused on finding a scapegoat.

The key components of this framework are outlined in Figure 15.1, and summarized below.

IDENTIFYING THE IMPORTANT COMPONENTS

The key to being able to make an objective judgement when a project fails lies in understanding the components that must be assessed in order to make that judgement. Where a project is well run, this is straightforward, because the information required to make the assessment is readily available. Where projects are run incompetently, however, this can present major problems. Important project components are its objectives, principal deliverables and responsibilities of the key players, including the project manager, sponsor and team members – these form the basis of the specific assessment criteria against which a judgement can be made. The standard project components, such as risk, issue and change management, form the basis of the standard criteria – these are activities that

any project should perform. The specific criteria are those elements that are unique to the project.

GATHERING INFORMATION

When gathering information about a failed project, there are two types of data of interest, hard and soft. Hard information includes key project events, minutes from meetings and project data, such as plans, project deliverables, risk registers and so on. Soft data includes soliciting the views and perceptions from the principal stakeholders, and understanding from the stories they tell, how the project was managed and what caused it to fail. These stories enrich the process and allow some of the political, organizational and behavioural issues associated with the failure to be drawn out in an objective manner. To maintain a balance, and ensure that a considered judgement can be made, it is important to include the project manager and project team within this process.

ASSESSMENT

Having gathered information about the project

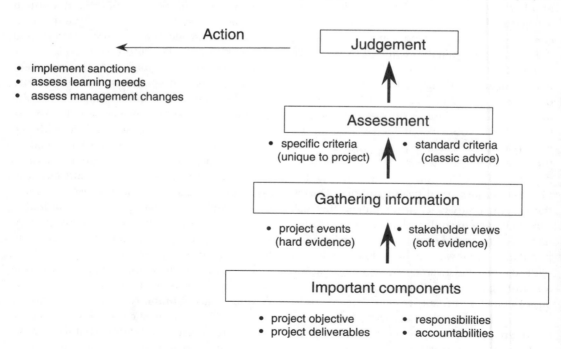

Figure 15.1   A framework for establishing accountability for a failed project

and how it progressed, the next stage is assessment. It is here that the accountability framework comes into its own. Designed to provide objectivity, it compares the project's performance against its own unique (project) criteria and that of a standard, which in this case is a mix of standard project management and software development activities.

As with health checks, it is advisable to make an independent assessment of the project because of the likelihood of irrational behaviour creeping in, principally ignoring and distorting the evidence. Depending on how they were affected by the project, people tend to distort events in order to protect themselves or divert the blame elsewhere. Thus to maintain objectivity, organizations have one of two choices:

1. Where an organization has a number of project managers, it can be useful for one of them to make the assessment. This can be valuable because it will sensitize the person conducting the review to the general reasons why projects fail, and provide important feedback into the wider project, business and IT communities.

2. Where suitably qualified people are not available, or it is difficult to maintain objectivity, an independent assessor should be employed to conduct the assessment. The assessor must have experience of managing information systems projects, methodologies and best practice, and have a deep understanding of why information systems projects fail.

The assessment should be made against what I have termed 'specific' and 'standard' criteria. The specific criteria relate to the project being assessed, and include the project data gathered during the information-gathering stage, whilst the standard criteria are composed of project activities which are found in any well-run information systems project. In assessing the project against the specific and standard criteria, it is essential to retain a neutral, and hence objective, stance, as this allows all the evidence to be judged on its own merits.

Unlike the health check and escalation tools introduced in the previous chapter, the accountability assessment tool illustrated in Figure 15.2 works in a slightly different way. The key difference is in how the questions are answered and scored. In this case, we are assessing accountability and whether negligence had a part to play in the project's failure. Therefore, it is necessary to make a wider, and arguably more qualitative, assessment taking into account any contingent factors that may have reduced the opportunity of the project succeeding. Each question can be scored as either having been fully met (there is evidence of full achievement of the activity/objective in question), partially met (there is evidence of some achievement of the activity/objective in question), or not met (there is no evidence of achievement of the activity/objective in question). Depending on individual project circumstances, and where in the life cycle the project failed, some questions will remain unanswered. Where a project was completed, but the software failed to function as planned, all questions should be answered, along with the questions relating to the implementation of the system and how it functioned once operational. These post-implementation performance questions have been included under the standard criteria.

When conducting the review, it is essential to be able to draw out whether due process was followed and hence whether or not there is a case of negligence. Where, for example, the project manager and their team have done the best they could, and applied best practice, it is unlikely there would be a case of negligence. Of course, to draw such conclusions requires an understanding of the context in which the project was run, and this is where the softer evidence is important. Also, where no standards for project management or software development exist within the organization, the likelihood of success would have been limited in the first place, and hence it would be unwise to hold the project manager accountable for the failure. This brings us back to Chapter 10, and mastering the basics.

Where an answer to a question is partially

met, or not met, it is necessary to understand why, as this is where there might be a case for negligence, and further evidence may be required to support the assessment.

JUDGEMENT

The purpose of the judgement stage is to make an objective decision about the level of competence displayed in the execution of the project, and hence whether anyone should be

Aspect	Fully met	Partially met	Not met
Project-specific criteria			
The project had clear, unambiguous and well-communicated objectives			
The project had clearly defined deliverables			
The project's stakeholder community were clearly identified			
The project team were in possession of the correct technical and business skills required to deliver the information system			
The project team had clearly defined roles and their workload was managed effectively throughout the project			
Recommendations from project health checks were followed			
Standard criteria			
The business community were fully involved throughout the project			
Project plans were created and maintained throughout the project			
Complete, coherent and consistent requirements (functional and non-functional) were in place prior to coding the system			
The organization's standard software development processes were applied within the project			
The organization's standard project management method was followed throughout the project			
Project progress was clearly reported throughout the project (including problems and issues requiring senior management attention)			
Project progress was made visible and unambiguous to all stakeholders throughout the project			
Project risks were identified and effectively managed throughout the project			
Issues, when they arose, were managed appropriately			
A reception strategy for the realization of the business benefits was in place and communicated to all stakeholders			
The business and IT community understood their relative roles in the project and any tensions between the two were adequately managed			
Politics around information was managed appropriately			
Any change that affected the final deliverables were controlled and their impacts on the project assessed and communicated			
The business community were fully prepared for the implementation			
The implemented information system met all of its functional and non-functional requirements			
The information system met all of its performance requirements			

Figure 15.2   Assessing accountability

held accountable for the failure. It should be remembered that, just as in a court of law, judgements should be made on the basis of evidence available. The judgement will be based upon a combination of:

- the hard evidence of the project, including plans, minutes and other documentary evidence;
- the soft evidence obtained from the stakeholders, project manager, team members and sponsor; and
- the results derived from the assessment using the tool shown in Figure 15.2.

Ideally, someone who is independent from the failed project should make the final judgement. However, where the failure is significant, it is likely that such impartiality would be difficult to find, and this may present the organization with a dilemma – without an impartial judgement, personal feelings are likely to creep into the decision. Once again, an independent judgement may be necessary to retain impartiality and could, if the IT professional bodies were capable, be provided by them.

Judgements will typically fall into one of three categories:

1. The project manager or key members of the project team failed to follow due process and complete the project in a competent fashion – including failing to follow the advice of health checks if they were conducted. As a result, there is likely to be a strong case for negligence, and therefore some kind of sanction should be applied.

2. The project manager and team worked as best they could within an environment that lacked effective project management and system development processes. In this case, there is no real argument for negligence; instead the focus should be on putting in place these fundamental components of project success.

3. The project manager and the team followed due process using standard project management and system development methods and tools, but other organizational

factors conspired to kill the project, including poor project sponsorship, limited senior management support, deliberate political manoeuvring, external events within the business environment, and so on.

ACTION

Having made the judgement, the final step in the process is to take action. The actions arising will naturally depend on the judgement made, but are likely to include:

- The application of sanctions where the project manager or members of the team have been found to be negligent in the execution of the project – Organizations typically respond differently when applying sanctions, and in many ways this reflects their underlying culture. Whereas some organizations will dismiss those that have been considered to fail, others will move them on to less important work – equally painful for those concerned. In others still, a period of rehabilitation occurs in which the person is able to redeem themselves by proving their capabilities elsewhere in the organization. Finally, there are those that avoid personal blame, instead focusing on the use of post-mortems as a means of building learning into the process at the personal and corporate level.[14] One could argue that the successful introduction of the CREST system at the London Stock Exchange was in part due to the lessons that had been learnt from the Taurus project's failure.

- Updating the project management and software development practices within the organization – Where no defined standards exist, these should be introduced as a matter of priority because they will instil consistency and are likely to have a significant impact in reversing the level of failure. Where standards exist, and these have been found wanting, it would be advisable to review their applicability within the organization and update them accordingly. In each case, it is essential that the project management community is fully trained in their application, and in the fundamental project management disciplines. The same thing applies to the software development practices, although in this case it might be necessary to introduce a small number of methods to suit the various types of project being executed.

- Making changes to the management structure that supports projects – In some instances, the supporting infrastructure is likely to be poor, with senior management taking little or no interest in the project. In others, the role of the sponsor is undefined, and hence inappropriate people may have been assigned to this very significant role – sponsorship is an important task, and one that should not be taken lightly.

The ultimate reason for taking action, once a judgement has been made, is to sensitize the organization to the reasons why projects fail and to make them more competent at running them in the future.

CREATING ACCOUNTABILITY IN THE WIDER IT PROFESSION

It is not enough to rely on the organization or a court of law to instil accountability and professionalism within the IT community, as the professional bodies that support it have a major role to play.

Since the 1980s, there has been some activity designed to instil ethics and codes of conduct within the IT profession. The stimulus for this interest has been the growing dependence on software within society, and its role in managing and controlling safety-critical events. For example, the Association for Computer Machinery (ACM) in the United States has developed a code of ethics and professional conduct, to which all members of the association were to sign up. The purpose of the code is twofold: first, to form the basis for ethical decision-making in the context of a member's professional work, and second, to serve as a basis for judging the merit of a formal complaint. Although a number of the code's 24 principles could be considered idealist, in that

members will contribute to society and human well-being, there are a number that are clearly worth embracing, including the need to acquire and maintain professional competence, and to know and respect the laws relating to the work they perform.[15] In addition, the British Computer Society have recently reissued their code of practice for IT professionals, which dates back to the 1980s. This provides guidance to all IT professionals regardless of their specialism, as well as sector-specific codes of practice governing practice in specialist areas.[16] It should be remembered that establishing a code of ethics is not easy, especially when many companies who insist on honesty in their dealings with others are infamous for breaking them.[17] For example, one only needs to consider the investigation by the United States Securities and Exchange Commission into the accountants PriceWaterhouseCoopers. The Commission found that they had broken the rules governing auditor independence more than eight thousand times in two years.[18]

The purpose of introducing such ethical principles is to embed the importance of accountability within a profession that typically lacks it. The other problem is that, unlike many of the older and more established professions, computing has never been regulated or maintained through a recognized professional body. Therefore, codes such as that introduced by the ACM are largely voluntary, and have no sanctions attached to them. That said, in the United Kingdom, IT professionals who are members of the British Computer Society are bound by their code of conduct, and if they have been found to be negligent, can be expunged from membership – however, I do not know of anyone who has. Moreover, if I was to compare this with the Royal Institution of Chartered Surveyors, of which I am a member, those expunged from membership are identified in the professional journal, for all to see. I believe that if the IT codes of conduct were as powerful as those of other professions, then we ought to be seeing the same thing in the professional journals affiliated to the IT profession.

Providing a framework in which the accountability for software allows both the practising IT professional and business user alike to have a mutual understanding of what is possible and impossible with technology is vital. It should also ensure that questions such as those below can be answered objectively:

● Who should be held accountable for software that, as a result of the bugs contained within it, gives rise to harm or loss?

● When a multi-million-dollar project is going off the rails, who should inform the client and advise them of the consequences?

● When a multi-million-dollar project fails, who should be held accountable, and how can this be established?

● Who should inform the business community, and wider general public, of the risks associated with the increasing dependency on IT?

In answering these and similar questions, it is hoped that IT professionals would be sensitized to the need to avoid those behaviours and practices that cause the profession to be held in disrepute. Recognizing that it is difficult to establish controls in a profession that is largely unregulated, the professional bodies that administer it would do well to adopt some of the principles for assessing accountability discussed within this chapter, since establishing accountability means recognizing the importance of IT to the organization and the wider business and social communities.

As a final thought on accountability, a 1999 survey sponsored by Bull in the United Kingdom which looked at individual's views on the Information Age found that:

● Over 33 per cent were concerned at the speed at which technology was changing.

● 53 per cent believed that automation posed a real risk to society.

● Only 12 per cent trusted the computer industry to regulate the advances of technology.

● 63 per cent believed computerization had already taken over too many people's jobs.[19]

The IT industry should take these concerns to heart, as they indicate an underlying angst about technology and its impacts on the workplace and society. By instilling a sense of social responsibility and accountability within the profession, people may become less concerned about what is in essence an unregulated environment, and become more comfortable with IT's place in an increasingly automated and turbulent world.

CHAPTER SIXTEEN

Avoiding the silver bullet syndrome: choosing the right tools and techniques

It's human nature to look for an easy way out, and it's entirely rational to look for the cheapest, fastest, easiest solution. But it's hard to believe that trained professionals would continue to act against their best judgement for 30 years, which is what we as an industry have done.

For 30 years we've been told that the magic that will enable us to slay giant schedules and budgets is just around the corner. For 30 years it hasn't come … There is no magic. There is no point in waiting for it. The more we wait, the more we deprive ourselves of valuable, incrementally better solutions to many of our problems.[1]

The two quotes above, from Steve McConnell's book *Rapid Development*, sum up the problems that the silver bullet syndrome presents to organizations. The constant rush of technological change has resulted in two tensions, both of which make the rational thinking process associated with sticking with tried and tested methods difficult. The first is the need to remain competitive. Here, organizations find themselves having to adopt the latest technology in the belief that this will provide them with the advantages they seek. The second is the need to be as productive and successful as possible in implementing technology. The first tension tends to impact the second, as with no time to fully test new methods prior to rolling them out, organizations often find themselves accepting, at face value, the claims made by the vendors of new products. In both cases, it is only once the new method or technology has failed to give the competitive advantage sought, that organizations realize the error of their ways. But, instead of stepping back and learning from this, they search for the next silver bullet to solve

their problems. McConnell is correct in stating that there are no magic bullets and there is no point in waiting for them – common sense is needed, but not just from the IT community.

Avoiding the silver bullet syndrome takes courage and care, because it takes time to make sense of the options available and put those that are likely to yield results to work. When I say time, I do not mean large amounts, but an appropriate amount in which to make a logical decision and establish realistic expectations. Each tool, technique and method has value and each can be used to generate improvements within the information system development process. But to do so means they must be carefully selected and modified to meet the needs of the particular organizational setting. Avoiding the seductive silver bullet requires three actions:

1. Ensure that senior business and technology management are aware of what impact the addition of new tools or technologies will have to the software development process.
2. Understand that if organizations want to be successful in the execution of their software projects, they must be predictable in the way they apply their methods and tools.
3. Assess each new tool in a way that is able to determine exactly what benefit it provides.

The remainder of this chapter looks at each of these in a little more detail.

DON'T FALL INTO THE FOOL'S GOLD TRAP

Managers often seek out and follow myths because they are desperate for answers. And, because most are frightened by ambiguity and uncertainty, they tend to follow the advice of the experts if they believe it will help them. This prevents creative thought, and plays into the hands of those peddling the latest theory that promises to bring home massive benefits from IT, or to radically improve the development process. Part I of this book deliberately set out to explode the myth that the failure of information systems projects can be resolved through the application of a single method or tool. In any case, the reasons why software projects are so ineffective, unproductive and poor at delivering benefits, has very little to with the actual tools used. It has far more to do with the culture gap, escalation, poor appraisal and benefits realization processes – in fact, the environment itself. Introducing something like CASE tools will not solve these problems. Tackling the issues detailed within Part I will.

The key step that senior managers, directors and IT professionals need to take is the recognition that without a suitable environment – in the widest sense – software projects will continue to fail, overrun and deliver poor benefit returns. This recognition must include the knowledge that introducing new tools and methods into a project is likely to have a detrimental effect on the productivity of the project team – time is needed to unlearn what they currently do, and relearn the subtleties of the new tool. This takes time, and one or two projects to achieve. Many organizations make the mistake of introducing a new tool on a mission-critical project, which they hope will be delivered faster as a result. The reverse is often the case.

Senior business and technology management also need to be more realistic in setting the expectations for these new tools and they need to be more sceptical of the vendor's claims. Introducing a realistic method for assessing new tools is essential if they are to avoid the quick-fix approaches used in the past. As McConnell points out, incremental improvements are what the profession needs: software development staff are under enough pressure as it is to deliver; adding additional tools without first giving some thought into how they might impact the process is dangerous.

Avoiding the fool's gold trap is really quite simple – it needs senior managers and technology experts to:

1. not over-estimate the savings achievable with the introduction of a new tool;
2. not give up on a new tool on its first application;
3. not switch tools mid-way during a project – this only serves to compound the problem; and
4. not apply new tools on mission-critical projects.

To ensure avoidance of the fool's gold trap, it is necessary to know what to expect when introducing a new tool. In reality, there should be plenty of anecdotal evidence of what happens around any organization, but because so few collect project metrics, it remains hidden from view.

KNOWING WHAT TO EXPECT

One of the key problems faced by organizations when they are offered the latest technique that is going to transform their software development process is whether they can trust the figures. In many cases, they are led to believe that the benefits are instantaneous, and because of the need to minimize uncertainty, they buy into it.

It is, of course, far better to go into the process with open eyes, and seek out information that is often publicly available, or gain some professional advice before committing. At the very minimum, it is essential for organizations to understand what factors can impact the productivity of their projects. Boehm's work has proved to be extremely beneficial in this respect.[2] He found that the introduction of new tools, programming languages and so on, could lead to a lengthening, not shortening of project schedule. For example, introducing a new tool could mean the specific tasks to which the tool is to be applied taking up to 50 per cent longer. This is important to know, especially if there is an expectation from senior management that application will be faster. Naturally, over a period of time, the tool will have a positive impact on a typical project's schedule, but expecting immediate improvements has been proven to be wrong. This is why organizations need to give a tool at least two or three projects to bed in. As more staff become familiar with the tool, productivity will increase. This is no different from introducing a new information system into the business – it takes time for the staff to become fully competent at using it. Moreover, research from 1996 clearly indicates that some of the commonly used techniques for improving productivity and software performance are not necessarily the best. The majority of organizations opt for the technology-based solutions, such as CASE tools, and higher-level languages, and yet things like defect prevention, general problem-solving techniques, improving the estimating skills and improving employee morale can have a much higher impact.[3] For those interested in gaining a more detailed understanding of what is involved with these technologies, or a wider discussion on improving software schedules, I would recommend *Rapid Development* by Steve McConnell, and *Patterns of software systems failure and success* by Capers Jones.[4]

Figure 16.1 highlights some of the approaches that are known to improve the effectiveness of software projects.[5] The model has two dimensions:

1. The first is the tool's ability to improve the effectiveness of the project. Effectiveness may mean many things, and is not just restricted to productivity improvements. It is wrong to think that delivering information systems faster will be a cure-all. For example, during the mid to late 1990s, we witnessed the introduction of rapid application development and, in the United Kingdom, the Dynamic Systems Development Method (DSDM), both of which purport to speed up the development process. They do, in the right hands, and after an appropriate time to bed in, but in the wrong hands, such methods can translate to disaster faster. Clearly, introducing some of the basic software development and project management disciplines will in themselves make the

process more effective and it is always best to start by mastering the basics (see Chapter 10). Getting the foundations right in any project will go a long way to improving the likelihood of success, but many organizations fail to get the basics right, before seeking out the silver bullet to solve their IT problems – it is always best to begin by looking internally.

2. The second is the time taken to bed the new tool or approach into the development or project management processes. No method is effective from day one (see Figure 4.1 in Chapter 4). Indeed, one of the reasons why third-party vendors offer first-time support using their gurus is to ensure the benefits claimed at the time of the sale come through. This is fine if the guru is with you all of the time, but this is rarely the case. Therefore, before rejecting the new approach, tool or method, it is essential to give the staff expected to use it, time to understand how best to apply it.

The other component to knowing what to expect is to apply the tools and techniques of project management and software development consistently and appropriately. Many organizations purport to apply a single method on all their projects, but on further investigation this is often far from the truth – inconsistent application, incomplete knowledge of the approach and so on render this method impossible. This makes it very difficult to gain the repeatability they seek. Such inconsistency is also the result of the haphazard way in which new tools and programming languages are introduced. It is clear, therefore, that organizations can improve some of their basic processes, which once again is likely to yield improvements in productivity and success in their projects.

ASSESSING NEW TOOLS AND TECHNIQUES

It is, of course, seductive to believe in the claims made about the impacts of new tools and techniques within IT. With the need to deliver systems faster, any tool that is able to deliver the

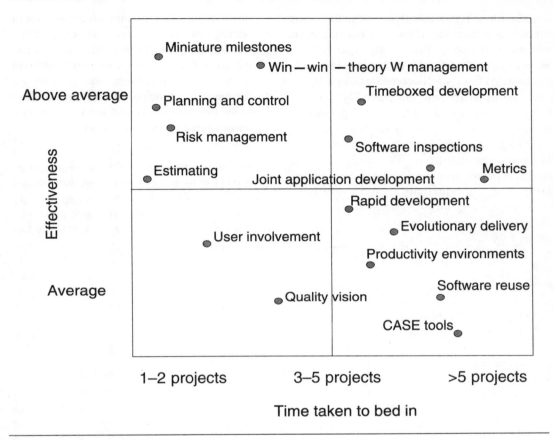

Figure 16.1 Knowing what to expect

speed that is looked for is usually adopted. Unfortunately, with the immediacy of the benefits not meeting expectations, these are prematurely rejected.

What is needed is a degree of realism and the application of a simple method for assessing any new productivity and software development support tool. I believe if organizations abide by the principles set out below they will experience more success in avoiding the silver bullet syndrome:

- Principle 1 – Ensure the fundamental processes of software development are in place, including development life cycles, quality reviews, testing and so on, and ensure all development staff know how to use them.
- Principle 2 – When discussing new tools and techniques with vendors, challenge them on

how immediate the improvements will be. When doing so, talk in terms of the number of people who need to be trained up in the method to reach critical mass, and the number of projects on which it should be used before the productivity improvements will materialize. Ask for evidence.

- Principle 3 – Treat the introduction of a new tool like an information systems project, and, like any project, ensure the benefits realization process is managed carefully.
- Principle 4 – If you are using a tool for the first time, increase the project's schedule and testing window.
- Principle 5 – When introducing a new tool on a project, work closely with the business to manage their expectations. If they believe it will improve the speed or quality of delivery immediately, there will be problems

down the line. It is better to be realistic and manage their expectations – never assume they are comfortable.

- Principle 6 – Do not use a new tool on a mission-critical project – instead apply current best practice. Use non-mission-critical projects to gain the necessary expertise before applying the tool to strategic initiatives.
- Principle 7 – If you will be using an expert supplier/consultant on a project, ensure their knowledge and expertise is transferred to your staff during the project. It is only through using the tool that they will learn about its strengths and weaknesses, not from a glossy brochure or slick presentation.
- Principle 8 – If you have used an expert on one project, expect the next two to three projects to take longer – give your staff time to become experts themselves.
- Principle 9 – Don't take the tool at face value: consider how it should be used in your organization, and where necessary consider how its use should be tailored.

In adopting these principles, organizations should start to remove some of the mystery associated with new tools and techniques, and as a result will limit the detrimental effect that the silver bullet syndrome has had on the IT profession and information systems projects.

PART III

OPTIMIZING INFORMATION SYSTEMS PROJECTS

Information technology doesn't support the business; it is the business.[1]

The key part of an alcoholic's treatment is to ensure they do not lapse into their old ways. This requires changes in their attitude towards alcohol and also the environment in which they live. Equally, organizations wishing to rid themselves of the problem of information systems project failure too must change their attitude to IT and enhance the environment in which projects are executed. Achieving the environmental changes requires organizations to bring the solutions outlined in Part II together so that they can be implemented in concert, and the environment in which information systems projects are executed, optimized. The changes in attitudes may take a little longer, but if the environment is enhanced, attitudes will follow:

- Chapter 17 details how organizations can optimize their information systems projects.
- Chapter 18 provides advice to the principal stakeholders who have a vested interest in the success of information systems projects, including the chief executive, the chief information officer, the IT project manager, the software developer and business user.
- Chapter 19 gives organizations the bottom line.

Optimizing the delivery of information systems projects

Software problems are not natural disasters like earthquakes or tornadoes in which human actions are more or less inconsequential. In fact, software disasters are entirely man-made, and we also have the ability to prevent them from occurring if we choose to do so.[1]

There are no quick fixes to the solution, no fast-track methods available, and no amazing management techniques that will make the difficulties with IT vanish into thin air. Making the shift from a situation in which IT is considered:

- erratic at delivering its systems and associated benefits;
- poor at communicating its value and purpose to the business;
- too focused on technology;
- not focused enough on the business and organization; and
- unable to deliver the value expected of it

to one in which it is viewed as:

- consistent at delivering its systems and associated benefits;
- in tune with the business, that is, understanding and communicating in their language;
- smart at balancing business and technology needs;
- focused on the business and organization at all times; and
- providing value each time, every time

requires organizations, IT professionals, and the wider IT-support mechanisms to comprehensively bite the silver bullet. The purpose of this book has been to make organizations realize that this shift is not an overnight affair, and also to provide some suggestions about what can be done to rectify the problems highlighted. The next step is to address these problems collectively by optimizing the project delivery environment.

The best way to achieve this is to have a blueprint that is capable of taking the organization from where it is now to where it should be, harnessing IT so that it enriches the functioning of the organization in every respect. If we adopt nineteenth-century mathematician Jules-Henri Poincaré's four-stage model of completing a creative act,[2] it is possible to develop an approach that can provide the organization with such a blueprint (see Figure 17.1). The four stages of this process are:

1. Preparation – This involves understanding the problem in detail, and gathering data about it. Organizations typically know they have problems with IT, but either cannot articulate them, or are unable to understand why they are so severe. Part I of this book should have given them the ability to do both, and therefore, the important work within this stage is to assess the specific organizational context and gather data associated with the issues they face, using Part I of this book as the template. It is likely that project management, or the lack of it, will feature quite heavily, but organizations should not believe this to be their only problem. Therefore, the best way to undertake this analysis is to take each issue raised within Part I and assess its severity. From this, it will be possible to identify where the biggest areas of concern lie and where the focus of the subsequent project activity should be directed. It should be stressed that true optimization will only come if all of the issues are tackled together: believing the problems of software project failure can be addressed by resolving just the highest priority issues is missing the point and falling into the silver bullet trap.

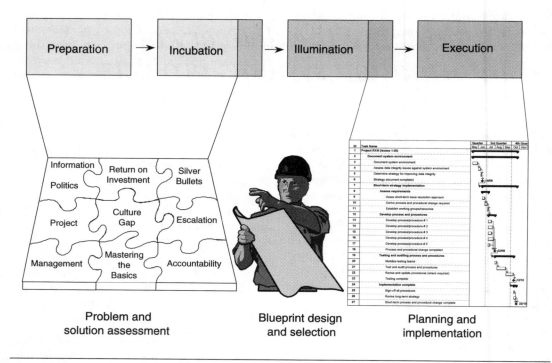

Figure 17.1 The four-stage optimization process

2. Incubation – Here, possible solutions to the individual problems are explored. Although Part II of this book has provided some solutions that can be employed in the resolution of the issues, it is important for organizations to assess these and determine their viability before their adoption. Therefore, if a solution outlined in Part II is not considered applicable to the specific organizational setting, alternatives should be explored and the most applicable selected. The secondary purpose of the incubation stage is to link each of the solutions together to create the basis of the projects that will feed into the illumination stage and the creation of the blueprint.

3. Illumination – Here, the blueprint is fully developed and the project streams refined. During this stage, it is likely that more than one blueprint will be created, as organizations explore how best to address all of their problems associated with information systems projects and IT in general. Once the blueprint has been finalized, the top-level planning required to implement it should commence. This will involve preparing the organization for the task ahead, and setting the vision for the optimized environment and the programme required to implement it. The former should comprise a series of statements that describe the various components of the optimized environment, whilst the latter should be a unifying mission statement which is capable of tying the project activity together. The other activity within the illumination stage is to prepare the programme and project teams, and start to generate the necessary commitment required to make the programme a success, in essence, ensuring there is sufficient support from the board, and engaging the principal stakeholders – itself a standard project activity.

4. Execution – This involves following through with the implementation of the blueprint and monitoring its success once in place.

Viewing this as a programme rather than a single project is important because it is likely to be a mixture of short- and medium-term activity, IT and non-IT project work, requiring significant cross-functional collaboration, and third-party involvement. And, like any project or programme, it is necessary to apply solid project and programme management disciplines throughout.

At the end of the execution stage, the organization should begin to see improvements in the delivery of its information systems projects. It should also see some of the worst excesses of the culture gap and information politics reduced. The changes to the technological infrastructure, particularly those related to the introduction of the information life cycle, should alleviate the problems of information overload, poor data integrity, and the productivity paradox.

The remainder of this chapter looks at each of these stages in more detail. It should be noted, however, that this optimization process is directed at the organization only. Wider issues, such as those associated with changes to the legal and education systems, are largely outside the direct control of most organizations. These need to be taken up by professional bodies such as the British Computer Society, or the Association of Computer Machinery in the United States, as they are more likely to have the lobbying power required to stimulate the debate necessary to make changes in these areas.

PREPARATION

The key focus of the preparation stage is to make an assessment of the specific problems faced by the organization and understand their severity. Clearly, with Part I of this book already providing sufficient information on which to base any analysis, there is little point in repeating it here. However, in order to facilitate the assessment, it is a good idea to summarize each of the key issues, together with their relevance to, and impact on, the organization. Table 17.1 has been completed for one of the organizations involved

with my initial research,[3] and is not therefore indicative of all organizations; this assessment must be organizationally specific to be of value. The assumption that 'one size fits all' is wrong, and it is clear from the classic advice discussed in Chapter 2 that generalizations are ineffective at resolving the problems with information systems projects.

When assessing an issue's impact, it is advisable to review it across a number of dimensions (see Table 17.2). This allows the full extent of its impact on the organization to be established, and serves to extend the assessment beyond the typically narrow project view.

When considering the impacts, a combination of hard and soft data would be needed to support the assessment. In this instance, hard data would include statistical information around project outcome (for example, percentage of projects that fail, and typical overruns as a percentage of project schedule), as well as financial data (for example, average return on investment and average project costs). Soft data will include people's perceptions about IT and IT staff, general beliefs about the effectiveness and applicability of technology and so on. This information also serves to describe the current environment in detail, which is important when considering the benefits of the optimization process.

The purpose of Table 17.1 is therefore to articulate the size of the problem the organization has with its information systems projects and IT in general, but more importantly, how severe these impacts are. This will probably be the first time the organization has understood the full scale of its IT problems since, in the past, it will have only ever tackled these on a piecemeal basis by reacting to events. As well as assessing the impact of specific issues on the organization, this summary has a number of additional uses:

1. It provides the basis for setting the performance targets of the optimized environment.
2. It helps to frame some of the critical success factors of the programme and the principal benefits of optimization.

Table 17.1 Issue applicability and severity summary

Issue	Applicable	Impact		
		Minor	Moderate	Severe
late delivery of information systems projects	✓		✓	
failure of information systems projects	✓		✓	
effectiveness of project management	✗			
inappropriate investment appraisal processes	✓	✓		
poor return on IT investments	✓			✓
limited or no benefits tracking	✓			✓
productivity issues with IT staff	✓		✓	
business productivity issues (related to the use of IT)	✓			✓
culture gap between the business and IT	✓			✓
culture gap between board level directors	✓		✓	
techno-illiteracy of non-IT staff	✓		✓	
business illiteracy of IT staff	✓			✓
information politics	✗			
no information strategy	✓	✓		
over-commitment within projects	✓			✓
limited learning from failure	✓	✓		
limited, or inappropriate, accountability mechanisms	✓		✓	
acceptance of management fads	✓		✓	
acceptance of silver bullet solutions	✓			✓

3. It provides a baseline against which the results of the optimization process can be compared.
4. It forms a baseline against which the benefits can be tracked.
5. It feeds into the incubation stage by providing a clear description of how issues manifest themselves within the organization.
6. It highlights those areas that are causing the most problems to the organization, and hence provides the basis for prioritizing the project work required to resolve them.

INCUBATION

The incubation stage is all about deriving solutions to the individual problems. Part II of this book has highlighted a number of approaches that can be used to resolve each of the issues, and these, along with any others, should be assessed for their applicability. Whilst deriving the solutions, other options should be considered, for example:

● the application of software improvement techniques such as the Capability Maturity Model to enhance the general quality and repeatability of information systems projects;
● modelling the success of other organizations who are largely unaffected by the issues or who have resolved them; and
● engaging professional services organizations who are able to provide

Table 17.2   Example impact definitions

Impact dimension	Minor	Moderate	Severe
Financial	Limited bottom-line impact. Some costs will be incurred but these are not considered to be excessive and can be covered by existing operational budgets. Little, if any, impact on revenue streams, as customer needs can still be satisfied.	Moderate financial impact. Costs will be incurred, and these may break existing operational budgets. Sufficient organizational funds are available to cover any shortfall. Moderate impact on revenue as the ability to maintain levels of customer service deteriorates.	Significant bottom-line impact. Additional costs will be incurred due to loss of operational efficiency. Revenue streams are likely to be severely impacted as the ability to conduct business transactions degrades.
Operational efficiency (internal)	Considered a minor disturbance. Will not impact day-to-day activity to any great extent.	Medium level of disruption. Level of downtime will lead to some backlogs, but these can be reduced through overtime.	Operationally, a disaster. Inability to conduct day-to-day activities because of excessive issues that need to be addressed. Likely to have major cross-functional and customer impact.
Customer service	Negligible impact on customers. Any fallout can be managed on a contingent – case by case – basis. Unlikely to have a significant impact on customer perception.	10–20% of customers impacted. Inability to service customer needs correctly, and backlog of complaints likely to cause some concern. Problems can be managed by existing staff, although some loss of customer confidence is inevitable.	In excess of 20% of customers impacted. Very difficult to maintain levels of customer service – level of complaints very high. Additional staff may be needed to cope with backlogs. Loss of confidence is quite high, and a public relations exercise may be required to address the risks and settle customer concerns.
Project delivery	Limited impact on the project. May cause minor problems, but these would not result in any significant delays in project schedule or increase in costs.	Considerable impact. Likely to cause major delays and slippage in project schedule. Costs are likely to escalate, and the project's benefits will be affected.	Severe impact. The project is likely to stall and fail to hit major milestones. Costs will spiral, and the danger of de-scoping and failure are very real without immediate action.

specific expertise, including training agencies; professional bodies, such as the British Computer Society, or the Association of Computer Machinery in the United States; niche consultancies, such as those offering advice on investment appraisal techniques or benefits realization processes, and, in particular, institutions like the West London Institute who may help in the removal of the culture gap.

When choosing individual solutions, it is essential that they are both achievable and workable within the organizational setting – accepting them at face value, or not assessing them in enough detail, could lead to their failure during the execution stage. It is advisable, therefore, to assess their applicability against a solid understanding of the individual issues (established during the preparation stage) and rank them against the following criteria:

- the ability to solve the problem – not at all, partially, or comprehensively?
- the ability of the organization to deliver the solution – training required, or skills present?
- the need for third party involvement – yes or no?
- the capability of the third party to deliver the solution – limited capability, strong capability with supporting evidence?
- the speed of implementation – slow, moderate or rapid?
- the level of cross-functional involvement required to complete the work – less than two functions or greater than three?

These criteria can allude to the solution's validity, viability and associated implementation risk. When ranking solutions, a simple scoring mechanism should be introduced based upon the criteria above. For example, if the speed of impact is slow, it should be assigned a value of 1, if moderate, 2, and if rapid, 3. Similar scoring mechanisms can be applied to each of the criteria, and in this way it should be possible to order the solutions based on their individual scores. Intuitively, those solutions with the highest scores should be adopted, although further judgement will need to be applied when making the final decision.

Once the individual solutions have been selected, the next step is to link these together to form the basis of the project activity. The simplest way to achieve this is to derive top-level categories which are impacted by the solutions. Table 17.3 gives one such categorization, based on the typology of people, process and technology – itself a fairly common and effective way of assessing the impacts of change. When considering how each of the categories are impacted, it is worth taking a broad view: when addressing information politics, for example, there are likely to be impacts in all three categories because of the need to enhance the IT infrastructure, change and introduce new process, and re-educate and realign people to the federal model of information management discussed in Chapter 13. In the example illustrated in Table 17.3, the solutions are high

level and generic, but are sufficient to illustrate the concept. It should be clear from this summary that the majority of the solutions fall into the 'process' and 'people' categories, as this is where the problems associated with information systems projects predominately lie.

Having derived the solution set and tied these together, the next stage of the optimization process is illumination.

ILLUMINATION

Activity within this stage is directed at the creation of the blueprint designed to optimize the project environment. Like other blueprints, this should describe the environment in some detail, and in this case can be achieved by using the outcome of the incubation stage as the starting point. Continuing with the people, process and technology theme, it is possible to describe the blueprint, as the following examples illustrate.

Process blueprint

- An investment appraisal process capable of fully assessing the costs and benefits of all information systems and IT investments will be introduced. This will entail linking the appraisal mechanism to the type of investment, conducting a sensitivity analysis around project outcome, and monitoring the business case as the project progresses.
- An information life cycle will be introduced in which the value of information can be assessed on an ongoing basis. Where information is not adding value to the organization's activities, it will, along with the information systems that support it, be retired.
- A robust benefits realization process will be introduced that links project deliverables to their benefits and this will include assigning accountabilities for the realization of the benefits within both the project team and the operational line. In addition, benefits will be tracked until such time as they have been fully realized, and the results will be used to update the investment appraisal process.

Table 17.3   Categorizing solutions

Solution	Impact		
	Process	People	Technology
implement robust project appraisal processes	✓	✓	
implement a robust benefits realization process	✓	✓	✓
develop productivity measures linked to technology	✓		✓
resolve the culture gap at board level		✓	
resolve the culture gap at working level		✓	
provide company-wide technology briefings	✓	✓	
provide business briefings for IT staff	✓	✓	
implement the federal model of information management	✓	✓	✓
develop tools to assess escalation and over-commitment	✓	✓	
establish feedback mechanisms within and across projects	✓	✓	
establish an objective accountability mechanism for assessing failed projects		✓	
develop thorough assessment processes for all new IT methods and tools	✓		

People blueprint

- IT staff will have the opportunity to enhance their business understanding through the provision of business-related training. In addition, career routes which provide IT staff with the opportunity to cross over to the business domain will be offered. For those staff who wish to remain in a technical discipline, a suitable career ladder will be made available that links their breadth of technical understanding to seniority and remuneration.

- Business people will be given regular technology briefings in which the full extent of the technology (including the benefits, costs, risks and organizational implications) will be explored. A balanced view of technology will be established and maintained – techno-illiteracy and techno-worship will be eliminated.

- Project staff will be given every opportunity to raise concerns they may have with their projects, especially when they consider them to be suffering from escalating commitment. In addition, when projects fail, every effort will be made to learn from the experience rather than indiscriminately blaming others for the failure.

- Information sharing will be actively promoted and those who exhibit these behaviours will be rewarded. Where people fail to share information and knowledge, suitable sanctions will be applied – information politics will not be tolerated. To facilitate the effective management and sharing of information, every employee will have suitable objectives set as part of their annual appraisal.

Technology blueprint

- The IT infrastructure will be based around information need, with the information value cell and associated information life cycle forming the hub. New systems will be implemented that are capable of supporting the rapid dissemination and application of information to support organizational, as well as functional, needs. Systems that are not capable of supporting this will be retired.

- Systems capable of measuring the benefits derived from information technology will be introduced. In addition, desktop solutions to support project and benefit tracking will be made available to all project managers. Where information systems are not improving the productivity of operational staff, they will be investigated and either enhanced or retired.
- The implications of the introduction of a new information system will be fully explored prior to its development. This will involve assessing its impacts on the working environment in its widest sense, including job design, work organization, team working and so on. Technological solutions that can add value to the operational staff will be favoured over those that relegate them to machine minders.

These blueprint statements can be used to link the specific problems and solutions together and, more importantly, the projects designed to optimize the environment. Figure 17.2 shows this relationship at its highest level.

EXECUTION

The final part of the optimization process is the execution stage. This is all about planning and executing the programme of work required to implement the blueprint designed under the illumination stage. Although the sequencing of the various activities will depend upon the individual organizational circumstances and choice of solution, a number of these will be the same no matter what solution is chosen. As a starting point for this process, Table 17.4 highlights some of these activities and identifies the project stream (people, process, technology) that would be responsible for its execution. The remainder of the work involves the execution of the programme itself and, as stated many times in this book, I will not go into the detail of how to run a programme – it is assumed that the organization will appoint an appropriately qualified individual to complete the task.

Optimizing the environment in which information systems projects are delivered is imperative if organizations are to achieve repeatable project success. As the quote at the beginning of this chapter suggests, the problems that we face are of our own making, and we hold the key to their resolution. Following an optimization process in which the problems with IT are solved collectively will yield results. But it requires organizations to make the necessary effort and, just as importantly, it needs the principal players to change their attitudes. This is the subject of this book's penultimate chapter.

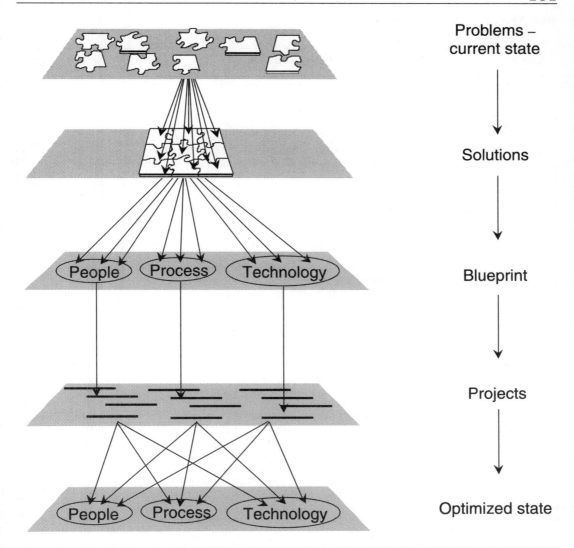

Figure 17.2 Linking the future state to the current state

Table 17.4   Principal project activities

Aspect	Primary activities	Project stream
Mastering the basics	• widen the project appraisal mechanism to include a sensitivity to project outcome	Process
	• develop robust project management selection and training processes	Process
	• implement project management tracking tools and processes, including a standardized reporting mechanism	Technology
	• implement a metrics gathering and dissemination process capable of capturing information about projects, including estimates, costs, benefits and resourcing	Process
Investment and benefits	• establish a rigorous challenge process for all IT investments	Process
	• develop a benefits realization process and roll out across the entire organization	Process
	• establish a link between people's objectives and the realization of project benefits	People
Culture gaps	• assess the scale and severity of the culture gap	People
	• establish target models for the working-level and board-level culture gaps	People
	• implement immediate and ongoing solutions to close the culture gap (aiming for the proactive, or integrated state)	Process
	• develop processes to eliminate the level of business illiteracy in IT staff, and IT illiteracy in business staff	People
	• establish links to education establishments and research institutions as a way of keeping abreast of changes in IT	Process
Information politics	• establish the information value cell	People
	• implement the information life cycle	People
	• assess the current information political landscape and create short-term solutions to counter its worst excesses	People
	• develop an IT architecture to support the federal model of information management	Technology
	• implement the new IT architecture, including retiring of systems that no longer support the information requirements of the business	Technology
	• establish data integrity levels covering currency, accuracy and availability, and link this into the information life cycle and information value cell	Process
	• establish processes for the retirement of information no longer required by the business	Process
	• create links between people's objectives and information sharing	People
Over-commitment	• implement project health checks that can fully ascertain the ability of projects to deliver	Process
	• establish and implement mechanisms for assessing the degree of over-commitment within large projects	Process
	• establish communication channels beyond the immediate project to allow concerns about escalation to be aired and assessed objectively	People
Accountability	• review and revise contract management processes for third-party software suppliers	Process
	• institute an internal contract management process for in-house system development projects	Process
	• establish an objective accountability assessment mechanism for internally executed projects	Process
	• establish an objective accountability assessment mechanism for third-party projects, as a first step in any contractual dispute	Process
	• educate internal project managers in the basics of computer law	Process
Silver bullets	• introduce a robust process for assessing new IT methods, tools and techniques	Process

CHAPTER EIGHTEEN

Changing attitudes towards IT and information systems projects

Biting the silver bullet means taking concerted action to make an organization's relationship with IT, and information systems projects, a healthy and productive one. Part II and Chapter 17 have highlighted these actions in some detail, and it is essential for organizations to consider these very carefully when deciding how they will tackle their own set of problems.

But, actions on their own are insufficient to create a long-lasting improvement, as it is necessary for those involved with the process to change some of their attitudes towards technology, information systems, and each other. Changing beliefs about IT and information systems will not be easy for some, because the legacy of poor performance, low return on investment, and failure have ingrained their beliefs about the inability of IT to deliver. However, without an acceptance that to achieve a successful information system project requires all of the key parties to have the right attitudes towards it, long-lasting success may be impossible. So after all the research I have conducted into why information systems projects fail, what advice can I give the principal players? I think the following.

ADVICE FOR THE CHIEF EXECUTIVE AND THE BOARD

- Don't abdicate responsibility for IT to the technologists. With the success of the organization increasingly dependent on IT and information systems, it is irresponsible to ignore the consequences by burying your head in the sand and believing that it has nothing to do with you. With 73 per cent of directors believing IT is of little strategic value,[1] it might be prudent to be one of those who believes it is. IT is here to stay, and it should be seen as a long-term enabler, rather than a short-term fix to business problems.

- Before you invest in any major information systems project, or one that involves a significant IT component, challenge the business case. If you are uncomfortable with it, ask that it be revisited. You should only bet your company on those projects that are realistic in their objectives and realistic in their outcomes.

- If you don't have time to investigate the viability of an information systems project, employ an independent person who can.

- At the time of the business case, consider the implications on the organization of late delivery and failure. In doing so you will automatically consider the risks.

- Before you embark on any major information systems project, ask yourself this one question: is the environment in which this project is going to be executed conducive to success? If it is not, then it is your job to ensure it is. If it is, ensure it stays that way.

- Take an active interest in the costs of your major IT projects, especially the benefits. Don't take benefit claims at face value, demand concrete reasoning to justify them, and ask that the impacts of any slippage and change in the projects are reflected in the benefits case. This will help to make any decisions about termination easier and avoid the temptation of believing in jam tomorrow.

- Be prepared to pull the plug on a project that is spiralling out of control. It doesn't matter if it is an internally or externally run project, the outcome will still be the same: failure. It is far better to terminate it early, when you still have some money left to finance other projects.

- Embrace technology and take the trouble to gain a basic understanding of some of its upsides and downsides. The technologists and salespeople only ever talk in upsides. Recognizing there are downsides adds balance and allows you to challenge the technologists rather than accepting what they have to say at face value. This should force the technologists to be more realistic in their claims.
- Don't believe that any problem can be solved by technology alone – most cannot.
- Take with a healthy pinch of salt any claims that suggest a new technology will radically improve your organization's prospects. Many are unfounded, unjustifiable and lead to disappointment.
- Introduce real accountability for the success of information systems projects, and make this effective across the whole organization, including the board. This means being prepared to implement sanctions where project personnel have deliberately lied about the status of their project, and where third-party suppliers have kept progress hidden from view. Unprofessional behaviour should be penalized, not accepted.
- Accept that some projects will inevitably fail and, when they do, learn from them. Do not react by blaming, sanitizing or forgetting. But when there is a need for accountability, enforce it.
- Expect the best of your project managers, and don't compromise. Project management is a crucial element to any project, particularly an information systems project. Make sure your project managers are suitably trained to meet the challenge. And, if you use third parties, make sure they are too.
- Don't always believe the advice of the experts, and if you consider their advice to be suspect, then you are probably right.

ADVICE FOR THE CHIEF INFORMATION OFFICER/IT DIRECTOR

- Refuse to become the whipping boy for every technology ill that befalls the organization. Your job is to steer the organization through the turbulent technological times ahead.
- Demystify technology for the rest of the board, and make them aware that technology can be of benefit to the organization, but can also create problems.
- Make the board aware of the impacts of IT dependency, and make them aware of their role in ensuring the application of technology is successful in their organization.
- Be brutally honest about the costs and benefits of major information systems projects. Try to avoid window-dressing and double-vision techniques that will enable projects to gain approval. If a project cannot be properly justified, then it may not prove to be beneficial to the firm.
- Take the time to really understand other parts of the business. Taking a genuine interest in the other key disciplines within the organization can only improve your credibility amongst your fellow board members. As the impacts of technology within the economy continue to rise, the criticality of your role will increase. Don't believe that CIO translates to 'career is over'. Instead use your combined business and technology understanding to guide the organization.
- Don't be lured into the leading edge. Just because you are perceived to be a technical expert, don't fall into the trap of hyping the benefits of the latest technology. One of the key skills you bring to the board is your ability to assess technology and provide a balanced argument as to its acceptance or rejection within the organization. Use it.
- Ensure that IT in its entirety is aligned to the organization's objectives and that it is sufficiently flexible to change as the organization changes.
- Ensure the organization's information is current, relevant and accessible. Information in all its constituent forms is essential for the smooth running of the firm. One of your jobs is to ensure the underlying technology is supportive of information

needs, and sufficiently flexible to change as the information needs change.

- In these turbulent times, the ability to apply technology successfully is critical to the organization. Use your skill, knowledge and judgement to ensure the organization uses IT wisely and profitably.

ADVICE FOR THE INFORMATION SYSTEMS PROJECT MANAGER

- Commit to applying best-practice project management techniques throughout the project. Getting the basics right will go a long way to achieving an effective outcome.
- Where historical project data exist (project size, budgeted costs, actual costs at completion, baseline schedule, actual schedule at completion, benefits achieved and so on), use these to aid in the planning of your project. Where they do not exist, start collecting them, and share them amongst the wider project community.
- Understand the dynamics of large projects, particularly escalation and over-commitment. If you can see the warning signs in yourself, then you will be able to see them in others.
- When a project is escalating out of control, do something about it before it is too late.
- Don't pay lip-service to user involvement, and ensure your communication skills are up to par.
- When discussing the merits of a new system with the business, avoid using technical jargon. Put yourself in the business professional's shoes and talk in his language.
- Make the project's progress visible and easy to interpret. Make reporting simple and focused; there should be only four things management should need to know about your project: have you completed what you said you would when you would, have you spent what you expected to spend, will you complete the project on time and to budget, and will it provide the organization with the benefits promised in the business case? Where the answer to any of these questions

is 'no', provide additional information and highlight the impacts.

- When progress has deviated from the plan, understand why this is the case. If it is a random problem, make sure it does not happen again. If it is a systematic problem, revisit the plan. But whatever you do, make sure the slippage is visible and its impacts known.
- Never believe that you and the project team can make up for lost time. Once time is lost, it is lost, and project heroics do no one any favours in the long run. Project heroics reduce productivity, and increase the likelihood of errors.
- Be honest if the project is going off the rails. Honesty early on can allow most situations to be rectified, and provide sufficient time to consider the alternatives.
- use the five project outcomes as a visibility tool, that is:

  * The project runs to time, budget and delivers all that is expected of it.
  * The project is late/over budget but delivers all that is expected of it.
  * The project is on time and to budget but has been de-scoped to meet these two constraints.
  * The project is late/over budget and delivers a reduced functionality.
  * The project fails.

Assess the probability of each of these outcomes at regular intervals and use it as an additional tool to manage and report on the project.

- Recognize that politics within information systems projects includes the dimension of information. With less opportunity for the attainment of positional and status power, people will look to information as a source of power. Being able to broker between opposing camps will be an important skill in the future. Therefore understand the principles of win–win negotiations.
- Ensure that adequate time is given to testing the software. If the schedule is slipping, do not compress the time allocated to testing.

Failing to test software thoroughly can have major, and very expensive, implications.

- Where unrealistic pressure is being brought to bear on the project, use the enhanced business case (see Chapter 12) to remind the board of the consequences of such pressure.
- Track the benefits of the project meticulously both during the project, and once completed. You may not believe this is part of your job, but it is, and its success is down to your ability to work with the business line to help them understand their role in delivering the benefits.
- Ensure you have the correct mix of technical and business skills within the project team, and consider the team's capabilities when drawing together the plan and making the estimates.
- Always ensure the team are aware of the bigger picture and keep them up to date with the overall status of the project.

ADVICE FOR THE BUSINESS USER

- Avoid confrontation with the technologists. Recognize, that, just like you, they have their own set of tensions to manage. In many cases they are trying their best – you should too.
- Take an active interest in all projects that will impact you and your colleagues. Don't abdicate your responsibility for the success of the project to the technologists – success of the project is dependent on your involvement as much as theirs.
- Don't just complain about the poor performance of information systems: work with the technologists to improve them.
- Take an active interest in technology, not for technology's sake, but rather to understand what its implications might be on the function or business in which you work.
- Play an active role in realizing the benefits. Take the trouble to understand the impacts the information system will have once

implemented and ensure you are adequately prepared.

ADVICE FOR THE IT EXPERT (SOFTWARE DEVELOPER, ANALYST)

- Avoid confrontation with the business users. Recognize, that, just like you, they have their own set of tensions to manage. In many cases they are trying their best – you should too.
- Apply your craft with professionalism. Professionalism means, amongst other things, taking the time to understand the business in which you work, not just the technology.
- Never assume that you know more than the end user does about their job. When determining how a job can be improved through computerization, ask the users whether the improvement would be of benefit. In many cases, they may have already considered the same idea and rejected it.
- When developing systems, always engage the subject matter experts within the business departments in which the systems will be implemented and use them as a basis for establishing sound business requirements.
- Commit to producing excellent documentation.
- Try to avoid making the software overly complex – where possible, see how it can be simplified.
- Help the business community to understand how technology can assist them.

Subscribing to the principles outlined above should go hand in hand with the specific changes discussed in this book, and in my mind are essential if the organization is to achieve what it really wants from its information systems. I commend all of them to you.

The bottom line

In less than forty years, we have gone from manual methods of controlling our lives and civilization to becoming totally dependent on the continued operation of our computers. Many people are comforted by the fact that we still have our hand on the 'plug', that we can turn our computers off if they get too uppity. In actuality, it's the computers that have their figurative hands on our plug.[1]

As we enter the next century, it is worth reflecting on how information technology has changed our working lives since its birth shortly after the Second World War.

- We have seen a remarkable shift in the importance of IT over the last fifty years. In the early 1950s, IT played an insignificant, back-office role in organizations, focusing on repetitive financial accounting and payroll activities. Contrast this with the 1990s, where IT plays such a significant role that many organizations cannot survive without it, and an increasing number of people are dependent on it for the smooth operation of their working lives. For example, in October 1993, the United States Census Bureau assessed the level to which people were reliant on computers in the execution of their work. They found that almost 46 per cent of all American workers used a computer at work.[2] Six years on, and with the increasing significance of electronic commerce, this percentage is probably much higher.

- The amount of computing power available on the average desktop is 25 million times greater than it was in 1948. This power is likely to increase by many billions when the scientific community break through the constraints imposed by the silicon chip.

- Computer software has proliferated to such an extent that there is a software tool for almost every business need.

- Organizations have become dependent on software to process an ever increasing amount of data and to cope with the significance of a globalized economy. This increasing dependence means that many organizations, and especially those within the financial sector, could not survive long without their computer systems. In some instances, because of the volume of transactions, this survival can be only a matter of days. Even for those organizations that can be considered less dependent on information systems, the survival time is still quite limited – even back in 1980, this was put at 101–102 days.[3]

- The volume of information available to the average person is incredible. With the explosive growth of the Internet, this volume is increasing daily, and with it comes the problems of information overload and poor data integrity.

- The complexity of the information systems has increased markedly. Organizations no longer have to contend with just systems, they are increasingly having to cope with systems within systems.

This massive change has not been without its problems, many of which still persist today:

- Very few information systems projects succeed. We are still witnessing high levels of failure and wastage. Although investment trends are rising, the level of failure has remained static, pointing to an increasing, not decreasing problem.

- Organizations are still grappling with the impacts that IT is having on the way they conduct their business. The speed of technological change, which is outstripping the organization's ability to cope with it, represents a major challenge, and one which can only be resolved through the appropriate and considered application of information technology.

- The culture gap between technologists and business people remains as solid as ever and represents a major barrier to success.
- Boards of directors fail to understand the role of IT in their business, and in many cases are frightened by its power to transform their companies.

The bottom line is that IT-enabled change will continue unabated, and this will have a profound effect on our working and personal lives. One only needs to look at the increasing number of books that discuss these impacts. For example, here are a small number of recent titles: *The Death of Distance, Going Digital, New Rules for the New Economy, Blur, Future Revolution, The Digital Economy, Faster*. Each is very similar to the others in that they expound the underlying theme that technology is changing everything, old rules no longer apply, and the speed of change is increasing. There is no doubt that every advance in the computer chip will bring more power and with it the ability to produce more complex software capable of automating another piece of business activity. Because organizations have to manage the tensions that are created by this technological change, they see information technology as the only way to cope. As a consequence, a greater number of organizations will become dependent on IT for their smooth and efficient running.

If we accept this continuous technological change as given, then it would be very wise to be smart in its application. Being smart means understanding why information systems projects fail, why benefit returns are poor, why the relationship between business and IT is troublesome, why large projects spiral out of control, why there is no real accountability for poor software, and why organizations adopt short-term solutions only to see them fail. Being smarter still means comprehensively tackling these issues and biting the silver bullet. But we must recognize that there will still be failures, and as long as we learn from them, then their number and frequency will reduce. In this way, organizations will be more capable of harnessing IT more effectively.

This book has provided chief executive officers, chief information officers/IT directors, business professionals and IT professionals alike with enough of a head start to take action to resolve these issues. But, with the increasing significance of IT and information systems, there is no time to stand on the sidelines – it is time for action and commitment. In the words of US statesman and Republican President Theodore Roosevelt (1858–1919):

> It is not the critic who counts, nor the man who points out how the strong man stumbled or where the doer of deeds could have done better. The credit belongs to the man who is actually in the arena; whose face is marred by dust and sweat and blood; who strives valiantly; who errs and comes up short again and again; who knows the great enthusiasms, the great devotions, and spends himself in a worthy cause; who at the best knows in the end triumph of high achievement; and who at worst, if he fails while daring greatly; so that his place shall never be with those cold and timid souls who know neither defeat or victory.

Seize the day, take action and turn failure into success. Bite the silver bullet.

Epilogue

As organizations wake up to the need to address their increasing problems with IT and information systems projects, it is vital that knowledge is shared and best practice transferred. It is also essential that as new problems arise, they are aired, and appropriate solutions developed and adopted. In this way, organizations will be able to enhance their capability in delivering information systems projects, but more importantly maintain it.

With advances in technology becoming more wide ranging, the future is as uncertain as ever. Key to survival is ensuring organizations are in a position to harness this and future technologies competently. To do so means biting the silver bullet, and to aid in this process, I have created a website where organizations can:

- find out about the latest ideas and solutions to the problems identified within this book;
- raise new issues, and co-develop solutions that are capable of resolving them;
- involve themselves in discussions about the problems that IT presents, and issues with their information systems;
- share case studies and swap ideas with other organizations; and
- get in contact with other organizations who are able to help improve their capability in managing an increasingly complex web of technology.

I invite you all to participate and help to make information systems project failure a thing of the past. Visit the website:

http://www.bitingthesilverbullet.co.uk

Notes

INTRODUCTION

1. Coombs, R. (1993), Organisational Politics and the strategic use of information technology, Programme for Information and Communication Technology, Brunel University.
2. Forester T., and Morrison, P. (1994), *Computer Ethics*, London: MIT Press, p. 107.
3. International Data Corporation, quoted in *Computing*, 'Global Innovators' Series, April 1997, p. 7.
4. Foremski, T. (1999), 'Technology spending set to surge when crisis wanes', *FT-IT Review*, 3 November, p. 11.

PART I: THE PROBLEM WITH INFORMATION SYSTEMS PROJECTS

1. Lyytinen, K. (1987) 'A taxonomic perspective of information systems development: theoretical constructs and recommendations', in Borland, R.J., and Hirschheim, R.A. (eds), *Critical Issues in Information Systems Research*, Chichester: John Wiley & Sons.
2. Tenner, E. (1996), *Why Things Bite Back: New Technology and the Revenge Effect*, London: Fourth Estate.

CHAPTER 1 – A FIFTY-YEAR CONTEXT

1. For a fuller description of the impacts which IT has had on the organization over the last forty years, see Somogyi, E.K., and Galliers, R.D. (1987), 'From Data Processing to Strategic Information Systems – A Historical Perspective', *Journal of Information Technology*, March.
2. '50 Years of Computing', *Computer Consultant*, November 1998, p. 27.
3. Kurzweil, R. (1999), *The Age of Spiritual Machines*, London: Phoenix, p. 130.

4. Saren, C. (1999), 'Beginning of the end for the silicon chip', *Computer Weekly*, 22 July, p. 3.
5. 1993 figure: *Price Waterhouse Technology Review*, 1992/93. 1999 figure: 'The Big Spenders', *Information and Strategy*, December 1998/1999.
6. Gibbs, W.W. (1997), 'Taking Computers to Task', *Scientific American*, July, p. 70.
7. Nolan, R.L. (1979), 'Managing the crisis in data processing', *Harvard Business Review*, March–April.
8. Gibbs, W.W. (1994), 'Software's Chronic Crisis', *Scientific American*, September, p. 76. For a fuller description of the Capability Maturity Model see Zahran, S. (1994), 'The software process – what it is, and how to improve it', in Ross, M. et al. (eds) (1994), *Software Quality Management II* – Vol. 1, 'Managing Quality Systems', Computational Mechanics Publications. Herbsleb, J. et al. (1994), 'Benefits of CMM-based software process improvement: Initial results', Technical report CMU/SEI-94-TR-13, Software Engineering Institute, Carnegie Mellon University, Pittsburgh, Pennsylvania.
9. Gibbs, W. W. (1994), 'Software's Chronic Crisis', *Scientific American*, September, pp. 72–81.

CHAPTER 2 – WHAT HAVE WE LEARNT FROM FAILURE SO FAR?

1. Camier, D.T. (1958) '… And how to avoid them', *Computer Journal*, **1** (1).
2. DeMarco, T. (1982), *Controlling Software Projects*, Southampton and Boston Massachusetts: New Yourden Press.
3. Gladden, G.R. (1982), 'Stop the life cycle I want to get off', *Software Engineering Notes*, **7** (2), pp. 35–59.
4. Charette, R.N. (1989), *Software Engineering Risk Analysis and Measurement*, McGraw Hill.

5. Szlichcinski, K. and Howarth, C. (1994), *Understanding why Systems Fail to Deliver*, London: Pagoda.

6. Gallagher, K. (1995), 'Chaos', *Proceedings of Information Technology and Project Management*, 19–20 September, pp. 21–36.

7. Clegg. C. (1996), 'Failing to Deliver: The IT Performance Gap', in *The Performance of Information Technology and the Role of Human and Organizational Factors*, OASIG, University of Sheffield.

8. *Computer World*, 24 February 1997.

9. 'IT projects failing to reach for the sky', *Computing*, 10 December 1998, p. 12.

10. IT World Consultants (1996), *Department of Trade and Industry BuyIT Guidelines*, London: ITWorld Consultants.

11. Pinto, J.K. (1994), *Successful information system implementation; the human side*, Upper Darby, Pennsylvania: Project Management Institute, pp. 51–89.

12. For a detailed analysis of the failure of the London Ambulance Automated Dispatch System see Flowers, S. (1996), *Software Failure: Management Failure*, New York: John Wiley & Sons, pp. 47–93; Page, D., Williams, P., and Boyd, D. (1993), *Report of the Inquiry into the London Ambulance Service*, London: South West Thames Regional Health Authority, February; Beynon-Davies, R. (1995), 'IS failure and risk assessment: The case of the London ambulance service computer-aided dispatch system', in *Proceedings of Third European Conference on information systems*, Greece, 3–5 June, Vol. II, pp. 1153–1170.

13. Oz, E. (1994), 'When professional standards are lax: The CONFIRM failure and its lessons', *Communications of the ACM*, **37** (10).

14. See Kennedy, S. (1992), 'What went wrong with CS90', MIS May; and Coleman, S. (1992), 'CS90: Could have cost $10 million?', *Computer Weekly*, 20 September.

CHAPTER 4 – HIGH INVESTMENT BUT LOW RETURN

1. *Information Strategy*, December 1998/January 1999, pp. 34–35.

2. Ibid., p. 30.

3. 'IT and telecoms show sustained growth for year', *Computer Consultant*, 2–15 April 1999, p. 19.

4. Ibid.

5. Foremski, T. (1999), 'Technology spending set to surge when crisis wanes', *FT-IT Review*, 3 November, p. 11.

6. Gibbs, W.W. (1997), 'Taking Computers to Task', *Scientific American*, July, p. 64.

7. Gallagher, K, (1995), 'Chaos', *Proceedings of Information Technology and Project Management*, 19–20 September, p. 26.

8. Quoted from Wiener, L.R. (1994), *Digital Woes: why we should not depend on software*, Harlow, Essex: Addison-Wesley, p. 70.

9. Quoted from Lucas, H.C.J. (1999), *Information technology and the productivity paradox: Assessing the value of investing in IT*, New York: Oxford University Press, p. 30.

10. Franz, D. (1996), 'B of A Plans for Computer Don't Add Up', in Kling, R. (ed.), *Computerization and controversy* (2nd edn), London: Academic Press.

11. For a full description of the Operational Strategy project failure, see Collins, T. and Bicknell, D. (1997), *Crash: ten easy ways to avoid a computer disaster*, London: Simon & Schuster, pp.195–205.

12. Bicknell, D. (1999), 'High cost of IT leadership crisis', *Computer Weekly*, 19 August, p. 19.

13. For a description of the project, see Flowers, S. (1996), *Software Failure: Management Failure*, New York: John Wiley & Sons, pp. 143–47.

14. Collins, T., (1999), 'Lessons not learnt from last passport disaster', *Computer Weekly*, 8 July, p. 10.

15. Comptroller and Auditor General (1999), *The passport delays of Summer 1999*, London: National Audit Office, October.

16. Timmins, N. (1999), 'An Explosive Mixture', *Financial Times*, 22 July.

17. Pike, A. (1999), 'Post Office heading for £200 million full year loss', *Financial Times*, 1 December, p. 2.

18. Farbey, B., Land, F. and Targett, D. (1993), *How to Assess your IT Investment – A Study of Methods and Practice*, Oxford: Butterworth Heinemann, p. 7.

19. Grindley, K. (1991), *Managing IT at Board Level: The Hidden Agenda Exposed*, UK: Longman.

20. Price Waterhouse (1993), *Information technology review 1992/93*, pp. 24–26.

21. Humphrey, W.S., Snyder, T.R. and Willis, R.R. (1991), 'Software process improvement at Hughes Aircraft', *IEEE Software*, July, pp. 11–23. For other examples, see Herbsleb, J. et al. (1994), 'Benefits of CMM-based software process improvement: Initial results', Technical report CMU/SEI-94-TR-13, Software Engineering Institute, Carnegie Mellon University, Pittsburgh, Pennsylvania.

22. For an outline of some of the specific problems relating to the introduction of software process maturity, see Thompson, K. and McParland, P. (1993), 'Software process maturity (SPM) and the information systems developer', *Information and Software Technology*, **35** (6/7), June/July.

23. For some detailed discussions on the productivity paradox, see Attewell, P. (1996), 'Information Technology and the Productivity Challenge', in Kling, R. (ed.), *Computerization and Controversy* (2nd edn), London: Academic Press.

24. King, J.L. (1996), 'Where are the payoffs from computerisation? Technology, learning and organisational change', in Kling, R. (ed.), *Computerization and Controversy* (2nd edn), London: Academic Press, p. 240.

25. Landauer, K.L. (1995), *The Trouble with Computers: Usefulness, Usability, and Productivity*, Cambridge, Massachusetts: MIT Press, pp. 45.

26. Quoted in Gibbs, W.W., (1997) 'Taking Computers to Task', *Scientific American*, July, p. 68.

27. Ibid., p. 70.

28. Ibid., p. 70.

29. Quoted in Forester, T. and Morrison, P. (1994), *Computer Ethics*, London: MIT Press, p. 106.

30. 'Firms struggle with the Net', *Computer Weekly*, 1 July 1999.

31. Quoted in Forester, T. and Morrison, P. (1994), *Computer Ethics*, London: MIT Press, p. 107.

32. Collins, T. (1999), 'Nirs2: an IT success or failure?', *Computer Weekly*, 4 February, pp. 16–17. See also Timmins, N. (1999), 'MPs call new benefits computer "a shambles"', *Financial Times*, 26 January, p. 1.

33. 'IT consultants burning goodwill', *Global IT Consulting Report* (1999), November, p. 1.

34. 'Firms struggle with the Net', *Computer Weekly*, 1 July 1999.

35. Szathmary, P. (1994), 'Technology fatigue enters the mainstream', *Computing Canada*, **20** (5), 2 March.

36. Forester, T. and Morrison, P. (1994), *Computer Ethics*, London: MIT Press, p. 208.

37. Ibid., p. 209.

38. For a description of the productivity paradox and the various arguments concerning its existence, see Gibbs, W.W. (1997), 'Taking Computers to Task', *Scientific American*, July, p. 67; Landauer, K.L. (1995), *The Trouble with Computers: Usefulness, Usability, and Productivity*, Cambridge, Massachusetts: MIT Press, p. 85; and, Brynjolfsson, E., and Hitt, L., (1993) *Is Information Systems spending productive? New evidence and new results*, Center of Information Systems Research, Sloan School of Management, Massachusetts Institute of Technology.

CHAPTER 5 – BUSINESS AND IT: THEY JUST CAN'T COMMUNICATE

1. 'Why IT staff are losers with an attitude problem', Cranfield School of

Management, August, 1997, cited in *Interface*, 27 August 1997. See also 'IT staff remaining loyal to their craft but not their company', *Computer Consultant*, 19 March–1 April 1999.

2. 'Ad hoc recruitment methods blamed for IT skills shortage', *Computer Consultant*, 6–20 August 1999.

3. Whitley, E. and Darking, S. (1994), 'Information systems: social technology in social systems', unpublished paper, London School of Economics.

4. Woodruff, C.K. (1979), 'Data Processing People – Are they really different?', *Information and Management*, **3**, pp. 133–39.

5. For example, see Ferratt, T.W. and Short, L.E. (1986), 'Are Information Systems People Different: An investigation of motivational differences', *MIS Quarterly*, December, pp. 376–85.

6. Brooke, C. (1995), 'Analyst and programmer stereotypes: a self-fulfilling prophecy?', *Journal of Information Technology*, **10**, pp. 15–25.

7. 'Contractors make the most of IT boom as demand sees sharp increase in rates', *Computer Consultant*, 26 November–9 December 1999, p. 19.

8. Johnson, G. (1992), 'Talking about computers: from metaphor to jargon', *AI and Society*, **3**, pp. 263–93.

9. Stoll, C. (1996), *Silicon Snake Oil: second thoughts on the information highway*, New York: First Anchor Books.

10. Wang, C. (1994), *Technovision: The executive's survival guide to understanding and managing information technology*, New York: McGraw-Hill, pp. 31–32.

11. Rzevski, G. (1994), 'Design for Quality' (lecture notes), Open University, Milton Keynes, January.

12. Hales, M. (1991), 'A human resource approach to information systems development, the USI (information systems use) design model', *Journal of Information Technology*, **6**, pp. 152.

13. For a general introduction to systems dynamics and systems theory, see Senge, P.
(1990), *The Fifth Discipline: The Art & Practice of The Learning Organization*, London: Century Business.

14. For a full discussion on the ETHICS methodology, see Mumford, E. (1983), *Designing Human Systems*, Manchester: Manchester Business School.

15. 'Why IT staff are losers with an attitude problem', Cranfield School of Management, August, 1997, cited in *Interface*, 27 August 1997.

16. Price Waterhouse (1993), *Information technology review 1992/93*, pp. 24–26.

CHAPTER 6 – INFORMATION POLITICS: THE NEW ORGANIZATIONAL BATTLEGROUND

1. Machiavelli, M. (1997), *The Prince*, London: W.W. Norton.

2. Simmons, A. (1998), *Territorial Games: Understanding & Ending Turf Wars at Work*, New York: Amacom.

3. Greene, R. and Joost, L. (1998), *The 48 Laws of Power*, London: Profile Books, pp. 37–43.

4. Brown, A. (1995), *Organisational Culture*, London: Pitman Publishing, p. 128. For general discussion on change, and resistance to change, see Moss Kanter, R. (1983), *The Change Masters: Corporate Entrepreneurs at Work*, London: Routledge.

5. For some excellent discussion on the effects of economic change and downsizing on the working population, see Downs, A. (1995), *Corporate executions: The ugly truth about downsizing – how corporate greed is shattering lives, companies and communities*, New York: Amacom; Elliot, L. and Atkinson, D. (1998), *The Age of Insecurity*, London: Verso: Deal, T. and Kennedy, A. (1999), *The New Corporate Cultures: Revitalising the workplace after downsizing, mergers and reengineering*, London: Orion Business Books.

6. Rzevski, G. (1994), 'Design for Quality' (lecture notes), Open University, Milton Keynes, January.

7. 'IT consultants burning goodwill', *Global*

IT Consulting Report (1999), November, p. 1.

8. Micklethwait, J., and Wooldridge, A. (1996), *The Witch Doctors*, London: Heinemann, p. 30.

9. Ibid., p. 36.

10. Nicolle, L. (1998), 'Marooned by an island mentality', *Interface*, 4 November.

11. Fran, A. (2000), 'Staff hide skills from bad bosses', *The Times*, 7 January, p. 11.

12. Davenport, T.H., Eccles, R.G. and Prusak, L. (1992), 'Information Politics', *Sloan Management Review*, Fall, pp. 52–65.

13. 'IT chief slams suppliers as "immature"', *Computer Weekly*, 28 April 1999.

14. See Davenport, T.H., Eccles, R.G. and Prusak, L. (1992), 'Information Politics', *Sloan Management Review*, Fall; Marchland D.A. (1995), 'What is your company's information culture?', 'Mastering Management' supplement, *Financial Times*.

15. For a detailed review of the London Stock Exchange Taurus Project, see Drummond, H. (1996), *Escalation in Decision-making: The Tragedy of Taurus*, Oxford: Oxford University Press; Collins, T. and Bicknell, D. (1997), *Crash: Ten easy ways to avoid a computer disaster*, New York: Simon & Schuster, pp. 174–93.

CHAPTER 7 – OVER-COMMITMENT WITHIN INFORMATION SYSTEMS PROJECTS: WHEN FAILURE IS THE ONLY OPTION

1. Drummond, H. (1994), 'Escalation in organisational decision making, a case of recruiting an incompetent employee', *Journal of Behavioural Decision Making*, **7**, pp. 43–55.

2. Flowers, S. (1996), *Software failure: management failure*, New York: John Wiley & Sons, pp. 23–24.

3. The basic irrational behaviour types have been derived from Sutherland, S. (1992), *Irrationality: The enemy within*, London: Penguin Books.

4. Adizes, I. (1989), *Corporate Lifecycles: How*

and why corporations grow and die and what to do about it, Paramus, New Jersey: Prentice Hall, p. 69.

5. Keil, M. (1995), 'Pulling the Plug: Software Project Management and the Problem of Project Escalation', *MIS Quarterly*, December.

6. For some general background to escalation, see Drummond, H. (1996), *Escalation in Decision-making: the Tragedy of Taurus*, Oxford: Oxford University Press; Keil, M., (1995) 'Pulling the Plug: software project management and the problem of project escalation', *MIS Quarterly*, December; Keil, M. et al., (1994–95) 'Understanding runaway information technology projects: Results from an international research program based on escalation theory', *Journal of Management Information Systems*, Winter; Keil, K., Truex, D. and Mixon, R. (1995), 'The effects of sunk cost and project completion on information technology project escalation', *IEEE Transactions on Engineering Management*, **42**(4), November.

7. Newman, M., (1996), 'Determinants of commitment to information systems development: A longitudinal investigation', *MIS Quarterly*, March, p. 25.

8. Gallagher, K. (1995), 'Chaos', *Proceedings of Information Technology and Project Management*, 19–20 September, pp. 21–36.

9. Cant, L. and Evans, C. (1995), 'Commissioning of the automated baggage system at the new Denver International Airport', *Proceedings of Information Technology and Project Management*, 19–20 September, pp. 9–15.

CHAPTER 8 – WHERE IS THE ACCOUNTABILITY WHEN INFORMATION SYSTEMS PROJECTS FAIL?

1. Forester, T. and Morrison, P. (1994), *Computer Ethics*, London: MIT Press, p. 105.

2. Jacky, J. (1996), 'Safety-critical computing:

Hazards, practices, standards, and regulation', in Kling, R., *Computerization and Controversy* (2nd edn), San Diego: Academic Press, p. 775.

3.   Wiener, L.R. (1994), *Digital Woes: why we should not depend on software*, Essex: Addison-Wesley, p. 5.

4.   Collins, W.R. et al. (1994), 'How good is good enough? An ethical analysis of software construction and use', *Communications of the ACM*, January, **37** (1), p. 82.

5.   Ewusi-Mensah, K. and Przasnyski, Z. (1995), 'Learning from abandoned information systems?', *Journal of Information Technology*, **10** (1), March, pp. 3–14.

6.   Dutton, W.H. et al. (1995), 'Computer Power and Human Limits: Learning from IT and Telecommunications Disasters', Brunel University PICT Policy Research Report No. 31, February.

7.   Nissenbaum, H. (1994), 'Computing and accountability', *Communications of the ACM*, **37** (1), January.

8.   Wiener, L.R. (1994), *Digital Woes: why we should not depend on software*, Essex: Addison-Wesley, pp. 8–9.

9.   'Brief Encounter', *Sunday Business*, 21 April 1996.

10. Bicknell, D. (1996), 'Miami Blues', *Computer Weekly*, 11 January.

CHAPTER 9 – THE SILVER BULLET SYNDROME: EXPECTING THE PROBLEMS WITH INFORMATION SYSTEMS PROJECTS TO BE SOLVED BY A SINGLE-SHOT SOLUTION

1.   Brooks, F. P. (1995), The Mythical Man Month (20th anniversary edn), Essex: Addison-Wesley, p. 208.

2.   For some interesting discussion on management fads, see Micklethwait, J. and Wooldridge, A. (1996), *The Witch Doctors*, London: Heinemann; Shapiro, E. (1996), *Fad Surfing in the Boardroom: Reclaiming the courage to manage in the age of instant answers*, Oxford: Capstone. In addition, a good book that highlights the need for predictability in the execution of business is Stevenson, H. and Cruikshank, J. (1998), *Do Lunch or Be Lunch: The Power of Predictability in Creating Your Future*, Cambridge, Massachusetts: Harvard Business School Press.

3.   Clarkson, P. (1995), *Change in Organisations*, London: Whurr Publishers, pp. 27–33.

4.   Clegg, C. et al. (1996), *The performance of Information Technology and the role of human and organizational factors*, Sheffield: Institute of Work Psychology, University of Sheffield.

5.   Strom, J. (1993), 'Executives pushing IT panic button', *IT Magazine*, **25** (11), p. 42.

6.   Wiener, L. R. (1994), *Digital Woes: why we should not depend on software*, Essex: Addison-Wesley, p. 14.

7.   'IT chief slams suppliers as immature', *Computer Weekly*, 29 April 1999.

8.   'Office 2000 promises real productivity gains', *Computer Weekly*, 22 April 1999.

9.   McConnell, S. (1996), *Rapid Development: Taming Wild Software Schedules*, Redmund, Washington: Microsoft Press, p. 365.

10. For a general discussion and analysis of software development methodologies and approaches, see Avgerou, C. and Cornford, T. (1993), *Developing Information Systems: Concepts, Issues and Practice*, London: Macmillan.

11. Jones, C. (1994), *Assessment and Control of Software Risks*, Yourdon Press.

12. Martin, M.P. (1995), 'The Case against CASE', *Journal of Systems Management*, January/February.

13. Turley, R.T., and Bieman, J.M. (1995), 'Competencies of exceptional and nonexceptional software engineers', *Journal of Systems Software*, **28**, p. 20.

14. Goleman, D. (1998), *Working with Emotional Intelligence*, London: Bloomsbury, p. 37.

CHAPTER 10 – MASTERING THE BASICS: IN FOUR, NOT SO EASY, STEPS

1. Wiener, L. R. (1994), *Digital Woes: why we should not depend on software*, Essex: Addison-Wesley, pp. 1–15.
2. Ibid., p. 4.
3. Forester, T. and Morrison, P. (1994), *Computer Ethics*, London: MIT Press, p. 108.
4. Collins, T. (1999), 'Lessons not learnt from last passport disaster', *Computer Weekly*, 8 July, p. 10.
5. Timmins, N. (1999), 'An Explosive Mixture', *Financial Times*, 22 July.
6. Tomkins, R. (1999), 'Software glitch cuts off Tesco internet shoppers', *Financial Times*, 'Weekend' magazine, 28–29 August, pp. 22.
7. Forester, T. and Morrison, P. (1994), *Computer Ethics*, London: MIT Press, p. 121.
8. For a general discussion on the testing of safety critical software, see Gardiner, S. N. (1998), *Testing Safety Related Software*, New York: Springer Verlag.
9. Forester, T. and Morrison, P. (1994), *Computer Ethics*, London: MIT Press, pp. 113–114.
10. Wenk, E. (1996), 'New principles for engineering ethics', in Kling, R. (ed.), *Computerization and Controversy* (2nd edn), San Diego: Academic Press, pp. 942–43.
11. Wiener, L. R. (1994), *Digital Woes: why we should not depend on software*, Essex: Addison-Wesley, pp. 195–206.
12. 'The business', *Financial Times*, 'Weekend' magazine, 1 January 2000, p. 22.
13. 'The rising cost of integration', *Computer Consultant*, 12 May 1999.
14. 'IT consultants burning goodwill', *Global IT Consulting Report* (1999), November, p. 14.
15. Cant, L. and Evans, C. (1995), 'Commissioning of the automated baggage system at the new Denver International Airport', *Proceedings of Information Technology and Project Management*, 19–20 September, pp. 9–15.
16. 'Millennium survey', *Project Manager Today*, January 2000, pp. 4–6.
17. Thamhain, H.J. (1996), 'Best practice for controlling technology-based projects', *Project Management Journal*, December.

CHAPTER 11 – GUARANTEEING THE RETURNS FROM HIGH-INVESTMENT INFORMATION SYSTEMS PROJECTS

1. Parker, A. (1999), 'Government to probe its IT failures', *Financial Times*, 9 September.
2. Lucas, H.C. (1999), *Information Technology and the Productivity Paradox: Assessing the Value of Investing in IT*, New York: Oxford University Press.
3. Willcocks, L. (1992), 'Evaluating information technology investments: Research findings and reappraisal', *Journal of Information Systems*. See also Farbey, B., Land, F. and Targett, D. (1993), *How to Assess your IT Investment – A Study of Methods and Practice*, Oxford: Butterworth Heinemann, pp. 119–33.
4. For a comprehensive grounding in the balanced scorecard, see Kaplan, R.S. and Norton, D.P. (1996), *The Balanced Scorecard: Translating Strategy into Action*, Cambridge, Massachusetts: Harvard Business School Press.
5. Farbey, B., Land, F. and Targett, D. (1993), *How to Assess your IT Investment – A Study of Methods and Practice*, Oxford: Butterworth Heinemann.
6. Sutherland, S. (1992), *Irrationality: The Enemy Within*, London: Penguin Books, pp. 289–308.
7. For a general discussion on information economics, see Wiseman, D. (1992), 'Information Economics: a practical approach to valuing information systems', *Journal of Information Technology*, **7**, pp. 169–76.
8. For an example of a product to benefit model, see Bartlett, J. (1998), *Managing programmes of business change*, Wokingham, UK: Project Manager Today Publications, p. 113.
9. For some general background on

stakeholder analysis and management, see Pinto, J.K. and Kharbanda, O.P. (1995), *Successful Project Managers: Leading Your Team to Success*, New York: Van Nostrand Reinhold, pp. 27–40.

CHAPTER 12 – ELIMINATING THE CULTURE GAP: BUSINESS AND IT WORKING TOGETHER

1. Tannen, D. (1998), The argument culture: changing the way we argue and debate', London: Virago Press, p. 297.
2. 'IT gets makeover to catch high-flyers', *Computer Weekly*, 27 May 1999, p. 4.
3. For some general concepts in branding, see Aaker, D. (1996), *Building Strong Brands*, New York: The Free Press. Also, for the link between brand and professionalism, see Maister, D. (1997), *True Professionalism: The Courage to Care About Your People, Your Clients, And Your Career*, New York: Touchstone Publications, pp. 103–14.
4. 'Rebranding is only the first step', *Computer Weekly*, 27 May 1999, p. 25.
5. LaPlante, A. (1993), 'Does CIO title translate to "career is over"; IS professionals face high turnover, communication gap with upper management, *InforWorld*, 9 August, **15** (32), p. 56.
6. Sauer, C., Sharma, R. and Potter, B. (1997), 'Are general managers well prepared to manage IT? The role of IT in general MBA programmes in Australia', *Journal of Information Technology*, **12**, pp. 261–76.
7. 'Wise up or be wiped out, warns ICI boss', *Computer Weekly*, 27 March 1997, p. 3.
8. 'UK boardrooms claim IT is not their concern', *Computer Contractor*, 15 October 1999, p. 9.
9. 'Bridge over troubled water', *Computer Bulletin*, November 1999, pp. 16–17.
10. Kaletsky, A. (2000), 'The bug that never was', *The Times*, 6 January, p. 18.
11. Young, J. (1993), 'Let's all avoid the feeding frenzy on IS departments', *Macweek*, **7** (35), 6 September.
12. The West London Centre is located in Hounslow, West London and can be contacted on 0208-814 3629.
13. Garrett, B. (1996), *The Fish Rots from the Head: The crisis in our boardrooms: Developing the crucial skills of the competent director*, London: Harper Collins Business, p. 29.
14. Coulson-Thomas, C.J. (1991), 'IT directors and IT strategy', *Journal of Information Technology*, **6**, pp. 192–203.
15. Ibid., p. 196.
16. Wang, C. (1994), *Technovision: The Executive's Survival Guide to Understanding and Managing Information Technology*, New York: McGraw-Hill, p. 88.
17. Taylor-Cummings, A. (1998), 'Bridging the user–IS gap: A study of major information systems projects', *Journal of Information Technology*, **13**, p. 30.
18. *profit for information* can be contacted on 01932 248027, e-mail: business@proinfo.co.uk.
19. Nicoll, A. (1999), 'Radio project faces more delays', *Financial Times*, 15 September, p. 9.
20. Taylor-Cummings, A. (1998), 'Bridging the user–IS gap: A study of major information systems projects', *Journal of Information Technology*, **13**, p. 33.
21. Ibid.
22. Adler, P.S., McDonald, D.W. and McDonald, F. (1992), 'Strategic Management of Technical Functions', *Sloan Management Review*, Winter.
23. Taylor-Cummings, A. (1998), 'Bridging the user–IS gap: A study of major information systems projects', *Journal of Information Technology*, **13**, p. 44.
24. Hofstede, G. (1994), *Cultures and Organizations: Intercultural Co-operation and its Importance for Survival*, London: Harper Collins Business, p. 202.
25. Virgo, P. (1994), 'The Collapse of Traditional IT Career Structures', NCC briefing, No. 37.
26. Goleman, D. (1998), *Working with Emotional Intelligence*, London: Bloomsbury, p. 17.
27. Kling, R. and Allen, J.P. (1996), 'Can computer science solve organisational

problems? The case for organisational informatics', in Kling, R. (ed.), *Computerization and Controversy* (2nd edn), San Diego: Academic Press, pp. 262.

28. 'Computing Curricula 1991', in Kling, R. (ed.), (1996) *Computerization and Controversy* (2nd edn), San Diego: Academic Press, Appendix B.

29. This story was raised during an interview with Shan Shanthakumar of the Executive Studio.

CHAPTER 13 – SHORT- AND MEDIUM-TERM SOLUTIONS TO INFORMATION POLITICS

1. McKean, J. (1999), *Information Masters: Secrets of the Customer Race*, New York: John Wiley & Sons, p. 3.

2. Wind, J.Y. and Main, J. (1998), *Driving Change: How the best companies are preparing for the 21st century*, London: Kogan Page, p. 158.

3. Newing, R. (1999), 'Taking the paranoia out of knowledge acquisition', *Financial Times*, 28 April.

4. McKean, J. (1999), *Information Masters: Secrets of the Customer Race*, London: John Wiley & Sons, p. 2.

5. Voyle, S. (1999), 'M&S to split into seven business units', *Financial Times*, 22 December, p. 17.

6. Marchland D.A. (1995), 'What is your company's information culture?', 'Mastering Management' supplement, *Financial Times*.

7. Davenport, T.H., Eccles, R.G. and Prusak, L. (1992), 'Information Politics', *Sloan Management Review*, Fall, pp. 52–65.

8. McKean, J. (1999), *Information Masters: Secrets of the Customer Race*, New York: John Wiley & Sons, p. 111.

9. Model derived from Arya, V. and Ottmann, B. (1994) 'Information Management 2001', Draft publication for the 1994 Information Management Conference, p. 11.

10. Black, G. (1997), 'Information overload: It will get worse before it gets better', *Financial Times*, 7 May.

11. Taylor, R. (1999), 'The pressure continues to rise', *Financial Times*, 21 October.

12. Hammer, M. (1996), *Beyond Reengineering: How the Process-centred Organization is Changing our Work and our Lives*, London: Harper Collins Business, p. xiii.

13. Wentworth Research (1997), *Exploiting Intranets*, London: Wentworth Research, February.

14. Dauphinais, W. and Price, C. (eds) (1998), *Straight from the CEO*, London: Nicolas Brealey, p. 184.

15. Clarkson, P., (1995) *Change in Organisations*, London: pp. 32.

16. Davenport, T.H., Eccles, R.G. and Prusak, L. (1992), 'Information Politics', *Sloan Management Review*, Fall, p. 65.

17. Adams, J. (1999), *The Next World War: The Warriors and Weapons of the New Battlefields in Cyberspace*, London: Arrow Books, pp. 35, 36.

18. Pfeffer, J. and Sutton, R. (2000), *The Knowing–Doing Gap: How Smart Companies Turn Knowledge into Action*, Cambridge, Massachusetts: Harvard Business School Press, p. 210.

CHAPTER 14 – STOPPING THE ESCALATOR: ENSURING YOUR INFORMATION SYSTEMS PROJECTS ARE SUCCESSFUL

1. Stone, D., Patton, B. and Heen, S. (1999), *Difficult Conversations: How to Discuss what Matters Most*, London: Michael Joseph, p. 12.

2. Jones, C. (1996), *Patterns of Software Systems Failure and Success*, Boston Massachusetts: International Thomson Computer Press, pp. xxvii.

3. One of the few project health checks that can be considered effective is the Project Implementation Profile developed by Pinto and Slevin, and marketed by Xicom Incorporated. Examples of project health checks can be found in Turner, R., Grude, K.V. and Thurloway, L. (1996), *The Project Manager as Change Agent: Leadership, influence and negotiation*, Maidenhead, UK: McGraw Hill, pp. 204–22.

4. McConnell, S. (1996), *Rapid Development: Taming Wild Software Schedules*, Redmund, Washington: Microsoft Press, pp. 379–84. This provides a very useful set of actions that ought to occur when recovering a project.

5. Brooks' law states that adding manpower to a late software project makes it later. See Brooks, F.P. (1995), *The Mythical Man Month* (20th anniversary edn), Essex: Addison-Wesley, p. 232.

6. Abdel-Hamid, T.K. and Madnick, S.E. (1990) 'The elusive silver lining: How we fail to learn from software development failures', *Sloan Management Review*, **32**(1), pp. 39–48.

CHAPTER 15 – REHABILITATING ACCOUNTABILITY

1. Adams, J. (1999), *The Next World War: The Warriors and Weapons of the New Battlefields in Cyberspace*, London: Arrow Books, p. 248.

2. Wenk, E. (1996), 'New Principles for Engineering Ethics' in Kling, R. (ed.), *Computerization and Controversy* (2nd edn), San Diego: Academic Press, Part VIII, pp. 848–944.

3. 'IT consultants burning goodwill', *Global IT Consulting Report* (1999), November, p. 1.

4. Taylor, C.L. and Beeman, C.E. (1992), 'Evaluation for Accountability: An Overview', Fact Sheet PE-27, University of Florida Co-operative Extension Service, Institute of Food and Agricultural Sciences, p. 1.

5. Ibid., p. 2.

6. Ibid., p. 1.

7. For a general, well-explained and comprehensive introduction to computer law for the non-legal expert, see Bainbridge, D. (1996), *Introduction to Computer Law* (3rd edn), London: Financial Times, Pitman Publishing.

8. The article by John Ramsey was found on the Internet. Ramsey, J. (1999), 'Software licensing primer'. The author can be contacted by e-mail: calgary@macleoddixon.com .

9. Bainbridge, D. (1996), *Introduction to Computer Law* (3rd edn), London: Financial Times, Pitman Publishing, p. 151.

10. Collins, T. (1999), 'Do users court disaster when they sue suppliers?', *Computer Weekly*, 4 March, p. 22.

11. Pritchard, J. (1986), *The Penguin Guide to the Law* (2nd edn), London: Guild Publishing, p. 506.

12. For some general explanations of the Sales of Goods Act 1979, the Unfair Contract Terms Act 1977, and the Supply of Goods and Services Act 1982, see Pritchard, J. (1986), *The Penguin Guide to the Law* (2nd edn), London: Guild Publishing, pp. 507–49. For an outline of the Consumer Protection Act 1987, see Bainbridge, D. (1996), *Introduction to Computer Law* (3rd edn), London: Financial Times, Pitman Publishing, pp. 157–58.

13. For more detail on the St Albans City & District versus ICL case, see Collins, T. and Bicknell, D. (1997), *Crash: ten easy ways to avoid a computer disaster*, New York: Simon & Schuster, pp. 273–81; Bainbridge, D. (1996), *Introduction to Computer Law* (3rd edn), London: Financial Times, Pitman Publishing, p. 164; Walker, C. (1994), 'Court tears £1m hole in ICL's liability safety net', *Computer Weekly*, 6 October, p. 1; Jarvis, J. (1996), 'ICL loses its appeal to limit liability for faulty software', *Computing*, 1 August, p. 1.

14. To see how organizational culture can impact the treatment of failure see Schein, E. (1999), *The Corporate Culture Survival Guide*, San Francisco: Jossey-Bass Publishers, pp. 38–40.

15. For the set of principles, see Forester, T. and Morrison, P. (1994), *Computer Ethics*, London: MIT Press, pp. 261–70. For further discussion on the ethical issues and dilemmas facing the IT profession, see Kling, R. (ed.) (1996), *Computerization and Controversy* (2nd edn), San Diego: Academic Press, Part VIII, pp. 848–944.

16. Kavanagh, J. (1999), 'BCS issues latest code

of practice for IT professionals', *Computer Weekly*, 2 December , p. 88.

17. Deal, T. and Kennedy, A. (1999), *The New Corporate Cultures: Revitalising the workplace after downsizing, mergers and reengineering*, London: Orion Business Books, p. 204.

18. Jones, A. (2000), 'PWC broke rules 8,000 times', *The Times*, 7 January, p. 27.

19. 'Automation comes of age amid rife ethical concerns', *Computer Consultant*, 26 November–9 December 1999, p. 22.

CHAPTER 16 – AVOIDING THE SILVER BULLET SYNDROME: CHOOSING THE RIGHT TOOLS AND TECHNIQUES

1. McConnell, S. (1996), *Rapid Development: Taming Wild Software Schedules*, Redmund, Washington: Microsoft Press, p. 368.

2. Boehm, B. (1986), *Software Engineering Economics*, Englewood Cliffs, New Jersey: Prentice Hall.

3. Goodhew, P. (1996), 'Ensuring profitable investment in software process improvement', in *Proceedings of Encouraging Leadership in IT*, 17th April 1996, London.

4. Both of these books provide the reader with an excellent understanding of how the various techniques and tools available can be used to improve the software schedule: McConnell, S. (1996), *Rapid Development: Taming Wild Software Schedules*, Redmund, Washington: Microsoft Press, pp. 390-607; Jones, C. (1996), '*Patterns of Software Systems Failure and Success*', Boston, Massachusetts: International Thomson Computer Press, pp. 111–50.

5. The information used to populate this model has come from the three main sources used for this chapter and which have already been quoted (see above). McConnell, for example, reviews best-practice techniques by considering their potential to reduce the nominal schedule, their ability to improve progress visibility, their effect on schedule risk, their chances

of first-time success and their chances of long-term success. Goodhew assesses the effectiveness of typically non-tool based techniques which mainly fall into the common project management activities, whilst Capers Jones concentrates on both project management activity and software development practices. Combining each of these sources provides a comprehensive review of what can be done to improve the effectiveness of software projects from an execution-view perspective.

PART III: OPTIMIZING INFORMATION SYSTEMS PROJECTS

1. Wang, C., (1994) *Technovision: The Executive's Survival Guide to Understanding and Managing Information Technology*, New York: McGraw-Hill, pp. 188.

CHAPTER 17: OPTIMIZING THE DELIVERY OF INFORMATION SYSTEMS PROJECTS

1. Jones, C. (1996), *Patterns of Software Systems Failure and Success*, Boston, Massachusetts: International Thomson Computer Press, p. 151.

2. Goldman, D. (1998), *Working with Emotional Intelligence*, London: Bloomsbury, pp. 100–01.

3. Holmes, A. (1994), 'Information Systems Failure: Diagnosis, Prevention and Cure', MSc dissertation, London School of Economics and Political Science.

CHAPTER 18: CHANGING ATTITUDES TOWARDS IT AND INFORMATION SYSTEMS PROJECTS

1. Saran, C. (1999), 'No room for IT at strategic level', *Computer Weekly*, 1 December, p. 13.

CHAPTER 19: THE BOTTOM LINE

1. Kurzweil, R. (1999), *The Age of Spiritual Machines*, London: Phoenix, p. 199.

2. Deal, T. and Kennedy, A. (1999), *The New Corporate Economy: Revitalising the workplace after downsizing, mergers and reengineering*, London: Orion Business Books, p. 132.

3. Ellis, S. (1980), 'Computer failure could pull plug on many firms', *Business Insurance*, **14** (32), pp. 34–35.

Index